WITHDRAWN
UTSA LIBRARIES

UTSA DT LIBRARY RENEWALS 458-2440
DATE DUE

Tampering with Tradition

NEW DIRECTIONS IN CULTURE AND GOVERNANCE

Series Editor: Terry Nichols Clark
The University of Chicago

This series has a combined focus on innovation in local governance and new developments in the field of cultural policy. Culture functions, much like society itself, as a complex system of elements that often acts to strengthen attachments to place. New Directions publishes scholarship that is thematically diverse—examining culture, for example, as a trigger for economic renewal or as a tool for intercultural understanding—and while books in the series may use differing methodologies, we are especially interested in creative applications of social science research.

TITLES IN SERIES
Tampering with Tradition: The Unrealized Authority of Democratic Agency
   Edited by Peter Bogason, Sandra Kensen, and Hugh T. Miller

Tampering with Tradition

The Unrealized Authority of Democratic Agency

Edited by Peter Bogason, Sandra Kensen,
and Hugh Miller

LEXINGTON BOOKS
Lanham • Boulder • New York • Toronto • Oxford

LEXINGTON BOOKS

Published in the United States of America
by Lexington Books
An imprint of The Rowman & Littlefield Publishing Group, Inc.
4501 Forbes Boulevard, Suite 200, Lanham, Maryland 20706

PO Box 317
Oxford
OX2 9RU, UK

Copyright © 2004 by Lexington Books

All rights reserved. No part of this publication may be reproduced, stored in a retrieval system, or transmitted in any form or by any means, electronic, mechanical, photocopying, recording, or otherwise, without the prior permission of the publisher.

British Library Cataloguing in Publication Information Available

Library of Congress Cataloging-in-Publication Data

Tampering with tradition : the unrealized authority of democratic agency / edited by Peter Bogason, Sandra Kensen, and Hugh Miller.
   p. cm. — (New directions in culture and governance)
Includes bibliographical references and index.
ISBN 0-7391-0748-8 (cloth : alk. paper)
1.   Democracy. 2. Local government. I. Bogason, Peter. II. Kensen, S. (Sandra), 1968-   III. Miller, Hugh T. (Hugh Theodore), 1953- IV. Series.

JC423.T283 2004
321.8—dc22   2004006464

Printed in the United States of America

∞™ The paper used in this publication meets the minimum requirements of American National Standard for Information Sciences—Permanence of Paper for Printed Library Materials, ANSI/NISO Z39.48–1992.

Contents

Preface		vii
1	Introduction: Extra-Formal Democracy *Peter Bogason, Sandra Kensen, and Hugh T. Miller*	1
2	Deliberative Governance: Renewing Public Service and Public Trust *James K. Scott, Guy B. Adams, and Barton Wechsler*	11
3	Local Democratic Governance: Allocative, Integrative, or Deliberative? *Peter Bogason*	23
4	Making Local Democracy Work: Neighborhood-Oriented Reform in Los Angeles and the Dutch Randstad *Frank Hendriks and Juliet Musso*	39
5	Democratic Consequences of Urban Governance: What Has Become of Representative Democracy? *Karina Sehested*	63
6	Entrepreneurship in Community Development and Local Governance *Lars Hulgård*	87
7	Democratic Governance and the Role of Public Administrators *Eva Sørensen*	107

8	Mediated Negotiation, a Deliberative Approach to Democratic Governance: Theoretical Linkages and Practical Examples *Gary S. Marshall and Connie P. Ozawa*	131
9	Interaction Research: Joining Persons, Theories, and Practices *Sandra Kensen and Pieter W. Tops*	149
10	Democratic Epistemology *Hugh T. Miller*	173
11	Extra-Formal Democracy: A Reflection *Hugh T. Miller*	185
References		197
Index		215
About the Contributors		223

Preface

Changes in contemporary Western democracies are easy to perceive but difficult to assess. The title of this book was inspired by a car theft alarm—it delivered the usual toots and howls, but then an electronic voice added: "Help, I'm being tampered with." Bystanders shook their heads and walked on.

Is traditional democracy being tampered with? And if so, can we shake our heads and walk on? This book delivers ample evidence that we see new forms of democracy, but rather than shake our heads we should consider the accusation of tampering. Tampering indicates that something not acceptable is going on, and that is what traditionalists in democratic theory believe. They are content with good old representative democracy, and if changes are necessary, political parties and parliaments are the ones to take action.

The authors of this book have another view. Democracy is changing toward more involvement of ordinary citizens in various quasi-political roles, and hence the borders for political action and democracy are being changed. Citizens increasingly face possibilities to become involved outside the traditional turf of political parties, and such changes deserve more analytical attention—also to probe the sincerity of politicians in such change. The book delivers evidence that there are differences both across and within countries, so "democracy" is not so easy to generalize about.

The task of this book is to call attention to what the changes involve, and to suggest how we can analyze them to better understand them. The task of the reader, then, is to assess if we are successful and, of course, to participate in on-going debates about the state of our democracies and the attempts to change them. There is no one solution to democratic challenges, but we believe that by discussing them openly, we can help empower everyone to be part of determining where we are going. So we hope that people will stop being bystanders and instead participate in the changes, to make them theirs.

The book is written by a group of scholars from Denmark, the Netherlands, and the United States, all participating in Demo-Net, a scholarly network on democratic governance. The book is our first accomplishment to be presented to the general public. We hope that more will follow, and that our analyses will create discussions among scholars and students of democracy, as well as the general public.

The network is financed by a three-year grant from the Danish Social Science Research Council, which we thank for making our deliberations and writing possible across borders and waters. The support made it possible to arrange scholarly workshops, participate in conferences, and to visit one another's home bases—thus combining research with personal acquaintance, an invaluable treat in sustainable scholarship.

Roskilde, Tilburg, and Fort Lauderdale, August 2003
Peter Bogason, Sandra Kensen, and Hugh T. Miller

Chapter 1

Introduction: Extra-Formal Democracy

Peter Bogason, Sandra Kensen, and Hugh T. Miller

This book presents a collection of chapters which deal with emerging patterns of democracy at the local level. We see these patterns as challenging traditional forms of democracy, both in theory (second section of this introduction) and in practice (third and fourth section of this introduction).

Research into the political systems of Western democracies has mostly been composed of analysis of formal systems and at the nation-state level. The point of departure typically has been a constitutional perspective, traversing numerous electoral and parliamentary processes that regulate access to political participation. When research focused on the exercise of power in government, the two main topics of inquiry have been political parties and parliamentary process. Regarding citizens, researchers have been preoccupied with voting behavior and opinion polling based on surveys.

In repudiating the naïveté of much of this research, it has been concluded that the "representative democratic accountability feedback loop" model of electoral politics does not perform as advertised (Fox and Miller 1995). Representational systems face numerous problems as political parties decline in membership, the voter turnout falls, the need for political campaign money increases, and mass media and media consultants insinuate spectacle into the vote accumulation process.

Another pattern of investigation, this time at the local level, has been to understand the influence of citizens from the point of view of representative democracy, but with some added ingredients. In addition to voting, citizen activities have been understood as protest movements against local town hall powers, for example, or as mobilizations for specific purposes, to some degree in opposition to rulers in public office. For the most part, however, formal systems of government (e.g., city charters, council-mayor forms of government, or special voting districts) have dominated local-government research. As a consequence of these patterns of investigation, the citizen has been of research interest mainly as a voter and as a determinant of coalition or party politics in local government councils.

New democratic practices at the local level challenge scholars because, in order to investigate these practices, new theories and ways of doing research are needed. In addition, these new local democratic practices also challenge democracy at higher levels of abstraction because they open up the range of possibilities and go beyond the institutionalized practices of representative democracy. In this chapter we argue for situational, relational and pragmatic alternatives to formal, representative, overhead democracy.

We think that in many cultures understanding democracy is undergoing change. Representative democracy is only one source of democratic inspiration. Directly participative forms are often attempted, but such alternatives lack the institutionalized history and, hence, the authority and prestige enjoyed by the formal representative model. Authority is not granted automatically to participative forms of democracy. Political scientists often consider representative democracy as an ideal standard against which to measure and evaluate participative forms. However, representative democracy is itself subject to change as a result of experimenting with these new forms. And researchers look for other democratic rationales in order to value these new forms with other criteria (Kensen 2000).

The objective of this book is to argue for an extended view of democracy, which we in this introduction call extra-formal democracy. This extended view lacks a generalizable legitimacy, because its practice is always contextual. We argue that the legitimacy of extra-legal forms of democracy derives from their relevance to public issues or their effectiveness in making a difference in the local situation. Researchers who would investigate these new forms of democracy are challenged to find ways to conduct research that are in accordance with democratic ideals. In addition, theorists are challenged to find the authoritative justifications for extra-formal democratic practices. Our aim here is to propose ways in which research may be conducted into extra-formal democratic practices, and to propose frameworks for thinking about these practices as potential extensions of democracy.

Predecessors

We are not the first to be critical about the state of the art in public administration and policy analysis regarding democracy. A number of researchers have challenged the notion that policy is made by means of traditional political institutions and traditional ways of public influence only (Kooiman 1993; Milward and Provan 1992; Miller 1994; Rhodes 1997; O'Toole 1997). These researchers claim that societal governance is no longer adequately described as a government governing a society. It is more adequately described as a network activity in which governments participate in the governance process as one among several stakeholders. As a consequence, the line between society and state is difficult to draw, and a monistic rational model—a system of government characterized by elected policy makers and neutral administrators who, with cause-and-effect determinism as background, carry out a singular policy goal via hierarchical, instrumentally rational, legal-rational means—must yield to a dynamic model called muddling through (Lindblom 1959).

In 1959 Charles Lindblom published his classic didactic model of public policy called the "root" and the "branch" method, which is to say the rational model versus that of the "science of muddling through." The policy implications of muddling through, as opposed to rational action, later were spelled out in a book on policy making, originally published in 1968 (Lindblom and Woodhouse 1993). The rational model imagines that democratic influence is expressed by representative democracy only. Due to many factors, actors (governmental or not) cannot set up goals in ways that satisfy the demand for separation of goals and means; they cannot achieve full information necessary for rational decision making, and they cannot rank order possible solutions in a coherent way that retains any constancy across time or cultures. Instead, people behave based on previous experience and relatively unsystematic updating of certain elements of information that they can digest without too much effort. Hence, muddling through has other options.

"Muddling through" in an organizational context means that bureaucratic actors enact pluralism rather than monism. In their political dealings they keep some information back, they hide certain achievements, and they often conflict with other bureaus rather than cooperate toward a singular goal. This model accounts for the everyday type of politics whereby many actors in complex interaction—involving some politicians, some interest organizations, and some administrative agencies—enter into processes of negotiation where the necessity is to reach accommodation rather than to fulfill a singular, overarching political goal. The actors participate in a give-and-take process, assuming that what may be lost for now may be achieved at a later stage in a new process of bargaining. The process creates new information not available beforehand and not amenable to a priori rank ordering assumed under the norms of rationality.

Muddling through thus implies that, rather than being created by legislatively determined fiat, policy emerges. In the analysis of how policy emerges, citizens' influence can be counted along with that of stakeholders. Recall that in the original thinking about muddling through, citizens' influence was recorded when citizens had organized themselves into associations and special interest groups. Gathered together as a formal organization, citizens could count as an interest-group organization proper. This early focus on organized interests is understandable when taking into consideration the level of analysis, which usually was the level of national policies and politics. Since Lindblom (1959), more attention has been paid to the dynamics of situational policy making in local context. At the local level, loosely organized citizens, well-organized citizens acting together on a singular issue, and individual citizens were included in the analysis in order to explain policy processes and their results.

What happens to processes of public policy when citizen involvement in the public sector increases? Public policy making is mostly understood as a complex process at some distance from the people. New channels of popular influence are likely to further reorient theoretical perceptions, but how? Recent developments in various segments of social science theories may be relevant to guide us in a search for a theoretical rationale.

For example Michael Gibbons and associates' discussed knowledge production in "Mode 2," which is taking over from "Mode 1" (Gibbons et al. 1994). Mode 1 is the kind of analysis based on law-like generalizations as we find them within the traditional natural sciences. Within the social sciences, Mode 1 is the forum for the established scientific disciplines. The stance in Mode 1 social science has encouraged homogeneity in epistemology and has not allowed forces in the society to influence the research process. Researchers work with data in their offices, analyze society at a distance based on their theories, and present their results in a debate with other scientists. In contrast, Mode 2 is transdisciplinary, heterogeneous, nonhierarchical, and socially reflexive, involving practitioners who collaborate on a problem defined in a specific and localized context, and discussing results in such a context of application (Gibbons et al. 1994, 3).

Similar thinking has been found in the literature on "bottom-up" policy implementation. At one end of a continuum, approaches apply a Quasi-Mode-1 style. In this mode the researchers define the policy problems they wanted to analyze, but attempt to do so from the perspective of the policy problem they want to solve (Hull and Hjern 1982). At the other end, Quasi-Mode-2, problems are analyzed in close consultation with the objects of the research in order to grasp their various understandings of the policy problem to be illuminated (Pedersen 1999).

Analogous developments may also be found in the evaluation literature. Mode 2 has many overlaps with Guba and Lincoln's "fourth generation of evaluation" (Guba and Lincoln 1989), and it is present in the narrative turn of policy analysis (Roe 1994; see also Kensen and Bogason [1999] for an explication of the similarities and differences between more traditional and more reflexive evaluation practices). This literature discusses multifarious ways of taking many and diverse channels of communication into account when research is conducted. The underlying rationale for a parallel shift from structured hierarchical systems to the practice of collaborative network systems in public policy and administration has been informed by developments in many different disciplines.

Democracy as a Social Practice

When democracy is looked upon as a practice of voting and electing representatives as well as a practice in which citizens, politicians, public administrators, and other professionals act together on issues or problems that are defined as public, then democracy may take many new forms. As democracy takes new forms, the complexity of relations between members of the public and persons associated with institutions of governance increases. These new forms of democracy are mostly extra-formal in that they do not rely on the usual legitimating processes—charters, constitutions, formal bureaucracy, and the electoral representative overhead model of democratic accountability—for their authority.

Extra-formal democracy goes by various names. Coproduction, direct democracy, communitarianism, deliberative democracy, discourse theory, social constructivism, and citizen engagement have become increasingly recognizable as useful concepts. (See, for example Dryzek 2000; Fischer 2000; Forester 1999; Wenger 1998). Also, positive programs have been set forth, oftentimes variations on the themes of "social capital" (Putnam 2000) or "community capacity-building" (Chaskin 2001). Denhardt and Denhardt (2000) propose a facilitative role for public administrators aimed at the public interest. Bang and Sørensen (1999) used the concept of "everyday maker" to refer to a new form of political engagement. They documented the ad hoc political activism of neighborhood members in eliciting governmental cooperation with respect to local situational exigencies. Recent discourse theory (Fox and Miller 1995; Miller 2002) has treated the local, situation-regarding exchange as an achievable vision. Box (1998) valorizes "community governance" along the same lines, while King and Stivers (1998) offer communitarian ideals in public administrative settings. These sometimes dreamy visions lack formal, constitutional legitimacy that electoral and parliamentary processes enjoy. Yet these extra-formal styles of citizen involvement are sufficiently well documented that theories of governance cannot simply ignore them.

Hence many parties may participate in political and administrative processes. Policies are created not by rational deduction of principles but as an outcome of interaction among interested parties. This is when public action becomes public policy (Bogason 2000), the product of the shaping of meaning and identity (March and Olsen 1995), and composed of narratives about the nature of society (Bevir and Rhodes 1998) or public policy (Roe 1994).

Among the wide variety of approaches that focus attention on local and situational dynamics, pragmatism has the longest history. Recent years have seen pragmatism reappearing in the social sciences (see, for example, the September 2000 symposium in Administration and Society). These recent visions of pragmatism mostly look toward possible futures in an effort to imagine a hopeful path. John Dewey saw communication and education as the lifeblood of democracy. Pragmatists from the last century such as William James and Dewey placed heavy emphasis on experimentation and experience. Mary Parker Follett added a critique of ballot box democracy in proposing that we submit ourselves to the law of the situation instead of representational structures. The law of the situation implies contextualism, and immersion in activity with others.

The reappearance of pragmatism can be said to start with Thomas Kuhn's attack on absolute objectivity in science (Kuhn 1962). Kuhn's study was directed toward the natural sciences; it has been followed by several analyses of the social sciences, all of which undermine the generalizing capacity of social theories. These contrary interpretations of the explanatory and predictive power of the social sciences paved the way for both severe criticisms and sobering reformulations of the status of social theory and administrative theory in particular.

The pragmatic way of looking at things is uniquely American. In Europe, public administration has focused largely on national administration and to some degree on local government, but typically in terms of analyzing political and administrative leadership. However, if we ask what the central tenets of pragmatism are about—action orientation, democratic development, reflective participation, and experimentation—and apply those concepts to an examination of the discussions, we are more likely to find common ground between European public administration and pragmatism. That literature, however, is not much identifiable as public administration analysis proper; rather it is found in other discussions of topics that are relevant for public administration, notably policy analysis and evaluation, and also urban planning.

Where do pragmatism and practice lead us? Morone (1990, 336) suggests:

> The present challenge is to infuse our institutions with broad, workable forms of popular participation; rather than pursuing the ideal on the political fringes, linking it directly to the institutions that govern the political economy: the people indoors.

With Morone, pragmatists would likely seek to modify the practices of existing institutions. Others believe that democratic agency should reside outside of status quo institutions. There are no easy answers, and all of the answers proposed are contestable. Communitarian proposals (Etzioni 2000; Bellah, et al. 1992) challenge the prerogatives of liberty in a way that classic liberals and minority factions might find disturbing because of the pressures for conformance that are often insinuated into the mix. Formal government enables a strong government, but many participative democrats do not want that. Wherein, then, would the agency of democratic authority reside? The chapters in this volume confront the challenge.

Public Action and Democratic Research

Collective public action, then, no longer takes place solely in organizational forms formally defined by the public sector as bureaucratic or democratic. Under present societal conditions in the advanced Western societies it seems that few actors will accept such monopolies and strict limitations. The development of democratic practices within collective public action takes place within hybrid forms of organization across the boundaries of public and private, but backed to some degree by public powers. So public action becomes public policy when the action is recognized as being legitimate and when it has implications for the formulation and/or implementation of policy under the responsibility of a public body in terms of legal, financial, or expert resources (Bogason 2000). Stated otherwise, *Government Is Us* (King, Stivers, and collaborators 1998), citizens create various kinds of self-governance in cooperation with the public sector.

Such a development should please a revived Dewey and it certainly is important to pragmatist and Mode-2 conceptions of research in which theory, action, and research get intertwined in ways which might shock the value-neutral modernist. We are going to make no excuses. We see fact and value, objective and subjective, theory and practice, ends and means, analytic and synthetic as mutually dependent rather than separable. We stress the role of community because we are formed in interaction with other people, and so we also stress the role of discourse and inquiry, open communication and education by fiat. In that sense, we choose our society and way of life. Not that we do so completely freely, but we act within boundaries that may vary from place to place, from situation to situation. It is our task to learn from such circumstances. In research on public policy and administration, the consequences are that we cannot just observe how politicians make policies for the people based on their representative platform. Various interventions and active roles by diverse citizens are part of the democratic landscape perfectly legitimate and desirable, and researchers, too, may be part of the dialogues as long as they realize their changed role. This book discusses democracy in connection with public participation. In brief, the authors investigate the question:

> Which contemporary types of agency have democratic authorization in localities across West-Europe and the United States?

Chapters 9 and 10 deal with this question in relation to researchers. The other chapters do so in relation to other agents, and at different levels of abstraction. Portraits of individuals, relationships, networks of organized interests, institutions, and also systems are painted in these chapters, with the artists' eyes keen to perceive democratic agency and its authorization.

Most authors relate their discussions to models of democracy that can be interpreted as aggregative, integrative, or deliberative. Democratic agency is understood differently within each model. Within the aggregative model, each citizen is a democratic agent, at least every election day. Democratic agency within the integrative model is more demanding. Here citizens are involved in debating public issues and resolving public problems. The deliberative model is considered an alternative to either the self-interested citizen or the dreamy vision of a fully committed citizen who wishes to contribute to a state of consensus. In the deliberative model there is room for both self-interest and the common good, for both consensus and conflict, and for both ideal and workable solutions. The authors in this volume value these different kinds of democratic agency differently.

In chapter 2, James Scott, Guy Adams, and Barton Wechsler examine the theory and practice of deliberative democracy in the United States. In later chapters, deliberative democracy is put forward as perhaps the most promising strategy for renewing authorized democratic agency in contemporary local democracies. Scott, Adams, and Wechsler elaborate in detail on this still-emerging democratic governance system. Deliberative democracy, according to the authors, is a process-oriented form of democratic governance that requires quite a lot from democratic agents, among others, being able to deal with change, uncertain outcomes, and a high level of doubt. These characteristics are necessary for building an authentic learning community.

The next two chapters are on local institutional reforms in Denmark, the Netherlands, and the United States. Peter Bogason describes how local institutional reforms in Denmark have created a fragmented governance system. The reforms in Denmark are a mixture of aggregative voting, integrative talking, and competitive negotiation. The coexistence of different democratic models in practice raises complex issues for local governments, on how they can best deal with this diversity. Bogason's advice to local governments is to take on roles as intermediaries between the different actors in the fragmented system of governance instead of trying to use a hierarchical means of control to influence decision making.

Frank Hendriks and Juliet Musso describe neighborhood-governance reforms within two regions, Los Angeles, California, and Randstad, in the Netherlands. They describe how new institutions are organized and how things work differently in these two regions. In addition, Hendriks and Musso interpret their findings from the point of view of the different democracy models. They reach the conclusion that the reforms in Los Angeles are inspired more by protective democracy and the reforms in the Randstad are inspired more by developmental democracy. The difference is related to who the main change agents are in the respective regions: citizens in Los Angeles and professionals (among whom are public administrators) in the Randstad.

In chapter 5, Karina Sehested elaborates the fascinating idea of a network-based democracy. Local democratic networks can take different forms in practice. Networks may be centralist-elitist and based upon a corporatist tradition, but networks can also be pluralist and combine public participation with representative democracy. How networks are organized is an empirical question. Therefore, Sehested analyzes a case in a Danish city as an illustration. This case shows the gloomy consequences when representative politicians participate in only one of the networks instead of being able both to link different networks and to translate the different democratic ideals on which these networks are based into a third model.

In chapter 6, Lars Hulgård makes a case for social or civic entrepreneurs. Hulgård provides examples of American and Danish entrepreneurs who are able to deal with several demarcation lines in pragmatic ways, including the line between individual calculation and societal development. By being able to actually deal with these lines, these entrepreneurs become vital for the development of local democracies. These entrepreneurs are examples of citizens and public administrators who are good at organizing local governance structures and activities. In this sense these social and civic entrepreneurs define a new political identity.

Eva Sørensen paints five portraits of local public administrators in a Danish town. These five public administrators individually develop strategies to cope with the changes in democratic institutions. Sørensen then discusses these different "coping" strategies from the point of view of two models of democracy, aggregative and integrative democracy, and she discovers a number of problems. Sørensen's objective is to secure an equal distribution of influence among citizens. Obtaining this objective should not be a public administrator's individual problem. Instead, Sørensen makes a case for reorganizing democratic institutions.

Gary Marshall and Connie Ozawa describe in chapter 8 two successful mediated negotiation processes. According to Marshall and Ozawa, the success of mediated negotiation was related to at least three elements, namely, who could join (quantity), how they could join, what the relationships were like (quality), and what these relationships brought about (individual and societal development). The fact that mediation processes can be successful in the United States shows that there is no inherent incompatibility between getting the job done efficiently and allowing for a broad civic involvement at the same time. Marshall and Ozawa show that either a societal or a governmental actor may initiate mediated negotiation processes.

The atmosphere of experimentation felt in cities across the United States and Western Europe inspired the authors of chapter 9, and also their colleagues at Tilburg University, to try another way of conducting research. Sandra Kensen and Pieter Tops reflect upon their experiences with this interaction research and describe the lessons they learned. An effort was made to build relationships among a team of researchers, between researchers and various local actors, and among local actors from numerous cities. The authors show how the quality of these relationships was decisive for the extent to which interesting and relevant research-exchange activities could be created for local democratic practices.

Hugh Miller, the author of chapter 10, discusses, from a theoretical and philosophical point of view, what it could mean to conduct research in a democratic fashion. Miller builds up his argument on the basis of practice. He goes from listening as a researcher to interpretation by both researchers and other participants to joint action, new practices, and intervention. The result is democratic research as a knowledge-building activity. According to Miller, democratic research is based upon pragmatism more than realism because such research is a form of democratic solidarity concerned with real consequences to be felt by democratic agents, such as the reintegration of social relations and the redistribution of specific freedoms and authorities.

In the concluding chapter, editor Hugh T. Miller discusses the main issues which arise in this book. On the basis of the chapters in this book, what conclusion can be made when representative democracy and extra-formal democracy are confronted with one another? The following issues are addressed: the (problematic) relationship between hierarchy and democracy; the possibilities of a discretionary bureaucrat becoming a democrat; the relationship between discretion and facilitation; and facilitators and entrepreneurs as important democratic agents.

Chapter 2

Deliberative Governance: Renewing Public Service and Public Trust

James K. Scott, Guy B. Adams, and Barton Wechsler

This chapter examines the theory and practice of deliberative governance, a promising strategy for renewing public trust and involvement in democratic institutions. After exploring the tensions inherent in democratic systems (Fowler 1991), we develop a robust characterization of deliberative governance. We offer definitions of deliberation and deliberative, as well as a description of deliberative processes in action. Next, we draw preliminary lessons from the practice of deliberation in the public sector. These lessons suggest changes in the role and identity of public administrators that require broadening, deepening, and extending a distinctive skill set and approach to administration (Stivers 1990; Thomas 1995; Luke 1998; Box 1998). Finally, we outline a research agenda to inform the further development of deliberative governance in the public service.

Governance and Its Tensions

Two intertwining streams of thought regarding democracy (and by extension, citizenship) have influenced the American experience and practice of governance. The tensions between these different visions of the polity play themselves out in public life as "competing values," highly desired outcomes that may appear to be mutually contradictory (Quinn 1984). In democratic governance, we seek both accountability in government and the flexibility to take innovative and timely action; we want both to make use of expert knowledge and to allow citizens to participate in public decisions; we expect governmental bodies to make high quality decisions and simultaneously to reflect the agreement of competing stakeholders; and we try both to provide stability and to facilitate positive change. All approaches to governance (and public administration) involve some trade-off among these competing values. Traditional public administration, for example, has been known for an emphasis on accountability and procedural correctness. In contrast, most variants of new public management focus on flexibility and competition as ways of achieving efficiency and/or effectiveness. Some would argue that what is needed is a transformational approach to governance that builds the capacity of the governance system and the citizens participating in it across multiple dimensions. Such an approach would carry the promise of lessening considerably the trade-offs between competing values (if not resolving the tensions altogether), thus producing a higher level of performance across multiple dimensions. However, the prospect of achieving simultaneous resolution of all competing values and, therefore, optimal system performance should only be considered a remote, theoretical possibility.

Deliberative Governance

Understanding governance as central to the balancing act needed to manage the tensions in our system of democracy leads us to examine "deliberative governance." We seek to show how deliberation and deliberative processes add value in governance, mitigate the contradictory tensions described above, and renew both public service and public trust. We will not argue that all governance is or should be deliberative. Rather, we attempt to explain when and where deliberative processes are appropriate and to present useful methods for improving and strengthening governance. First, however, we need to explain what we mean by deliberation and deliberative processes.

In its simplest sense, deliberation is careful thought and discussion about issues and decisions. Deliberative processes comprise discussion and consideration by a group of persons of the reasons for and against a measure, or, put another way, consulting with others in a process of reaching a decision (Fishkin 1991). According to Dryzek (2000), deliberation is a process of social inquiry in which participants seek to gain understanding of themselves and others, to learn and to persuade. Thus, one of the cornerstones of deliberative processes is the nature of the communication involved: participants strive to rise above win-lose exchange; over time, they may aspire to dialogue, and even to become a learning community (Yankelovich 1999). Participants in deliberative processes are expected to be open to change in their attitudes, ideas, and/or positions. Changing perspectives through a process of learning and discussion is an expected, though not required, outcome of deliberation. It is a process that can, over time, grow citizens, fostering growth both in the capacity for practical judgment and in the art of living together in a context of disagreement. Tolerance is elevated to a central virtue in public life. Deliberative governance is the application of deliberation and deliberative processes to the activities of governance.

Many of the processes associated with public involvement have the aim of "bringing all parties to the table," and they utilize negotiation, mediation, or alternative dispute resolution—processes that may stop short of a willingness to modify judgments, preferences, or positions (Chaskin et al. 2001). That is, there is no built-in expectation that the process itself will change the perspectives and commitments of participants or that citizen building is a worthy goal in itself.

In contrast to other, more instrumental approaches, deliberative governance prefers a meaningful role for citizens in public decisions, although sorting out which citizens and what decisions are appropriate for deliberation represent ongoing problems.

While there is a considerable theoretical literature on both deliberative democracy (Gutmann and Thompson 1996; Dryzek 1990), and deliberative governance (Forester 1999; Hajer and Wagenaar, 2003; Fischer 2000; deLeon 1997), there is a second, large stream of writing on deliberative processes that draws on practice at all levels of government (although mostly at the local level) involving citizens in public discussion and decision making. Of course, not all of these instances of public participation have been deliberative. Indeed, insistence on "full" deliberation sets a very high standard that will be met only rarely in most settings, and then, only after multiple iterations. From our perspective, the most valuable lesson from current practice is to suggest when and where deliberative processes can add value to governance and, alternatively, when and where its costs are prohibitive.

Deliberative governance occurs within the public arena and, in that sense, overlaps the political domain that is the province of deliberative democracy. The domain of deliberative governance comprises those issues of public policy and public administration which can admit (or in some cases, must submit to) the meaningful engagement of citizens in discussions and/or decisions. Both deliberative democracy and deliberative governance share some sense of urgency in the face of our deteriorating civic culture (Yankelovich 1991).

We live in a time when politics has become more sharply partisan, when public discussion in many forums has degenerated well below hard-edged debate, when hyperpluralism underlines our differences perhaps beyond repair, and when the relentless pressure to entertain in the media has made even the somewhat thoughtful sound bite seem deliberative by comparison with the serial-monologue-by-interruption so common on television. In response, there have been growing calls for civic education, for the nurturance of civil society, for the rebuilding of social capital (Putnam 2000). There has also been a growing series of practices, particularly at the local level, that involve citizens in public discussion and decision (Dryzek and Torgerson 1993).

Lessons from the Practice of Deliberative Governance

Our own experiences with deliberative governance in practice cover a variety of settings, including rural communities where residents weighed competing visions of their future together (Scott and Cox 2001; Johnson, Cox and Kovalyova 1998; Scott and Cox 1999), public-private consortia brought together to consider the future of failing industries (Hamed 1998; Johnson and Hamed 1999), and a state-mandated consultation with local government, business owners, and citizens on the future of a highway interchange (Mundell, Kovalyova and Johnson 2002). Each of these projects took place in the public arena and was designed to directly inform a particular public decision. None relied exclusively on citizen deliberation to reach a decision and each achieved mixed results. The following vignette, drawn from the work of one of the authors in Saline County, Missouri, provides an illustration of the challenges and opportunities inherent in deliberative governance. We cite the Saline County study for two reasons. First, this was a lengthy and extended process, involving a diverse range of stakeholders and significant investment of public resources; it also addressed an active public dispute of significant concern to the community. Second, Saline County represents a case in which two very different approaches to deliberative governance were applied.

One approach to deliberation—advanced principally by the Kettering Foundation—relates to governance only indirectly. In this approach, deliberation is a scheduled, structured group discussion that compares different perspectives on a controversial public issue. Participants attend a public forum and agree to a prescribed set of rules to assure mutual respect and civility. The goal of this approach is not to negotiate particular policy solutions, but to help citizens consider views that differ from their own—thus preparing them to assume a more active role in democratic governance. The second approach, as proposed by Forester (1999), places deliberation directly in the public decision process. Public officials are actively engaged in public arenas with disputing parties to work out pragmatic, mutually satisfying solutions to public problems.

The Saline County Study

Saline County, Missouri, is a rural, agriculture-based community in mid-Missouri. Like many rural communities in America, it is facing land use conflicts and concerns about changes in agriculture, particularly, the industrialization of that sector. Residents are concerned about environmental issues, lack of economic opportunities, and the need for local public investments in infrastructure, education, public safety, and quality of life while avoiding high taxes.

In 1997, competing groups of county residents asked several University of Missouri faculty members to help them find solutions to the controversial issue of so-called CAFOs (confined animal feeding operations), in this case, large-scale hog farms and the odors they produce. One group contacted university scientists who could be expected to support large-scale hog operations. Another group sought experts who could "prove" that such operations caused irreparable environmental damage. Tensions between these groups escalated and, eventually, the Saline County Commission asked University of Missouri Outreach and Extension to intervene.

Ultimately, the county and the university agreed to collaborate in a community decision support project called the Saline County Study (http://saline.missouri.edu/). The project's mission was to "promote a rational, predictable and stable investment environment that identifies and protects key resources, personal rights and property rights through a process that involves and educates the citizens of Saline County."

As a first step toward achieving this mission, the County Commission appointed a citizen's advisory panel to serve as the Saline County Study steering committee. The panel comprised members from all sides of the issue, including the most vocal opponents of hog farms who wanted all new operations prohibited. From the beginning, this committee was asked to play a very active role in addressing the future of CAFOs in the county. The process, as planned, required the steering committee to work closely with university faculty to identify key issues, design and review research plans, oversee data collection, and interpret research findings. Ultimately, the committee accepted these responsibilities and embraced its work. However, it took time to achieve this outcome. Initially, suspicion, mistrust, and fear were so great that committee members placed a gag order on themselves to control public perception of the project. In response, one member of the committee (a leading representative of the antihog viewpoint) resigned. Subsequently, committee members invited him back, marking a turning point in the process, and, in 1999, that same member became chair of the steering committee.

In the second year of the project, the committee identified key tasks and assigned them to several subcommittees, including research design, modeling, and public communication. Together, the committee expanded the scope of the initial study to include land use planning, economic development, and housing issues. In consultation with university faculty, they chose a variety of techniques to engage these issues, including the use of regional economic and environmental systems modeling, a series of public meetings, and an adapted deliberative issues forum, drawing on methods developed by the Kettering Foundation (Matthews and McAfee 1999).

The steering committee later developed a strategic planning process that involves the whole community. They have charged a communications committee with informing all county residents about the issues and encouraging their involvement in the process. The steering committee has created a web site to keep citizenry informed, as well as an information leaflet and computerized slide presentation. Many of the committee members are now linked via e-mail, and, through participation in this project, learned how to use the Internet. The committee has expanded its membership to include high school students, who have been focusing on ways to increase the retention of a very important community resource, namely its youth. The county is considering such innovative alternatives as a county park system, voluntary land use restrictions, and universal fiber optics connectivity. Finally, environmentalists and hog farmers are working together to solve odor problems in a mutually acceptable way.

The Saline County study has generated a number of products and outcomes beyond those already mentioned. A geographic information system for the county was created, with several layers derived from "local knowledge" (location of hog farms, location and "value" of natural ecological sites, location of historical resources). At least four decision support tools have been developed: an economic impact model, a fiscal impact model, a land value determinant model, and a manure assimilative capacity algorithm. In addition, other tools are planned. Community residents have asked for and received various reports, demonstrations, training sessions (on Internet use, GIS, etc.), each of which has increased their decision-making capacity. Significant amounts of data, both secondary and primary, have been collected and added to the publicly available information system. A ten-year economic and demographic baseline has been produced, and profiles have been conducted for the agricultural sector and the health sector. A scenario subcommittee to develop meaningful scenarios for further study has been appointed. Finally, impact studies of the agricultural sector, the health sector, and land values have been conducted.

With the help of the university, the county developed a Land Use Public Issues Forum booklet consistent with the Kettering Foundation approach; the booklet lays out several views on rural land use and the arguments for and against each. The steering committee organized a leadership program, and in spring 2000 held five leadership programs in which peoples' preferences for land use change were elicited. In August 2000 the group compiled the results of the preference elicitations and the findings of the studies into a final report and recommendations to the County Commission.

Ultimately, the project produced mixed results. On one hand, the process allowed deeply divided community members to meet and discuss issues that were impossible to talk about previously. In the process, the dispute about CAFOs, which had precipitated the project, was largely diffused. The study informed citizens and local government officials on key environmental and economic questions related to industrial agriculture. The project produced new local knowledge related to broader economic and fiscal issues, and it fostered collective interest in long-term strategic issues, such as housing, information and communications technology, and the future of the regional economy.

On the other hand, using different—and sometimes conflicting—methods of deliberation confused participants as to the key objectives of the project. This mixed approach also prolonged public dialogue and debate on critical policy questions. Although the County Commission received recommendations from the steering committee, it ultimately chose not to adopt or apply them. In this case, extended deliberation did not lead to public action or the resolution of the specific issues facing the community.

Preliminary Lessons

Deliberative governance, then, is both descriptive of a growing set of processes that involve citizens in public issues, and a normative response to our currently depleted levels of social capital. To evaluate the benefits and costs of deliberative governance and to determine when and where it is appropriately employed, we turn to some lessons we have drawn from this still emerging practice. Many of these are still quite preliminary and require additional testing both in practice and through research.

Lesson 1: Deliberative Governance Is an Ongoing, Developmental Process

Deliberative governance should not be understood as a discrete event or a particular process or technique, but rather as a series of connected experiences evolving over time. Deliberative governance demands the commitment of more time and energy from participants, increasing the transaction costs associated with any decision, and, potentially, producing a less efficient or effective solution than might be possible through other methods. In the Saline County case, steering committee members met monthly for almost a year before their common interests and their genuine concerns could be counted on. Once they accepted responsibility for engaging their collective future, the members made decisions and took actions that were not always consistent with the interests of the county commissioners or their university partners. However, participation in the deliberative process builds social capital and makes possible decisions that are both more creative and more readily implemented. The citizens involved also came to appreciate the responsibilities and constraints faced by the elected county officials. In short, deliberative governance does not always proceed according to plan, and it emerges not out of discrete events or projects but out of long-term relationships and commitment.

Lesson 2: Deliberation Works Best When It Begins Early in the Public Decision Process

Again, in Saline County the chief conflicts over industrial agriculture and land use existed long before the county chose to admit it. By the time the government acknowledged that it was a public issue, many of the participants had little interest in achieving an equitable solution. This slow start made the project much more difficult and placed the outcomes of the project clearly in doubt. Deliberative processes are clearly more useful and better suited to the early stage of the policy or decision cycle, especially in agenda setting or in the formulation and evaluation of alternatives. That is, if the possibility of changing minds is characteristic of deliberation, it is far better to have that process occur as early as possible in the process so that changed minds can make a difference.

Lesson 3: Deliberation Requires Facilitation Skills, Management, and a Significant Investment of Public Resources

Deliberation is rarely something that just happens, particularly given the erosion of social capital in our society. Citizens come to deliberative processes with a wide variety of experiences—some perhaps inclined toward deliberation, but many not so inclined. The design of deliberative processes and the creation of settings in which deliberation can occur could prove to be an increasingly important responsibility of public administration. Similarly, for public administrators, deliberative governance requires astute listening, political reflection, and an appreciation of "apparently innocuous storytelling" (Forester 1993, 3). The vestments of professional expertise are put aside in favor of an appreciation of the collective public imagination. In the process, space opens up for individual minds to change and creative synergies to emerge (Forester 1999).

Many analysts have noted the transaction costs associated with participation in all aspects of public affairs (Couto and Guthrie 1999). Conditions of contemporary life allow fewer opportunities and less inclination to participate in deliberative processes, unless the stakes are understood to be high for the individual. Methods for lowering the transaction costs to participants in deliberative governance, without destroying the process of deliberation, are necessary for the value and viability of deliberative governance. Information technologies, including the Internet, provide new opportunities for creating virtual settings in which deliberative processes can occur (Clift 2002; Fountain 2000; Kamarck and Nye 2000; Levine 2001; Toregas 2001). However, the development and application of electronic media for deliberation is, so far, quite rare (OECD 2001), and it requires major investments in hardware, software, training, and support.

The Saline County project represented a public investment of over $200,000. The cost of deliberative projects will obviously vary according to interest and need. However, in a time of fiscal constraints, committing sufficient resources to adequately support deliberative processes will be increasingly difficult.

Lesson 4: The Outcome of Public Deliberation Is Always Uncertain

Despite the best of intentions and management practices, deliberative governance may lead to unexpected, poorer quality—or even ethically questionable—decisions. Deliberative governance can raise important ethical questions about who has access to deliberations and when and how access may be denied. For example, to what extent do recreational users and environmentalists who live outside a region have a right to engage in a local land use planning or strategic planning project? Deliberative governance should assist stakeholders in articulating their own interests and those of others, and it should seek to build mutual interests and "win-win" strategies. However, this outcome is by no means assured. Public policy makers, administrators and citizens involved in planning or implementing deliberative processes should acknowledge the possibilities of outcomes that are dissatisfying and anticipate the actions necessary to address those possibilities.

By opening governance to diverse stakeholders, deliberative processes can increase the transparency of public decisions, increase confidence in the decision makers, and provide new means of ensuring accountability to those most affected. However, these positive benefits can be lost if there is even remote suspicion that the deliberative process is in any way inauthentic or manipulative. Unless public officials are themselves open to learning from the deliberative process and to changing their course of action as a result, deliberative governance is likely only to increase citizens' incredulity and cynicism.

Lesson 5: Deliberation Produces Both Tangible and Intangible Benefits

As we have argued earlier, deliberative governance has the potential to positively affect social capital, that is, the wide variety of benefits that emerge from the trust, reciprocity, information sharing, and cooperation involved in collective endeavors. In a recent metanalysis of dozens of local environmental policy decisions that used public participation, Bierle (2000) found that public involvement improved citizen understanding and ownership of environmental issues. Public involvement also tended to improve the quality and effectiveness of the public decisions. Our own work with a variety of projects both in the United States and overseas demonstrates the powerful benefits to groups and communities that result from deliberative processes, including cohesion, mutual understanding, and willingness to work together to achieve collaborative outcomes.

Lesson 6: Deliberation Is Only Part of the Story

Deliberative processes should be placed in the context of a broader strategy for public involvement. A program in local public involvement could include public meetings and information exchanges, community advisory panels and task forces, collaborative research and evaluation, mediation and conflict resolution, and public referenda. A public involvement strategy would spell out local values, objectives, roles for key stakeholders, and principles to assist public administrators in deciding whether and how the different public involvement techniques should be used. The strategy would also outline the staffing, training, and other resources needed to affect this plan. Finally, the public involvement strategy would include a process for evaluation of deliberative governance and continuous quality improvement.

Few parties (individuals or groups) are well prepared to engage in deliberative governance. They typically lack the interpersonal and decision skills and/or the substantive knowledge to make good use of opportunities to participate in deliberative processes. Deliberation may best be accomplished with the neutral leadership of trained facilitators, who can establish and maintain a deliberative environment. Decision support technologies can also offer powerful facilitation tools that provide participants with relevant knowledge, new ways of thinking about their situation, and methods of reaching agreement on how to move forward. With appropriate decision support, deliberation can produce more informed decisions, a more level playing field, and increased confidence in the governance process.

Lesson 7: Practitioners and Scholars of Deliberative Governance Should Take Steps to Build a Learning Community

Deliberative governance should be regarded as experimental. Those interested in deliberative processes should seek guidance and information from others with knowledge and experience. Deliberative governance will not develop optimally in isolation, nor will it work if it is perceived as a program imposed by those in authority. One way that our understanding of deliberative governance and its implementation could progress is through informal alliances or networks that allow people to learn from each other's experience.

Despite the best efforts of scholars and practitioners to flesh out knowledge about the theory and practice of deliberative governance, our knowledge is both sketchy and preliminary. In a very real sense, we (speaking only for ourselves) have more questions than answers: What are the essential features and characteristics of deliberation and deliberative governance? How is deliberation different from other forms of citizen participation? What is its appropriate domain? What is required for authentic deliberation? How do we make participation in deliberation meaningful? Are there "cultural" or other factors that influence the feasibility of meaningful deliberation? What are the shared values and experiences that are prerequisites for deliberation? How do we give participants the skill and knowledge necessary for meaningful participation? How do we determine who has a stake in deliberation and ensure that all relevant stakeholders have meaningful opportunities for authentic deliberation? How does deliberative governance change our conception of the citizen?

Directions for Further Research

Clearly, much more formal research is needed on deliberative governance. Most of the published literature on the topic is theoretical or consists of reports on the results of a case study. This literature can inform important empirical analyses of the causes and effects of local deliberative processes. These studies then could be used to build theory and to assist in deciding when and how deliberative techniques should be used. This research also could examine how many communities are using deliberative processes and where these communities are located. In addition, research is needed on who plays what roles in local deliberative governance. (For example, what do local public administrators do? Do they receive assistance from regional, state, or federal government agencies? How are universities and funding sponsors involved? What can be learned from deliberative governance projects outside the United States?) Finally, efforts should be made to capture the learning that occurs during deliberations.

Drawing on the organizational learning and organizational memory literature (Argyris and Schon 1990; Scott, Johnson and Mundell 2000), we believe that the observations, experiences, and insights of deliberators involved in one project might be useful to participants in other projects as well. Public administrators could use a variety of technologies to design and implement community memory systems that could then be used to enhance the quality of deliberative processes and, potentially, reduce the time required for participants to work through the issues.

Conclusion

If implemented carefully, deliberative governance can generate a variety of tangible public goods (i.e., social capital, community learning, more informed public decisions, improved policy outcomes, broader and deeper ownership of public issues, civil society, enhanced democracy, among others). At the same time, deliberation will add to the cost of governance. It will take more time, more professional staffing, and higher transaction and opportunity costs. Not all public issues are amenable to deliberative processes. In some cases, deliberative processes will, despite best intentions and careful facilitation, lead to outcomes that are frustrating for many involved. For example, deliberative processes can result in impasse, communication breakdown, dispute, polarization, and dropout. They can also fail to engage the range of stakeholders needed to achieve meaningful public dialogue on issues.

Note

1. An earlier version of this chapter was prepared for the Paul Van Riper Symposium, American Society for Public Administration Annual Meeting, Phoenix, March 23, 2002. The authors wish to acknowledge the contributions of Dana Baker, Thomas Johnson, Lilliard Richardson, and Lisa Zanetti both to the earlier paper and to the overall research effort.

Chapter 3

Local Democratic Governance: Allocative, Integrative, or Deliberative?

Peter Bogason

Introduction

This chapter discusses the consequences of organizational changes for democracy in local government systems. Until 1970, the nonurban local government system in Denmark was fragmented into relatively small local governments which were to some degree dependent on third sector organizations for some services. Then, over a ten-year period radical changes were introduced: Local governments were merged, many third sector organizations were integrated into the new system of government, and a consolidated, rationalized system of bureaucratized municipalities was created. However, from 1985 onward, fragmentation again slowly set in, this time in terms of new organizational forms in local services.

Fragmentation, consolidation, and then new forms of fragmentation, how does local democracy fare under such changes? How may we understand a system which has developed into having several democratic rationales working at the same time? The concrete examples presented in this chapter come from Denmark but the trend toward more citizen involvement is found in many Western democracies.

The present result of the changes has been organizational fragmentation, but this does not necessarily mean a total lack of coherence. We shall see how these institutional changes (Bogason 2000 109-11) have created new roles and new scope for local action. We shall also see that the changes have created platforms which have induced clashes between different norms of democratic behavior. This chapter begins by describing the elements of change, and then goes on to discuss the consequences for democracy, first in individualistic terms, then from a more aggregate perspective. Finally, we shall see how the changes in institutional forms have resulted in a multifaceted system of democracy with which some actors find it difficult to cope.

Theory: Aggregation, Integration, and Deliberation

We shall begin with a theoretical discussion, for many quite familiar, of aggregative and integrative democracy. Disenchantment with the latter among Habermasian analysts has been the stimulus for an amended version, namely, deliberative democracy.

Aggregative and Integrative Perspectives

March and Olsen (1989, 117-42) discuss two ways—aggregative and integrative—of understanding democratic institutions. The former is based on liberal democratic theory and the latter on (Greek or urban) republican democratic theory. These two systems of governance stress, respectively, competition between conflicting interests with the aim of creating adversarial winning coalitions and the integration of interests into a common good or purpose based on the notion of community.

The *aggregative* perspective, in its modern version, is based on the enlightenment revolutions of the late eighteenth century in the United States and France, which inspired most Western democracies as they unfolded during the nineteenth and twentieth centuries, building up contractual relations between political actors. The aggregative perspective commences with the individual, giving him or her certain rights that protect him or her from undue interventions from the state, but those rights at the same time make it possible for him or her to have a say in how the state rules society. Participation in public affairs is mainly linked to material interests and mostly occurs ad hoc; political parties and interest organizations function as watch dogs for those interests, relieving the individual from the arduous task of continuously pursuing political goals. The political leadership is seen as an intermediary between competing material interests; however, they are restricted to decide only what is supported by a majority of the political actors. Institutions and procedures are organized so that they lead actors to perform according to their preferences, under the assumption that any action is countered by the action of others, thus creating a continuous process of weighing and counterweighing interests. Participation in political life is, therefore, partial, and linked to an active, and mostly personal, material interest in the allocation of goods and values; when the issue has been settled, one withdraws from the scene.

The *integrative* perspective is rooted in a (Greek) republican or communal understanding of the world, emphasizing the need for bonds between the members of the institution to secure supraindividual goals of survival, and the obligation for the participants actively to reinforce those bonds by participation in political life. So we start out with the collectivity, and individual action is judged on the basis of its contribution to the common good. In return, minorities have guarantees against systematic defeat by a majority. Politics in such a setting to a large extent deals with establishing and confirming the purposes of the collectivity and maintaining the support of members by securing their trust in the common good. Officials act on the basis of an ethic that goes beyond the individual, for example, by professional norms or organizational goals and procedures, as in Weber's conception of bureaucracy. Since the overarching issue is the persistence of the community, participation in political life is linked to continued membership of a deliberating community and participants are expected to voice their opinions on issues beyond their personal material interests. Important elements of these two understandings are summarized in figure 3.1.

Figure 3.1

	Aggregative Institution	Integrative Institution
The people:	cluster of individuals	a group
Will of the people:	bargained	deliberated
Base of order:	exchange	reason
Change:	instantaneous	adaptation
Leadership:	brokerage	trusteeship
Majority rule:	dominant	curbed by norms
Policy outcome:	allocation of resources	shared purpose and trust
Loyalty of agents:	incentive compatibility	professional integrity

Source: March and Olsen (1989, 118-19).

The democratic standard version of the aggregative institution is the national parliamentary democracy where representatives are elected for parliamentary sessions in order to decide on matters that involve allocation of scarce resources. The development of political parties and interest organizations as important intermediaries in such a system is well known by most readers and thus there is no need to go into detail here. The idea is that once representatives are elected, citizens need not continually worry about their interests as these are taken care of by the representatives. However, some activity by the electorate is possible and desired, for example via expressions of demands, the mass media and various organizations, plus personal contacts, if necessary, in constituency meetings. Too much activity on the part of the electorate may destabilize the functioning of the system because it becomes overloaded by communication. Elaborate discussions are to be held between representatives, not between representatives and the electorate. The voters are supposed to wait with their final judgment until next Election Day—when inattentive representatives are not reelected. There are instruments of communication besides the vote: mass media are supposed to serve as channels for the public at large and, in addition, the editorials of daily papers see to it that political actions are commented upon. Nevertheless, if the holders of parliamentary seats choose, they can stay in power for a relatively long period of time without really incorporating new points of view from the electorate. So, if a new majority takes over after an election, one must expect rapid changes in order to accommodate these alternative points of view.

The traditional, democratic, version of the integrative model is the Greek republic where citizens are vested, more or less, in turn, with public powers as trustees on behalf of the body of citizens. Carrying out these powers, however, presupposes that those who are affected by proposals for public action are invited to comment on and thus influence matters which concern them. At the same time, however, matters concerning an overarching good must also be furthered. The role of the trustees, then, is to secure continued deliberation between interests and thereby, step-by-step, help advancement toward collective action and understanding. In the aggregative system, changes may come swiftly with a new majority; in the integrative institution there will be fewer dramatic and instantaneous transformations. In small systems, members will be involved as often as possible; in larger systems, one must expect frequent checks of the citizens' sentiments, but, in addition, norms for political action are continuously linked to rationales that go beyond the party political ideologies. Thus professional norms may become important as carriers of public action over time, serving as determinants of what makes sense and what constitutes proper reason for intervention (or inactivity, for that matter).

The Deliberative Perspective

A number of theorists have developed a third model of democratic participation, inspired by Habermas's discourse theory. This is a so-called deliberative model representing a compromise between the aggregative and integrative models (Habermas 1996). It derives most of its thrust from the integrative or republican model, but, nonetheless, Habermas is very skeptical about it, and he fears that the integrationist stance can develop into a communitarian model where there is little room for tolerance towards people whose opinions diverge, and therefore it may turn into a somewhat authoritarian version of democracy.

In terms of the discussion above, the republican virtues of deliberation, processes of reasoning, and adaptive change are upheld. The people are not, however, seen as one group, and it follows that leadership, norms, trust, and professional integrity are understood in a somewhat more diversified manner than among (communitarian) republicans. Discourse theory underscores the need for a common understanding of procedure rather than of common values. Such a procedure also makes it possible to acknowledge internal differences of opinion and sets rules for their (temporary) solution e.g. by voting rules in cases where negotiation cannot lead to a compromise. Finally, discourse theory puts politics before morals and thus acknowledges the need for instrumental decisions in the present political realm (Eriksen 2000, 20-22).

Elements of Organizational Change

How do models of democracy fit practice? We would not expect any perfect fit. However, they can act as guidelines to lay bare the democratic consequences of local practices. So in the following pages we shall go through the most essential elements of local governmental systems and their patterns of change.

Let us briefly run through a few details of the first Danish reform. Like most North European countries, Danish local government in the 1970s went through a comprehensive series of administrative reforms which, in brief:

- merged small parishes into larger communes (i.e., municipalities)

- consolidated local governments in city areas into one commune

- consolidated various public and semi-private agencies placing social services and health care under the administration of the new enlarged commune councils

- created new budgetary and policy planning instruments

Details of the reforms are found in Bogason (1990). Danish local government is a two-tier system of communes (275) and counties (14). It is potent in that much of its revenue is based on income taxes with local rates set individually by each council, and it has considerable discretion within the limits of national legislation. Communes implement most public services but hospitals, environmental affairs, regional infrastructure, and high schools are run by the counties. Labor exchanges and law enforcement are run by the state.

The thrust of the consolidatory reforms of the 1970s was to make local governments efficient producers of welfare services, run by political parties and administered by a professional staff. Thus activities run by third sector organizations (e.g., sickness insurance and maternity assistance for young mothers) were integrated in the new administration system. To put it crudely, the reforms created strong town halls to run all the affairs of local government; cases were decided upon by a council of elected representatives drawn from the political parties. It can be said that this was the result of a modernistic approach to government, namely to centralize services in one professional organization in the locality. The creation of this local government system may be characterized as the apex of modernity (e.g., Hatch 1997, 328) within Danish government. It comprised a rationalized, centralized, formalized, and professionalized system of services with town hall servicing the locality.

Most of the reforms consolidating public services in the town hall were implemented over a brief span of years. Politicians and staff became active partners in the growing welfare state. More and more professionals were hired, creating a very efficient service organization with subsidiaries—schools, day care for children, homes for the elderly—delivering services in the localities. The service organizations were organized in a hierarchical system with town hall and its administrative subsections at the top. By 1980, the communes had gone through the necessary steps to become the local organizational centers of the welfare state. They were furnished with a bureaucratic staff capable of running a large system of public service providers in the localities, and capable of serving the politicians with analytical reports outlining alternative futures and setting up alternative long-term budgets. However, this centralized pattern of organization has gradually been changed over a period of roughly fifteen years, starting in the mid-1980s. We have seen a shift in processes away from centralized consolidation and toward decentralized organizational fragmentation, particularly in the case of local public services. Each step toward the decentralization of powers has had its own rationale instead of being implemented as part of an overarching vision, as was the case in the earlier reforms. I shall describe a series of organizational modifications which have, step by step, changed this consolidated system (Bogason 2001; see also Bogason 1996). The changes comprise—in chronological order—state grants for local experiments and demonstration projects; user boards of directors; new advisory bodies; and state mandated cooperation with third sector organizations.

Experiments and Demonstration Projects

From the mid-1980s, Danish public administration has increasingly used experiments and demonstration projects to try out new ways of delivering services in the locality as well as new ways of governing public activities. Well-known examples are the free commune experiments (also tried in the other Nordic countries), allowing communes to deviate from national laws when testing new ways of operation (Baldersheim and Ståhlberg 1994). In addition, various experiments in social service and in primary schools have been played out by the initiative of the state. Finally, the European Union (EU) has a number of funds which can be used for developing alternative ways of organizing local services.

These experiments and grants have supported local demands for diversity, and thus they have created more room for differentiation among local governments compared to past principles of control which led to, by and large, the same local services everywhere. Similarity was seen as necessary when the new, amalgamated communes of the 1970s were working toward the implementation of their new status; as time went by, stronger demands for personalized services followed, and local governments demanded more room for adaptation to particular local circumstances.

User Boards of Directors

National laws have mandated all primary public schools (in 1989) and day care organizations for children (in 1993) set up a User Board of Directors, elected by the users of the organization; consequently, such reforms may be seen as an empowerment of citizens—or rather users (Sørensen 1997). The board also includes members of the staff and representatives of the senior classes, but user representatives are in the majority. Their powers may differ from commune to commune, but mostly they include hiring and firing and the (re)allocation of budgetary items. The board cannot interfere with the pedagogic praxis of the individual teacher, but it should set up general principles for local education. The principal or his substitute acts as administrative secretary of the board, which has no further administrative resources.

Advisory Bodies

Since 1997, national laws mandate three types of advisory local bodies. The communes must establish an advisory council for the elderly, elected by the elderly of the area, to advise on the policies for the elderly in the commune. Furthermore, a commune (or several communes in unison) must appoint an advisory body on local labor market and social policy affairs to advise on the creation of jobs for the weakest members of the labor force. The appointees represent various labor market organizations and the commune(s) of the area. Finally, the commune must set up an integration council advising on the problems of integrating refugees in the area, if local citizens demand that such a body be established.

Communes are free to establish any other advisory body they wish to, and some have a fairly large number representing, for example, villages, users of particular public organizations (e.g., libraries), and so on. So there is great variance across the country regarding the organization of such advice.

Mandatory Cooperation with Third Sector Organizations

As we saw above, the local government reforms of the early 1970s nearly eliminated third sector organizations as welfare providers at the local level. In the late 1980s, some demonstration grants were used to test renewed uses of third sector organizations that deal with services typically found on the border of normal life—drug abatement, shelters for the destitute, and so forth (Flex 1993).

In addition, one particular organization, the Danish Red Cross, became widely used as a contractor in the running of refugee camps in Denmark.

A national law on public social services from 1998 mandates communes to cooperate with the third sector. The details of such cooperation are to be determined locally, so the pattern may vary among communes. Cooperation with third sector organizations in Denmark goes beyond the mandated fields defined by the law. Third sector organizations increasingly run local activities as contractors with the town hall—shelters, small cafés for people who need some personal assistance to strengthen their capabilities for (part-time) work, and so on.

The Overall Picture

The changes outlined above have altered the organizational pattern in the locality, from a centralized system of government, run from town hall, into a more fragmented locality of governance with more decisions to be taken locally, with new channels of participation for citizens in the area. One could speak of postindustrial or even postmodern trends creating possibilities for diversity and differentiation, especially in cultural terms (Hatch 1997, 229-31; Clark and Inglehart 1998); those might be analyzed from an institutionalist perspective with norms and roles at the center of the analytical interest (Bogason 2000). What happens to public participation and, hence, democracy under such institutional change? We shall discuss the consequences of organizational fragmentation for democratic participation, first from the perspective of the individual, then from a more systemic viewpoint.

Consequences of Fragmentation for Participation—the Individual Perspective

The four types of changes in the channels for democratic participation at the local level have had impacts on the form and scope of citizens' participation in public affairs, and this is reflected in the diminishing role of political parties in politics and policies at all levels. Locally, the reforms of 1970 had the effect that political parties were strengthened as platforms for local representative democracy. In the countryside, political parties existed before 1970, but often they meant less to voters than the qualities of particular individuals running for office. In the small parish communes, trust was more important than political party affiliation. Thus one could expect that anyone within the bourgeois group of parties could get votes from bourgeois voters, and correspondingly within the leftist parties. In many areas, special electoral lists across party lines were created for local elections. It would be fair to assume that such a voting pattern would benefit centrist candidates from both camps, and thus a pattern of consent-prone members of councils would be likely to emerge.

After the mergers of 1970, political parties came to dominate most of the new and larger communes. Most of the mayors were elected from political party groups, but few of the councils have one political party in the majority, so a compromise has to be reached between several parties. This pattern also encourages consensus policies.

Political parties still dominate the politics of the commune councils, but, in terms of the policy-making process, the role of the councils is undergoing change because of the new channels of influence we discussed above. Citizens no longer have to be members of parties to gain influence beyond the vote, but what does it take for people to become active through these channels? We shall take a closer look at activists, users of services, and members of third sector associations.

The Adhoc Democracy of Activists

Modernity with its need for scientific development has been part and parcel of raising the formal education of citizens to a very high level. With education follows strong individuals, knowledgeable and inquisitive, desiring experiments and changes of their world. They do not share the fear of most traditionalists that changes may hurt their interests. They have analytical skills and sophisticated knowledge about both local and global affairs.

Probably such people have always been around; what is new is that there are so many of them today because of the growth of (higher) education. These people want intelligent action, they do not accept traditional bureaucratic authority to make decisions on their behalf, and they want to be part of the action. We saw them in 1968 and its aftermath, when it exhibited a revolutionary character. Today the scope is different, the concern is at one level global (environmental concerns), but much is local, linked to everyday life. Most activists are interested in enhancing the conditions of their everyday lives—schools, day care, care for the elderly, involvement in local urban development projects, and so on, maybe as a reaction to other trends toward the uprooting or disembedding of people (Beck, Giddens and Lash 1994, 13), which many see as a consequence of late modernity.

Contrary to, for example, membership of political parties and associations, such involvement is often ad hoc and hence expected to last only until a better situation is obtained. A Danish—now internationalized—phrase is that of the "Everyday Maker," the person who is interested in local affairs, wanting to do this for the fun of it, but with an earnest purpose. They want to act together with other people and in concrete ways (Bang and Sørensen 1999). So it concerns not just maximization of individual preferences, but calculated action in cooperation with fellow souls in the locality. Dialogue and reflexivity are crucial for successful action.

Closely related is the local entrepreneur who is typically active within local projects based on various grants, often within human services (Hulgård 1995).

These actors cooperate with other people, but, compared with the everyday maker, their actions are more managerial in nature. The entrepreneurs are the ones working to secure grants from various sources; having done that they head the small organizations created by the grant. They have some specific ideas they want to try out as part of their life project. Therefore, their scope is larger than that of most actions of the Everyday Makers. They establish a formal organization and may hire people to work for them.

User Democracy

Users have been strengthened in general by an increased interest from political bodies in seeing that their constituencies are well served—but somewhat ironically, the move toward more information has been carried out by bureaucrats inspired by new public management. Service users, of course, enjoy the same rights as anyone else, so in general users have been put in a stronger position. At the organizational level, users have gained strength not only by user boards of directors running local service organizations but also through advisory bodies which have better access to the town hall.

These changes have raised concerns, especially among mayors, that the "special interests" of the locality become empowered, and logically it follows that the general voter has lost influence; the user dominates (Bogason 2001, 157). Such a statement, however, presupposes that we are speaking of a zero-sum game, and the perspective is advanced by those actors whose main concern is funds allocation in the annual budgetary process. Furthermore, they seem to forget or neglect that other social interests have always been organized to gain influence, so without user representation, these may dominate. In other words, the budgetary allocation will always be subject to various channels of influence, users and nonusers alike.

May user influence be understood as a version of a local corporatism (Villadsen 1986)? Basically, corporatism is a network of various organizational interests obtaining direct influence on political bodies by their sheer size and the degree of their skills in negotiating and exerting pressure. User democracy is rather modest in scope, and there are very few interest organizations involved. Apart from the advisory councils for the elderly, none are used as identifiers by candidates running for office.

Associational Democracy

Third sector associations are based on particular values. Many were created 150 years ago as a local, quasi-political reaction to the development of the newly established national parliament, which after a few years became dominated by the landed gentry and some bourgeois groups from the cities. The skilled workers and the farmers reacted by organizing their communities on the basis of particular interests: rights to establish labor unions and cooperative ventures of various kinds, including dairies and slaughterhouses, insurance, stores for groceries and many other activities. This was in accordance with the rise of associations in many other countries in the nineteenth century (Jansson 1988). The message to power holders in Denmark was that the localities could do without the central state, and the local effect was that civil society was strengthened, particularly in terms of meeting the adverse effects of the free market forces, unleashed by a comprehensive national deregulation by the parliament (Bogason 1992).

The present-day rationale for uses of associations by the public sector is that third sector associations will impart to the welfare solutions in the locality new values and hence widen the types of solutions offered locally. This may also be understood as a general widening of "social responsibility"; private firms are encouraged to create jobs for the less able, and third sector organizations are involved in the provision of social public services (Gundelach and Torpe 1997). They are dependent on individual preparedness to join. So more people share "the burdens" of socially responsible actions (Hirst 1994). This is close to the ideas of Tocqueville: local involvement strengthens social cohesion. The catch phrase of these years seems to be "social capital," the idea being that local involvement of citizens through third sector organizations will create among them a general understanding for the necessity of sticking together and helping out when necessary, as Robert Putnam and associates have analyzed (Putnam, Leonardi and Nanetti 1993). Such action becomes an investment and creates a social capital which may be drawn upon any time. The organizations may be seen as guarantees that involvement is maintained over time. So even though individuals may opt out, the organization will recruit new members to replace them.

Metaphors of Participation

If one takes the consequences of the changes indicated above at the individual level, one may draw some rather crude conclusions regarding what happens to a number of roles—voters, clients, actors in the third sector, and the activists. The changes are indicated by the labels or concepts increasingly used in the literature on democracy, as we shall see below.

The *traditional voter* still is present, but since voting has lost its role as virtually the sole way of voicing a political opinion, voters are increasingly becoming *spectators*, acting routinely when called for, but beyond that they mainly look for what may be of interest to them ad hoc. They rely on the traditional political parties and interest organizations to discuss the contents of local policies.

Activists are increasingly, conceptually, being "upgraded" as a sort of social capital. We may distinguish between two forms. The first are project managers, who are now being called *entrepreneurs*, comparable within the public sector to those who venture their capital in the private sector, creating a dynamic sphere. The second type comes from some of those who earlier demanded increased activity from governments. Those with a sense for compromise are now conceptualized as *everyday* makers who take an active local role within public institutions for a while and then go back to their normal chores.

Clients of public assistance have been changed into users, and as such they are treated with respect by politicians, who accept the need for user satisfaction. However, some politicians see the user representatives as threatening special interest advocates.

Members of associations are increasingly called upon to render services voluntarily for the public sector, and this group of active people is increasingly seen as a foundation for social *capital*, important for the cohesion of society.

These are some of the changes as seen from the perspective of the individual actor and groups of actors. There is a pattern of change from democratic action by individuals and political parties to action by various forms of organization; some very small (for the entrepreneurs), others more comprehensive within a particular policy field (boards of directors, third sector associations). Activism has been channeled into organized support for welfare state services. Let us shift the lenses to a bird's-eye view and see how these changes affect democracy at a more aggregate level.

Consequences of Fragmentation for Participation— The Systemic Perspective

The range of channels of democratic influence has become large if one compares the year 1970 (and even 1985) with 2001. Local democracy has expanded its mechanisms from basically one—representative government—to "many." Exactly how many depends on the perspective one wants to apply; above we saw the options from an individual perspective. We shall now turn to the "systemic view."

Diversification

The changes have diversified the foundation for democratic governance. The reforms of 1970 put representative local government in the driver's seat, and the political parties developed their local platforms for running the advanced welfare state. However, most of the channels which have materialized over a number of years do not take representative democracy based on political parties as their starting point. They have rationales which may include:

- lay "expertise": users know of the particular needs the service should fulfill

- otherness: experiments encourage alternative ways of thinking

- variance: local influence may alter the principles of the service

- social integration: political color is not decisive for the line of the service

One may understand each of the new phenomena as value premises of separate democratic institutions. The user boards of directors may be seen as a quasi-representative system, specialized for specific functions and having little party politicization. Together with the advisory councils they then border on a system of new corporatism vis-à-vis the commune councils since they represent special interests of the community. The involvement of third sector associations, and the opportunities for local entrepreneurial spirits to engage themselves in publicly financed projects, represent the same, namely, strengthening efficiency and especially effectiveness, that is, local application, of service delivery. At the same time, the associations infuse special values in their services and, hence, represent some sort of minority interests, and some of them, in addition, have their own democratic procedures.

Applicability of the Models of Aggregation, Integration, and Deliberation

The three democratic models discussed at the beginning of this chapter are each applicable to one or more of the phenomena we discussed above.

The aggregative form of democracy is present in any parliamentary model of governance, be it a national parliament or a local government council; such assemblies are based on contestations by political parties, and powers may change dramatically following the verdict by the voters on election day. It is elite oriented, many participants being spectators since not everyone can participate in politics of this kind all the time. Associations may coexist within the model, but then they are understood as phenomena taking care of activities relevant for civil society only, and, hence, outside the political sphere proper. At the individual level, some activism is desirable, but preferably in a version channeled by the political parties, not as nonorganized opposition to the (local) regime.

The integrative model is to some degree present in the user democratic systems of governance, particularly in the boards of directors elected by users of service organizations. However, associations have similar paths of participation. They all are dependent on deliberation and the absence of strong conflicts between factions trying to grasp the first available opportunity to take over control of the organization. At the individual level, the everyday makers are likely to follow the integrative tradition by quietly working for a betterment of local conditions without making much fuss about it.

The deliberative model is reflected in the patterns resulting from the interaction of the various new organizations. In the aggregative system, a bureaucratic apparatus is supposed to take care of the implementation of the policies of the body politic, and organizations are part of the hierarchical line of command. However, with the changed status of organizations, with user boards of directors, with the increased uses of third sector associations and local entrepreneurs doing things, the traditional bureaucracy may have difficulties in handling, there develops a greater need for negotiating—deliberating—conditions of local action between, for example, the town hall and new and revitalized organizations.

These ideas seem to be helpful in understanding the changes within local democracy, but discourse theory in the Habermasian version maintains a sharp distinction between the political, economic, and social spheres, or state, market and civil society. Such a distinction seems to be difficult to maintain if one looks at the peculiar mix of elements of all three spheres documented above. It is difficult to see political discourse as a very distinct activity from other discourses in the locality; on the contrary, they intermingle in new ways that, while they still require the concept of deliberation, permit us to analyze across the three spheres of state, market, and civil society.

In sum, we have elements of all three models present in the localities. None of those models adequately describes local democracy. On the one hand, this should cause concern. Our models do not apply strictly to the phenomena under study. On the other hand, we may be following a wrong track. If that is the case, we may try to understand local democracy from other perspectives than the models which tend to drive us into sharp conceptual distinctions, thereby excluding one another.

To move on, it may be helpful to start from the deliberative model of local politics. However, we should then try to break down the barriers between the state (public sector), the market, and civil society. These are difficult to maintain as separate spheres in contemporary society. So instead of taking this relatively static analytical position, we may have to understand how democracy is constructed and reconstructed, not as a process of maintaining some popular sovereignty but as processes of solving local problems requiring some type of collective activity (Bogason 2000). To do this, we may need to employ a process view, but first we have to establish a perspective to drive our questioning. That might be done from a "positive" understanding of power, such as power as a transformative capacity (Giddens 1984, 15), or from another angle which is central to democracy.

Which contemporary problems requrie concepts of democracy to be analyzed? One problem of the past was the establishment and perseverance of the nation-state based on popular support after the breakdown of the authoritarian regimes. This may still be the agenda in some parts of the world, but it certainly is not so in the Western democracies. They have developed into welfare states (with some differences in scope), so today, a major theme is the maintenance of local welfare institutions in the realization that if they break down, much of contemporary society would break down, too. At the local level, then, we must identify problematics that require collective action in some form, and ask ourselves how procedures for such action are established and maintained, how resources are allocated, and how positions are formed and filled. This is an approach within institutional analysis but without a presupposition that any particular value of (liberal) politics, local solidarity of civil society, or market forces must have precedence over the other. Precisely this question is an open one, and there is a distinct possibility that these values will be mixed.

Multifaceted View of Democracy

The discussion above has been based on an understanding of institutional change due to changes in norms and roles. New roles have been added at the local level, and the democratic norms they are based on possess a variety which goes beyond traditional representative democracy. We have then discussed the applicability of single models to democratic features of present-day society, and we found that none alone was usable. But why look for one model when the democratic norms indicate variance? Why the belief that there is one people asking for one solution to their demands for influence? Why believe that researchers may cook up the ultimate, right solution for everyone?

The questions may be seen as polemic, but they are not intended that way. The 1970s reforms of local government in Denmark were signposts of a belief that the best system of government was uniform across levels of government and regardless of particular local circumstances (Bogason 1990). The same pattern occurred in the other Scandinavian countries. All local governments were merged into systems having the same basic characteristics. It did not matter whether this was an urban or rural area, nor did size of population.

Denmark is not alone. The West European understanding of local democracy is to a large degree based on the consolidation solution; in particular, the northwestern European countries have gone through one or more rounds of mergers of local governments as responses to demands for efficient service delivery after the Second World War.

The 1990s, however, have seen some changes. In Northern Europe, subnational democratic development favors, in many countries, integrative institutions. We saw in this chapter such examples from Denmark. They are not clearcut integrative institutions involving the citizenship at large. Rather, they represent the involvement of particular groups which have a particular interest in certain public services. Special interests have a possibility to pursue those interests in relatively closed organizations, but they must also take into account the interests of the society at large.

This is where the deliberative understanding of democracy may become important as a basic ingredient. The horizon should be widened from individual participation to organizational participation. The point is to avoid creating a one-for-all model applicable to any situation. In Europe, politicians and administrators should avoid resorting to hierarchy, a solution very often resorted to during disputes. This is not to say that an authority really decides over the heads of disagreeing parties; rather, that the superior authority voices opinions which then become the solution reached by local contestants—this would be the solution the authority would reach if the case were referred to it. Local negotiations should be made in a freer spirit, if the deliberative ideal were to be reached.

Under such conditions of deliberation among many organizational actors as well as individuals, the core body of local representative democracy—the local council which exists in most Western democracies and which is elected in general elections—may find a new role. It was constructed to represent the people and to make decisions on their behalf. That role has been watered down, as we have seen above, by various interests which organize for action for rather specific purposes. However, there still is a community which is likely to demand some integrative measures instead of possibly becoming victim of adversarial interests fighting one another and creating cleavages in the community. If so, there is a role for a general council to face the challenge of integration and pursue a role of heading deliberations in the community in order to help create the desired picture of the whole in which the various parts must fit.

The task, then, is to strike a balance between various forms of democracy with differing forms of legitimation supporting them. In the Danish case, the political elite has been broadened from members of the commune council to members or governors of many more local organizations. They demand room for influence. The condition may be close to that analyzed by Eva Etzioni-Halevy, who speaks of elites and subelites; the subelites occupy the "middle rank of power structures" (Etzioni-Halevy 1993, 95), which in our terminology may apply to members of user boards of directors, local grant holders, members of advisory bodies, and the like.

Their capacity for influence is based on resources such as money, staff, and various symbols. The degree to which they control such resources alone delineate their degree of autonomy. In the cases we have discussed, the autonomy of the traditional politicians seems to have been reduced because, increasingly, control over resources is shared in a complex interorganizational pattern of interaction with new power holders in the localities. So actors from a commune council are required to abandon the role of the not so distant past—in which they increasingly came to act like the bureaucratic controller—and to adopt a role of an intermediary with a special responsibility for the aggregate community.

Such actors are required to act with tact and a certain sense of diplomacy, creating relations to ease communication between many organizations and interests (Bogason 1998). Actors are certainly not invited to proceed on the basis of feelings of superiority or attitudes of higher legitimacy. They have to coordinate the elements of the increasingly fragmented organizational system of the local welfare state. That may be quite time consuming, but it seems necessary if decisions are to be made. It also requires actors to actually visit the local organizations and get some hands-on experience with what goes on there. Insofar as a generation of local politicians has been raised to take upon themselves the general role of running their organization by policy principles and budgets—and this has been the general message at least in the Scandinavian countries—the challenges mentioned above require them to reassess their options and roles.

Chapter 4

Making Local Democracy Work: Neighborhood-Oriented Reform in Los Angeles and the Dutch Randstad

Frank Hendriks and Juliet Musso[1]

This chapter compares efforts toward neighborhood-based governance reform in two urban fields, the Dutch Randstad and the city of Los Angeles. Los Angeles and the Randstad are major metropolitan areas trying to deal with the challenges of a dynamic, diversifying environment. Both urban areas are subject to "glocalization"—the parallel occurrence of globalization and localization (Tomlinson 1999). Both are "global city regions," strongly influenced by international networks and developments (Scott 2001). At the same time, both urban areas are also witnessing patterns of institutional "localization," albeit in different ways. In Los Angeles, the administrative process is brought "down to earth" through the development of Neighborhood Councils. In the Randstad, the interaction with local milieux in neighborhoods is primarily sought through informal neighborhood-oriented reform. This chapter presents a comparative analysis of the varying patterns of institutional change, the democratic ideals inspiring the patterns of change, and the change agents driving the efforts at institutional reform.

We focus on institutional reform at the neighborhood level in Los Angeles and the Randstad: reform of the political institutions, both formal and informal, influencing neighborhood governance in the two urban areas. A political institution can be viewed as "an authoritative interaction network linked to a policy problem" (Bogason, 2000). In this case, the underlying problem or challenge is the management of neighborhood transformation. We are interested in the attempts to change the authoritative, neighborhood-focused, interaction networks. In general, we seek to answer the following questions:

- How does neighborhood-oriented reform take effect in the urban regions of Los Angeles and the Randstad? What are the common patterns and trends? Which differences come to the fore?

- Who are the change agents driving the attempts at neighborhood-oriented reform? Who are the "prime movers"?

- What are the democratic ideals driving the attempts at neighborhood-oriented reform? What kind of democratic logic is being pursued in the two regions?

Searching for answers to these questions is important and relevant for various reasons, both empirically and theoretically. Empirically, neighborhood-oriented reform is a trend observable in many city regions in the industrialized West. As major urban regions, Los Angeles and the Randstad deserve attention in their own right, but also comparatively as distinct—and presumably alternative—models of urban development and transformation. Theoretically, institutional change is a special case—the exception to the "rule" of institutional persistence and stability. The factors and the actors driving institutional change in the real world of urban governance are worth examining. The democratic logic behind neighborhood-oriented reform—and the alleged connection with "bottom-up" theories of democracy—is of special interest.

The first question listed above will be taken up primarily in the first section of this chapter. This section presents an empirical comparison of neighborhood-oriented reform in Los Angeles and the Randstad. Change agents, central to the second question, will be introduced in the first section, more or less in order of appearance. In the second section, the change agents will be dealt with more analytically, distinguishing three types of actors: politicians, professionals, and citizens (see figure 4.1). The same procedure applies to the democratic ideals central to question 3. They are part of the story line in the first two sections. The final section deals with them more analytically, distinguishing between different "democratic languages"—protective versus developmental—and different democratic models—radical, consensus, pendulum, and plebiscitary democracy (see figure 4.2). The three questions thus run across the various sections, with the analytic emphasis shifting sequentially from the first question to the second and the third. The final section presents conclusions.

Neighborhood Governance Reform in Los Angeles and the Randstad

Los Angeles and the Randstad in Perspective

Los Angeles and the Randstad are interesting cases for comparative analysis as they present an intriguing mixture of differences and similarities. Los Angeles is the quintessential American "edge metropolis," often characterized by its Northern California detractors as "sixty suburbs in search of a city," and portrayed in the film *Blade Runner*, as an urban dystopia, a "starkly divided, permanently depressed city wilting under a steady drizzle of acid rain" (Siegel 1997, 118; Garreau 1992). The city spans an area of over 466 square miles and contains a 2000 population of over 3.7 million. Not unlike Los Angeles, the Randstad is a large, pluriform, and "polycentric" urban field, connecting different edge cities (actually: the direct translation of the Dutch word "Randstad" is "edge city"). Amsterdam, Rotterdam, The Hague, and Utrecht—the "big four," at least in Dutch proportions—are the major centers of the Randstad-Holland. The combined agglomerations around these four cities comprise 3.9 million inhabitants, not far from Los Angeles' 3.7 million inhabitants.

Architectural Design Profile wrote in 1994: "Perhaps the best developed examples of the city as 'field' are the Randstad Holland and Los Angeles." They are both polycentric fields. They are both institutionally fragmented fields, but the type of fragmentation seems to differ tremendously. In Los Angeles, three factors characterize local governance: (1) intense fragmentation of local institutions; (2) the challenges of extreme population diversity and an "hourglass" economy, resulting in large part from rapid immigration over the past two decades; and (3) a turbulent institutional environment, including such reforms as term limits and city charter reform, and proposed secessions from the city of Los Angeles. The fragmented institutional structure in Los Angeles encourages exit over voice and loyalty, in some respects epitomizing the metropolitan area as a market place where people vote with their feet for the package of amenities most to their liking (Tiebout 1956; Ostrom 1991).

The "meshes" of the institutional net appear to be tighter in the Randstad: the governance framework is more "fine-grained," with much stronger institutions of comprehensive, territorial government. The institutional and cultural context encourages voice and loyalty, rather than exit. Where L.A. discusses secession, the Randstad discusses fusion and amalgamation in keeping with a strong (comprehensive) planning tradition that is focused on one particular part of the country: the most densely populated Randstad-region, which is also physically the most challenged (historically below sea level!). In contrast, the Los Angeles region is characterized by a laissez-faire approach to development, where white flight and the search for affordable homes has caused the city to "sprawl" from one valley to the next. As we will see, these differences in govemance and political culture are reflected in the approaches to neighborhood reform.

Neighborhood-Oriented Reform in the Randstad

In the Netherlands, attention to the neighborhood as a framework for democratic renewal has been developing in waves, with alternating periods of high tide and low tide. De Boer (2001) distinguishes, in the postwar era, three periods of high tide: (1) the early postwar period, when the neighborhood was propagated as an alternative (geographic) frame of reference for a society divided in (subcultural) pillars; (2) the 1970s, when neighborhood-based project groups were dealing with urban renewal in decaying neighborhoods, and when, more or less in the slipstream of this development, democratically elected area councils were developed in the neighborhoods of Amsterdam and Rotterdam; and (3) the 1990s, when the neighborhood was put on the forefront of democratic renewal more than ever.

In this chapter we will focus on the latter period, which extends to the early years of the new century. "We are all neighborhood workers now"—"peak hour in the neighborhood"—"neighborhood fixation": phrases like these, picked-up in present-day discourse on democratic renewal, signal the rediscovered importance of the neighborhood as a framework for governance in the Netherlands in general and the Randstad in particular (De Boer and Duyvendak 1999).

Recent attempts to "make democracy work" at the neighborhood-level in the Netherlands are covered under the headings of *Wijkaanpak* (neighborhood reform) and *Wijkgericht werken* (neighborhood-oriented governance). In this chapter, we use the contraction "neighborhood-oriented reform" as a container-concept covering various attempts at developing useful and meaningful institutions at the level of the Dutch neighborhood. In neighborhood-oriented reform Dutch-style, structure follows strategy. Neighborhood-oriented projects and programs ("strategy") form the experimentation ground for a different model of governance ("structure"): a model of governance closer to people's homes and demands, a model of governance inspired by a demand-orientation and a situational logic. In Randstad cities like Amsterdam, Rotterdam, The Hague, and Utrecht, there are high expectations in terms of democratic renewal and institutional innovation. Neighborhood-oriented reform is seen as a way to revitalize local democracy, a way to reorient public administration, and a way to produce policies and programs that are more responsive to diverse local needs and preferences.

Structure follows strategy, but not in the traditional sense of developing new formal structures of government at the neighborhood level. Neighborhood-oriented reform in the Dutch Randstad illustrates a trend from formal institutions to informal institutions, from fixed organizations to fluid networks, from "government" to "governance." Formal structures for neighborhood-government—

"area councils" (*deelgemeenten*)—were developed in Amsterdam and Rotterdam in the 1970s and 1980s, but since the early 1990s the byword has been "No New Formal Structures!" Nowadays, this sentiment is broadly supported. Network structures, more informal and fluid, are broadly sought, even in Amsterdam and Rotterdam.

The fact that Amsterdam and Rotterdam have developed formal neighborhood-structures in an earlier stage makes them a little different from cities like Utrecht and The Hague that have not developed such formal structures. The four Randstad cities thus represent two variants (1) the Amsterdam/Rotterdam variant; (2) the Utrecht/The Hague variant. These are, however, variants on the same theme. In each variant, a trend from "neighborhood government" to "neighborhood governance," from fixed organizations to fluid networks, can be discerned.

For Example: Rotterdam

The city of Rotterdam illustrates the first variant of neighborhood-oriented reform in the Dutch Randstad, a variant that can be found also in the city of Amsterdam. The major difference between this variant and the variant found in cities like Utrecht and The Hague is the existence of directly elected "area councils" at the neighborhood level. Both Rotterdam and Amsterdam have about fourteen area councils that cover the entire municipal territory. The area councils are part and parcel of city government. They are, literally, "submunicipalities" (miniature municipalities) with political and administrative institutions (a "submunicipal council" and an "executive board") that resemble the institutions of their municipal umbrellas (the cities of Amsterdam and Rotterdam).

The submunicipalities are institutional "copies" of municipalities at the neighborhood-level. They play a role in submunicipal service delivery, and they advice city government regarding issues that (also) affect their neighborhood. They are generally perceived as a mixed blessing. The belated establishment of an area council for Amsterdam city center in 2001 (Amsterdam and Rotterdam had excluded the city centers from area council formation) met with quite some opposition, also from actors that otherwise are very much in favor of social and political innovation. When other Dutch cities invest in neighborhood-oriented reform—and almost all Dutch cities are doing that one way or the other—they stay well away from "submunicipal" constructions. "Neighborhood councils? That's the infinite sadness, isn't it," says Hein van Oorschot, mayor of Delft, in an interview with Binnenlands Bestuur (5/10/2001).

The establishment of area councils is often viewed as a somewhat old-fashioned (mono-institutional) solution for problems that are rather tackled by (multiactor) networks. The preference for fluid networks over fixed institutions is widespread, even in Amsterdam and Rotterdam, where submunicipalities are nowadays subordinated to the respective neighborhood-focused initiatives. Neighborhood-oriented networks come first; submunicipalities come second.

The submunicipality is not the framework for action; it is merely part of the framework.

For example the framework of Rotterdam's Neighborhood Initiative (its Wijkaanpak) is a complex patchwork of institutions developed at different points in time. While the submunicipality is one of these institutions, it is not the prime actor; in line with Dutch administrative tradition, no single actor is dominant. An official called the "area manager" (*Gebiedscoordinator*) is expected to be the spider in the web that deals with public problems in his/her particular area. As primus inter pares, the area manager is responsible for the integration of the three relevant policy sectors or "pillars"—the "social pillar," the "economic pillar," and the "physical pillar" as they are called—into a variegated and effective Neighborhood Inititiative.

In any particular area, the Neighborhood Initiative is not only meant to integrate different sectors of public policy making but also different layers of decision making. In the current jargon: it is a matter of "horizontal coordination" and "vertical coordination." The latter is reflected in the steering committees that formally drive the Neighborhood Initiatives. In any given area these steering committees are a tandem of submunicipality (represented by the chairman) and central city (represented by an alderman). The area manager runs the secretariat of the steering committee, and is expected to be the "motor" powering the tandem with ideas and proposals coming from different directions.

The ambitions of the Neighborhood Initiative in Rotterdam can be subdivided into external ("societal") ambitions and internal ("organizational") ambitions. Bout-Saari and Groenewold (2001) describe the internal ambitions as follows: changing organizational structures and practices into a more "client-focused" and "demand-driven" type of cooperation. The organization should think and work "from the outside-in" rather than "from the inside-out." It is all about putting the client, the citizen, first, and about making the municipal supply side responsive to the demand side of local governance. The aim is organizational innovation, but one of the side effects of trying to connect everything to everything is certainly also organizational complication.

The external ambitions are described as "the integrative realization of structural improvements in the social, economic and physical domain in the various area's of the city" (Bout-Saari and Groenenwold 2001). The ultimate aim is social betterment. The social pillar is seen as the central pillar in an integrative multipillar approach. The key concept in Rotterdam's model for social betterment at the neighborhood level is called "Social Investing" (*sociaal investeren*), geared at stimulating the development of social capital. Neighborhood policy should be redressed "from steering to supporting" (that is, supporting the development of social and related types of capital needed to deal with problems and challenges in the lives of peoples in the neighborhoods).

A municipal brochure about Rotterdam's Neighborhood Initiative suggests that administrative priorities are as follows: "Supporting the initiatives of (groups) of citizens comes first. Formulating and implementing plans ourselves comes second." Most actors involved would support this order, at least in theory, but the actual practice of the Neighborhood Initiative is still a bit different (Hendriks and Tops 2001a). It is more the other way around: the networks of professionals involved in the Neighborhood Initiative formulate and implement plans. Citizens and groups of citizens are taken into consideration, and at certain points in time they are called in to respond to plans and proposals. It is interactive policy making, but of a particular sort, following from a long-standing Dutch administrative tradition. Most of the interacting is done by pluriform networks of professionals. Individual citizens are selectively called into the process, in some sense even committed, but this is not necessarily the same as being "involved" in the broader sense of the word.[2]

For Example: The Hague

The Hague illustrates the second variant of neighborhood-oriented reform in the Dutch Randstad, a variant that can also be found in Utrecht, the other member of the "Big Four." The second variant has much in common with the first variant, apart from the existence of area councils. The cities of The Hague and Utrecht are also subdivided into different parts—Utrecht into ten neighborhoods (*wijken*) and The Hague into seven wards (*stadsdelen*)—but these subdivisions do not have a formal political complement, such as the subdivisions in Rotterdam and Amsterdam. To compensate for the lack of political representation at the neighborhood level, the city councils of The Hague and Utrecht work with "area committees" (in addition to the functional committees that traditionally exist as subdivisions of the city council).[3]

Neighborhood-oriented reform in The Hague and Utrecht is inspired by the same "integrative" ambitions as neighborhood-oriented reform in Rotterdam and Amsterdam. Again it is all about the integration of the social, the economic, and the physical pillars of policy making at the neighborhood level. This ambition is central to the Main Cities Policy (*grotestedenbeleid*) advocated and subsidized by the national government. Combined with a reliance on multi-actor networks, the integrative ambition inspires institutional innovation throughout the urban field of the Netherlands. As a rule, integrative policy making for the neighborhood is made a matter of networks, not of single neighborhood-based institutions.

The example of Rotterdam highlighted the network-managing role of the area managers. A similar role is played by the area managers (*wijkmanagers*) in Utrecht—who head the ten administrative area's in this city—and by the area managers (*stadsdeelcoordinatoren*) in The Hague—who head the seven administrative areas in this city. It is the responsibility of these functionaries to bring together all the actors needed for the integration of physical, economic, and social policies geared at their particular neighborhoods. In Utrecht and The Hague, the area manager chairs an "area management team" (*wijkmanagementteam*), meant to provide a symbolic "round table" where professionals coming from different fields and disciplines can meet to discuss and tackle the problems of the area at hand. The various administrative departments are represented by account managers. Other professionals represent organizations such as housing corporations, welfare organizations, community work agencies, and community policing groups.

Taking a closer look at the ambitions of neighborhood-oriented reform in The Hague, we find two sets of ambitions—internal ("organizational") ambitions and external ("societal") ambitions—that resemble the two sets of ambitions found in the example of Rotterdam. Table 4.1 summarizes a detailed analysis of the ambitions of neighborhood-oriented reform in The Hague, unravelling different layers within both sets of ambitions (Hendriks and Tops 2001b).

Table 4.1. Ambitions of Neighborhood-Oriented Reform in The Hague

1) Neighborhood-Oriented Reform as "Solving" Organizational Problems

1a) improving the connection between the "hard" (economic/physical) sectors and the "soft" (social) sectors of municipal government through an integrated "de-sectoralized approach"

1b) improving the connection between the central and decentralized segments of municipal government through integrated "complementary administration"

1c) improving the connection between short-term projects and long-term policy objectives through an integrated "programmatic approach"

2) Neighborhood-Oriented Reform as "Solving" Societal Problems

2a) improving the service to the citizen—with all his interrelated "hard" (materialist) and "soft" (non-materialist) needs—through an integrated "demand-driven approach"

2b) improving citizen involvement in the public domain—in the "hard" (physical) sense as well as in the " soft" (political) sense—through comprehensive investment in "social integration and participation" at the neighborhood level;

2c) strengthening the urban fabric—both "soft" and "hard"—through "comprehensive investment" in social, economic, and physical infrastructure at the neighborhood level.

Source: Hendriks and Tops (2001b).

The administrative jargon is tenacious but also telling. The abundant use of adjectives such as "integrated," "integral," and "comprehensive" is characteristic of neighborhood-oriented reform in not only The Hague but in other Dutch cities as well. The copious use of such adjectives is functional in suggesting a bridge or a connection between disparate values and concerns. Administrative reformers in The Hague try to capture these disparate values under the dichotomous shorthand of "soft" and "hard." Neighborhood-oriented reform in The Hague is even labeled "The Operation Hard/Soft" (*de operatie hard/zacht*).

The hard/soft dichotomy reminds us of the three "pillars" distinguished in the national "Big Cities Policy" (*Grotestedenbeleid*): "hard" are all those values and concerns connected to the economic pillar and the physical pillar; "soft" are all those values and concerns connected to the social pillar. Administrative reform in The Hague is meant to bring a happier marriage of the "hard" and the "soft" at the neighborhood level. This requires better coordination of long-term and short-term policies, and of central and decentralized administration in the city.

As in Rotterdam, comprehensive investment in social, economic and physical infrastructure is assumed to be in the citizen's broadly defined interest. Administrative networks are moving closer to (groups of) citizens in their neighborhoods, attempting to produce more responsive, demand-driven urban policies. Special attention to social integration and participation is expected to further social capital and citizen involvement in the neighborhood. But again, as in Rotterdam, there is still a difference between the theory and the practice of neighborhood-oriented reform in The Hague. Empirical studies of this practice reveal that neighborhood-focused policies in The Hague are still to a large extent "bureaucracy-driven" and "supply-driven," albeit in a more or less "enlightened" way (Hendriks and Tops 2001b). Bureaucracy is getting closer to the neighborhoods, and is organizing round tables in which many different actors participate, but these actors are not very often ordinary, individual citizens. They are usually professionals and representatives of associations and organizations. These actors do a lot of reaching out, they do try to consult and commit as much as they can, but this is done on their own terms and initiative.

The Neighborhood Council Movement in Los Angeles

The city of Los Angeles is located within the fragmented governance structure of the Southern California metropolitan area. The region epitomizes the political and economic forces that have shaped many southwest American cities in the latter twentieth century: fragmentation and decentralization of governance, integration into the competitive global service/information economy, and rapid population growth and racial/cultural diversification. The metropolitan area spans five counties, with a complicated system of service provision by its counties, some 170 cities and 1,100 special districts, institutional fragmentation that perhaps encourages "exit" (migration between cities) over "voice and loyalty," (Hirschman 1972). In the past several decades the region experienced rapid population growth and tremendous racial and cultural diversification as a result of the region's status as an immigration hub. The region has an "hourglass" economy with most job growth at the high or low ends of the wage scale, and it has historically accommodated population growth by sprawling its predominately white middle class from one valley to the next, leaving the region's poorer and more racially diverse communities concentrated in the urban core (Siegel 1997, 153; Southern California Studies Center 2001).

As a consequence of these forces, the racial and cultural diversity of the city of Los Angeles has increased dramatically. Between 1960 and 1990, the foreignborn population of the city of Los Angeles grew from 9 percent to 40 percent (Siegel 1997, 145). Whereas as late as 1960, Los Angeles had much the character of a homogeneous Midwestern city, with the "largest percentage of native-born white Protestants of any major city in the United States" (Siegel 1997, 133), the city now contains a minority of non-Hispanic white residents, and a population that is 40 percent foreign born.[4] In the United States historically, the needs and interests of immigrant communities have been accommodated by the ward politics of political machines, which exchanged economic resources (jobs, aid) for political support. This has not been the case in Los Angeles, which is governed by a decentralized progressive political structure created by its 1925 charter.[5]

From Secession to Neighborhood-Council Formation

The progressive governance structures designed to serve the homogeneous populations and business interests of the early twentieth century are strained by the diversity of postmodern Los Angeles. Siegel (1997) characterizes Los Angeles as a "centrifugal city," buffeted by racial conflict and a crisis of governance expressed most particularly with regard to police/community relations, and a secession movement fuelled by white flight and dissatisfaction with city land use policies. In 1993, dissatisfaction with the city council contributed to the passage of a ballot initiative limiting the tenure of the mayor and city council to two four-year terms. Term limits have made political regimes much less stable; in 2001, the city replaced its mayor, along with more than half the city council. The other source of instability is the threat of municipal secession; three areas of the city, collectively containing more than one-half of its population, are threatening to detach and become independent cities. Hogan-Esche (2001) shows that while the secession movement is often understood to be an institutional manifestation of "white flight," it is more accurately understood as a reaction of homeowners and local businesses against land use and development policies on the part of the Los Angeles downtown political regime.

Unlike the Randstad, Los Angeles does not have a long history of neighborhood-based reform, although the issue has been debated and resisted by city policymakers for two decades. The creation of neighborhood councils became the mobilizing issue in a two-year process of charter reform catalyzed by the threat of secession. On June 8, 1999, voters in the city of Los Angeles approved a charter reform measure that did rationalize and streamline the 1925 charter, but did not substantially alter the dispersion of formal authority within the city's governance structure. The most popular provision of the reform, credited with its success at the polls, was a proposal to create a citywide system of neighborhood councils.

The neighborhood council concept only became successful when proponents decided to wrap it into charter reform, rather than enacting it by ordinance. The charter left vague the process for forming councils, the governance structure and territorial definition of the councils, mechanisms for their involvement in city governance, and the resources to be provided to them. The inclusion of neighborhood councils in charter reform, and the vagueness of the provision creating them, resulted in part from political expedience, in part an acknowledgment that no single model of neighborhood council would likely "fit" the diverse circumstances of all Los Angeles communities (Musso 1999).

Neighborhood councils are required to represent all stakeholders, who are defined as those who live, work, or own property in a community. While the councils have no formal powers, such as power over land use or budget allocations, the charter does contain several provisions expected to improve the influence of neighborhoods in the city policy making process, primarily through improved communication channels. For example, there is a requirement that the city implement an "early warning" system to provide advance notification of any city council actions that affect a neighborhood. In addition, the charter allows neighborhood councils to submit budget proposals, which must be communicated to the city council. The charter also provides for the neighborhood councils to meet together periodically as a "Congress of Neighborhoods" to debate issues of citywide significance.

The charter authorized a Department of Neighborhood Empowerment (DONE), and set into place a two-year process of implementing a plan for the system of neighborhood councils. The general model is one by which community stakeholders will "self-organize" into neighborhood councils across the city. This self-organization requires collective activity on the part of community members to establish boundaries, design a governance structure, create bylaws, and establish organizing and outreach procedures designed to attain inclusion or representation of all community stakeholders in the neighborhood council. Neighborhood councils must represent areas with at least 20,000 residents. With a few exceptions, their boundaries may not overlap with one another. As of March 2003, more than a hundred groups were organizing throughout the city, sixty seven neighborhood councils had been approved, and forty five had elected governing boards.

The existence of citywide mobilization of neighborhood stakeholders in the organizing process appears to be evidence of a nascent social movement in the face of grave obstacles that include lack of a unified political structure, limited resources, a challenging socioeconomic environment, and institutional obstacles. Perhaps the ambiguity of the charter and the apparent apathy and lack of direction on the part of city officials provided a stimulating opportunity for self-determination that motivated citizens to take reform into their own hands. While this neighborhood mobilization is encouraging, it has also drawn criticism on the grounds that it is largely a middle-class movement that does not represent historically disenfranchised residents such as people of color, recent immigrants, and the poor.

The Shaping of Neighborhood Councils

Given that neighborhood councils are not fully implemented at present, it may be premature to make definitive comparisons with neighborhood governance in the Netherlands. However, some initial observations can be developed based on the requirements embodied in the city charter and implementing ordinances, and in the shape of neighborhood councils that are under development. Clearly neighborhood councils do not resemble the submunicipalities created in the first wave of neighborhood reform in the Randstad. While Los Angeles neighborhood councils are formal institutions, and have a territorial rather than situational logic, they do not have any legal authority, and are not constitutionally representative bodies of government. At the same time, they are creations of government, and part of the local governance system, and as such have been found by the city attorney to be subject to state open meeting and ethics requirements.

Nor are neighborhood councils in Los Angeles functional networks like the neighborhood-oriented reform networks currently evolving in Randstad cities in the context of the Dutch Neighborhood Initiatives. The development of neighborhood councils in Los Angeles is not based in situational logic or strategically oriented toward instrumental goals. Whereas the Randstad reforms entail multiactor networks aiming to integrate the three "pillars" (social, economic, and physical), the Los Angeles neighborhood councils are described as structural reforms intended to connect neighborhood "stakeholders" more intimately to each other and to urban policy making in the neighborhood. Goals are not clearly articulated, and there is no agreement regarding the types of projects or programs that may be undertaken by these groups. Considering that there will likely be more than one hundred neighborhood councils, it is probable that form and function will vary considerably across the city.

Lack of specificity in the plan has supported a range of vision for the neighborhood council systems. Some view neighborhood councils as collaborative with city policymakers, implying a "co-production" model in which neighborhood councils work in partnership with the city on community improvement. A related vision articulated by some organizers stresses the civic and community nature of neighborhood councils, emphasizing self-governance and community-based problem solving. In contrast, some neighborhood council organizers appear to be working from a more overtly political or oppositional stance, stressing the importance of neighborhood councils as "lobbyists" for neighborhood interests in downtown political struggles with development and business interests. This perspective seems to acknowledge the role of neighborhoods as contested spaces in the American urban politics of growth and development (Peterson 1981; Mollenkopf 1983; Logan and Molotoch 1987). Neighborhood-based voluntary associations are an important component of city policy networks, often successfully challenging urban growth prerogatives that ignore neighborhood interests (Ferman 1996). At the same time there is a tension, as Ferman (1996) discusses, between the constructive civic role of neighborhood association and the potential for development of an "enclave consciousness" that promotes narrow parochial interests and maintains race and class divisions within the city.

The co-production vision perhaps bears the greatest similarity to the integrative nature of neighborhood reforms in the Randstad. Some supporters of neighborhood councils hope that they will become the coordinating entity for services provided by a balkanized city bureaucracy. At the neighborhood level, however, activists are much more likely to stress the political potential of neighborhood councils, and perhaps hopes that the "soft" social concerns around quality of life are not sacrificed to the "hard" interests of economic development. In other words, it would appear that rather than integrating material and social values, as is the aim of the Neighborhood Initiative in Rotterdam, the Los Angeles neighborhood councils represent an arena for articulation of neighborhood needs that historically have been ignored in the interests of business growth.

Change Agents in the Randstad and Los Angeles

In discussing change agents, a useful analytic distinction can be made between three general domains: (1) the political domain, where democratic decisionmaking is formally situated; (2) the professional domain, where administrative and technical expertise is traditionally situated; and (3) the citizen's domain, or public domain, where social wishes and expectations are articulated, and where urban government must gain legitimacy.

Figure 4.1. The Three Domains of Local Democracy

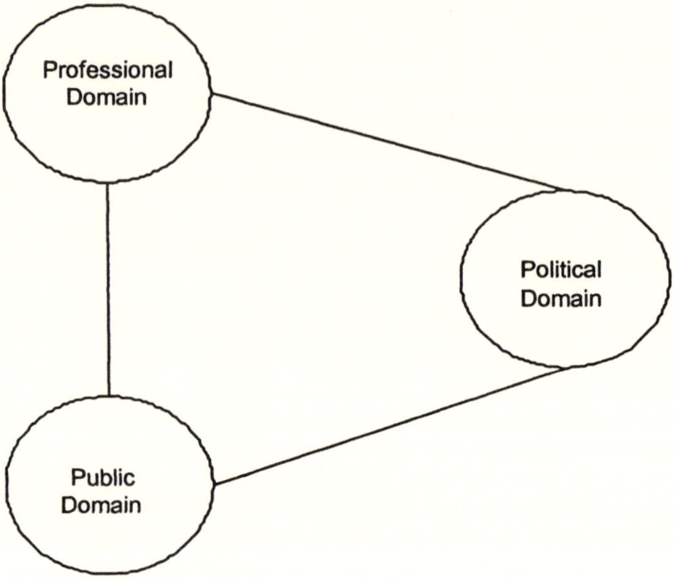

[Diagram: Three circles connected in a triangle — "Professional Domain" (top left), "Political Domain" (right), "Public Domain" (bottom left)]

Source: Hendriks and Tops (2002)

The analytic triangle (figure 4.1) can help in mapping the agents of change in Los Angeles and the Randstad. It can also facilitate the connection to theoretical discourse about institutional change, and the role of the various actors in that process. For example, Box (1998) argues that "citizen governance" requires reorientation in the traditional roles of citizens, public administrators, and political representatives. Citizens must be activists rather than watchdogs or free riders, while their representatives must "refer much policy authority to citizen bodies and [be] deeply involved in coordination and joint action" (121). For public administrators, the challenge is: how "to combine the practitioner's unavoidably subservient position in the hierarchy of public organizations with a proactive stance in relation to public policy formulation and implementation" (143). Box argues that public administrators should play a role as enablers or "helpers," assisting to create the conditions for informed citizen deliberation (146). King and Stivers (1998, 195) also argue, "Administrators and front-line workers can . . .work to change citizen perceptions by collaborating with citizens; they can, in effect, democratise public administration. Democratising public administration means creating the conditions under which citizens and public servants can join in deliberating about, deciding, and implementing the work of public agencies." Indeed, there is a call among administrative theorists for calls for ethical administrators to act as citizens in the interests of citizens (Cooper 1984; Box and Sagen 1998).

The three domains—that of the citizen, the politician and the professional—have played different roles in the evolution of community governance institutions in the Randstad and Los Angeles. The relative weight of individual citizens in the policy and reform communities that are active in developing neighborhood governance is relatively low in the case of the Randstad and relatively high in the case of Los Angeles. In contrast, the relative weight of the professional domain is relatively high in the case of the Randstad and relatively low in the case of Los Angeles. The relative position of the political domain is less clearcut and more refined, as we will elaborate below.

Comparing Change Agents

While neighborhood governance in the Randstad develops in relation to individual citizens, and is relatively responsive to citizen preferences, it is responsive in an indirect, associational way. The professional representatives of various groups and interests do the bulk of the work in the process of neighborhood governance. When they are not meeting each other at the proverbial "round tables" of neighborhood governance, these professionals spend a lot of time trying to stay in touch with societal needs and preferences. This is accomplished professionally through studies commissioned from universities, city surveys, and "user panels." Moreover, participants in neighborhood governance sit on boards of societal associations and have ongoing direct contacts "in the field." Another particularly important way in which citizen input enters the system is through interactions between neighborhood workers and citizens. Neighborhood workers are integrated into the fabric of neighborhood life, and they become advocates for the interests of citizens with whom they interact on an almost daily basis.

In terms of the political domain, while politicians have not played a tremendously prominent role in institutional change, neither can they be said to be irrelevant, as some authors in the "end of politics debate" seem to suggest is their fate. While politicians have not driven concept-development, which stems primarily from the professional domain, they nonetheless participate in particular ways. For example, aldermen and boardmembers from the district councils in Amsterdam and Rotterdam participate in neighborhood-based structures. Subcommittees of the city councils of Utrecht and The Hague are not only organized along functional lines but also along the boundaries of the various neighborhoods. In the Randstad, politicians appear to follow rather than initiate change in local institutions, change that is primarily initiated from the professional domain.

In the Randstad, citizen and societal inputs enter neighborhood institutions in a manner that is very often organized, mobilized, and channelled by professionals and public administrators, in keeping with Dutch political traditions of consociational democracy. Citizens are engaged interactively in "managing the life world at a micro level" through such processes as neighborhood inquests (*wijkschouw*), opinion panels, and neighborhood-oriented projects (Hendriks and Tops, 2002). There have also been local experiments with referenda, consumer surveys, and opinion polls, again, initiated primarily by government organizations. While this interaction approach has been lauded for its customer orientation and its unconventional approach that breathes life into policy making, it has also drawn criticism on the grounds that it is "repressively tolerant" and breeds passivity in citizens who generally follow, rather than lead, interactive practices (Hendriks and Tops, 2002).

In contrast to the "dynamic conservativism" of the Randstad, in which Dutch local bureaucrats work to stay one step ahead of other potential change agents, and citizens appear curiously absent, the design of neighborhood councils in Los Angeles could be characterized as constituting a more reactive dynamic between local activists and elected officials. The institutional reform process that has led to the creation of neighborhood councils in Los Angeles has embodied reactions and counterreactions between neighborhood activists—primarily middle-class homeowners—on the one hand, and on elected officials interested in preserving existing institutions of governance in Los Angeles. In contrast to the Randstad case, public service practitioners—city administrators and neighborhood workers—have played a relatively minor supporting role in the reform.

The neighborhood council began as a political initiative of an entrepreneurial city councilman, but it could not achieve political traction due to political resistance among members of the city council. The concept ultimately was wrapped into the broader charter reform process, which in turn had been initiated by the city council and mayor in response to a local movement toward secession of the San Fernando Valley, the largely "suburban" part of the city of Los Angeles. Hence while it would be a mistake to credit citizens with the concept of neighborhood councils, a secessionist movement on the part of valley homeowners and business interests was the catalyst behind the reform. Pressure from local activists prevented political control or cooptation on the part of the city and built momentum for reform through a noisy and often conflictual process of self-organization that helped to make the city planning effort more responsive to neighborhood preferences.

A majority of city council members opposed the new charter and neighborhood councils, while the mayor provided little financial or political support for system implementation. While infighting between mayoral appointments and the city council clearly hampered city support for implementation, it paradoxically may have created a space for neighborhood councils to develop out of the neighborhoods rather than being imposed from above in a repressive fashion. Because Los Angeles city politicians were either obstructive or passive, implementation was largely driven by local activism at the neighborhood level. It is truly remarkable that with virtually no city investment in neighborhood council organizing, there are more than one hundred neighborhood councils emerging in virtually every area of the city.

The prime movers in the reform have been middle class homeowners, neighborhood activists, and local business people. These neighborhood advocates appear to be American versions of the Danish "Everyday Maker" so vividly described by Bang and Sorenson (1999, 326): "Neither 'bowling alone' nor 'bowling together' is a feature of their day-to-day political engagement. . . . Their political engagement is directed toward concrete problem solving in everyday life more than it is related to the performance of government [per se]." In Los Angeles, Everyday Makers have formed loosely coupled policy networks to address a wide array of city policies, and they have been involved in the neighborhood council formation process from the beginning, many of them monitoring city council meetings as they began organizational efforts in their own communities.

The motivations of council organizers for involvement in neighborhood councils and their visions of the function of councils vary considerably. Some view neighborhood councils as collaborative with city policy makers, stressing what neighborhood councils can accomplish working in partnership with the city. A related vision articulated by some organizers stresses the civic and community nature of neighborhood councils, emphasizing self-governance and community-based problem solving. Others organize from an oppositional stance of anger toward what is perceived to be a distant and arrogant city policymaking structure and an unaccountable and faceless bureaucracy.

In contrast to the Randstad, Los Angeles city administrators or neighborhood workers have been less present in the reform movement. Perhaps part of the reason for this is the city's lack of a neighborhood orientation, which itself was an impetus for reform. While the implementing department did employ some neighborhood workers ("project coordinators"), during the formation process there were about seven workers for the entire city, implying that each was responsible for about one-half million city residents. To date, much of the administrative apparatus of the city has ignored the neighborhood council movement; it is unclear how neighborhood councils, once formed, will interact with the city. Most likely they will channel their activities toward city council members, planning commissioners, or the mayor rather than interacting directly with city administrators.

Citizen Governance?

In sum, neither the Randstad nor Los Angeles is fully developing the conditions of citizen governance described by Box (1998). Perhaps the Randstad is coming a bit closer, in that its public service practitioners are experimenting with different means of engaging citizens in service delivery questions at the neighborhood level. The question in the Randstad is whether this might constitute repressive tolerance—political appeasement rather than genuine dialogue—and whether citizens play the activist role contemplated by Box. In Los Angeles, there is a high degree of citizen activism evident within the reform. These active citizens are, however, a tiny minority of the city's population, which is more generally marked by high levels of disaffection and political apathy. Moreover, city representatives have generally been oriented toward preserving rather than sharing political power, and administrators have generally remained isolated from citizens and the community. The question in Los Angeles is whether neighborhood councils will be able to develop democratic legitimacy by representing a more diverse group of stakeholders. They need to transcend the "enclave consciousness" described by Ferman (1996) and become representative of the diversity of Los Angeles.

Models of Democracy and Institutional Reform

Democratic Languages

Both urban agglomerations, Los Angeles and the Dutch Randstad, illustrate the drive toward neighborhood-oriented reform in the face of urban diversification and transformation. At first sight, processes of institutional renewal seem to be inspired by, and tend toward, different models of democracy. Distinguishing protective democracy from developmental democracy (Held 1987), neighborhood-council reform in Los Angeles is heading more toward the first model of democracy, while neighborhood-oriented reform in the Randstad is heading more toward the second model. Building an "early-warning system," "challenging the growth machine," and protecting homeowner and small-business values seem to be more important to reform discourse in Los Angeles than in the Randstad. In the former, the context of reform is defined by secession threats, slow-growth sentiments, restrictions and individual protectionism. In the latter, the context of reform is defined by the long-standing quest for consolidation and fusion—"keeping things together"—and the long-standing quest for social betterment and social development—helping people in neighborhoods, especially difficult neighborhoods, to get ahead through "social investing."

But the picture is more shaded. Behind the "first language" of protectionism and individualism in Los Angeles's neighborhood council reform, there is a "second language" of co-production and communitarianism.[6] In neighborhood council reform throughout the city both languages are spoken. The neighborhood council movement displays a mixture of protective, oppositional, co-productive, and communitarian strategies, with different accents in different neighborhoods. Behind the first language of social development and social betterment in neighborhood-oriented reform in the Dutch Randstad there is also a second language, different from the one heard in Los Angeles. It is a second language of technocracy, paternalism, and repressive tolerance, supplementing the first language that suggests that neighborhood-oriented reform is driven entirely by the citizen. As said before, neighborhood-oriented reform may be quite focused on problems and needs of citizens in neighborhoods, but it is mostly the administrative professional and the associational representative who is doing the focusing, trying to solve problems "proactively," trying to stay one step ahead of discontent.

Democratic Accents

The democratic subtext of neighborhood-oriented reform in Los Angeles and the Randstad may be further appreciated in reference to basic democratic models, derived from two classic dimensions of democratic theory: the direct-indirect dimension and the majoritarian-consensual dimension:

Concerning the direct-indirect dimension, the core question is who, ultimately, makes the decisions? Are final decisions made by the members of a community themselves (the direct democracy option) or by representatives of sections of that community (the indirect democracy option)? Is it decision making "by themselves and for themselves" or is it "instead of others, on behalf of those others and for the whole"? (Dahl 1989).

Concerning the majoritarian-consensual dimension, the core question is how are decisions made? Is the process aggregative, meaning that a simple majority of 50%+1 is ultimately decisive even if relatively large minorities oppose it (the majoritarian option), or is the process integrative, meaning that efforts are made to reach a consensus that is as broad as possible (the consensual option)? Is it "winner takes all" or "accommodation and compromise"? (Lijphart, 1999)[7] The intersection of these two dimensions, which are usually viewed separately, produces the following four ideal typical democratic perspectives (Hendriks and Tops, 2002).

Figure 4.2. Democratic Perspectives and Institutions

How are public decisions made?

	Majoritarian institutions	*Consensual* institutions
Who makes decisions?		
Indirect institutions	I) Pendulum democracy	II) Consensus democracy
Direct institutions	II) Plebiscitary democracy	III) Radical democracy

Source: Hendriks and Tops (2002)

Obviously, democratic institutions are mainly indirectly democratic in large and complex urban areas like the Randstad and Los Angeles. Differences come to the fore when looking at the way in which the indirectly democratic institutions are constructed and the extent to which they are supplemented (and corrected) by directly democratic institutions.

Comparing the two urban regions, and arguing along the indirect-direct dimension, it is fair to say that directly democratic institutions are more important as a supplement (and a corrective) to indirectly democratic institutions in Los Angeles. There is clearly more direct citizen involvement in the policy and reform communities that are active in developing neighborhood governance in the California city than in the Randstad, where such communities are dominated by associational representatives and other professionals who act on behalf of (groups of) citizens.

Referring to the consensual-majoritarian dimension, consensual (or integrative) institutions are more prominent in the institutional setting of the Dutch Randstad and in neighborhood-oriented reform in the Randstad as a particular arena. The professionals and the representatives who dominate neighborhood-oriented reform in the Dutch Randstad meet each other at a multitude of interconnected "round tables," where they try to integrate various policy perspectives in a consensual way. To apply Elster's (1998) typology, the dominant coordination mechanism is (integrative) talking, not (competitive) negotiating or (aggregative) voting.

The combined tendencies toward integrative institutions and indirect institutions amount to an accent on consensus democracy, but that is not to say that neighborhood-oriented reform in the Dutch Randstad is fully confined to the "walls" of cell II in the matrix of democratic perspectives. There are also, but less prominent, hints to radical democracy (experiments with direct citizen involvement in service delivery and neighborhood management) and plebiscitary democracy (experiments with consumer surveys and with local referenda that witness a modest rise). Notions of pendulum democracy (indirect democracy through the aggregation of votes at the neighborhood level) have played a modest role during the inception of neighborhood councils in Amsterdam and Rotterdam. Nowadays, no one of influence would think of them as indirectly majoritarian "ward republics."

The echo of the "ward republic" seems to reverberate more in the policy and reform communities active in developing neighborhood councils in Los Angeles. The by-laws of some neighborhood councils show tendencies in that direction. But neighborhood council reform in Los Angeles is surely not confined to the "walls" of cell I in the matrix of democratic perspectives. There are also strong tendencies toward directly democratic institutions: plebiscitary tendencies evident in the town hall meetings organized in many parts of the city; radical tendencies evident in the action-committee model applied in quite a few neighborhoods. It is especially these tendencies toward direct democracy (direct citizen involvement unmediated by the professional domain) that are responsible for the contrast between the overall pictures of neighborhood-focused reform in Los Angeles and the Randstad.

The grass-roots nature of neighborhood council reform in Los Angeles is allowing greater opportunity for consensual practices in an institutional setting that traditionally would not be described as very consensual. But interestingly enough, it is mainly citizens who try to do the integrating (in action committees, in citywide alliances of activists, etc.) in contrast to the Randstad, where it is usually the professionals who try to seek consensus.

Conclusion

The Randstad and Los Angeles provide two examples of profound institutional change with regard to neighborhood governance within polycentric urban fields. While these reforms are in some respects quite different, they share the common goal of localization. In complex and diversifying urban fields, traditional government approaches do not suffice, and governance structures are reorienting themselves to connect to pluralization at the neighborhood level.

In Los Angeles, we see the creation of community-level governance institutions intended to connect neighborhood-level concerns within governance processes at the city level. These institutions are developing largely from the grass roots, with some regulation and minimal support on the part of the city. The goals for the system are as pluralistic as the individuals involved in their creation: neighborhood lobbyists; spaces for the development of community; institutions of self-governance. In Los Angeles, neighborhood activists seem to be driven into action by institutions that are generally perceived as distant and not very participation friendly. Passive resistance, apathy, and in-fighting on the part of the mayor and city council appeared to create space for a social movement supporting neighborhood council development. This advocacy-oriented structure is in keeping with the individualistic and pluralistic political culture of the region and that culture's impulses toward institutional fragmentation.

In the Randstad, neighborhood-based projects and programs provide the experimentation ground for a different type of governance: a type of local governance inspired by a situational logic. In Amsterdam, Rotterdam, The Hague, and Utrecht, neighborhood governance is seen as a way to revitalize local democracy, to reorient public administration, and to produce policies, programs, and projects that are more responsive to diverse local needs and preferences. The field offices in the various neighborhoods also serve as just one part of the neighborhood governance network. In many cases these field offices are primarily the meeting places or "round tables" for the reinvention of associational democracy at the neighborhood level: the places where representatives from various professional domains and interest groups meet to discuss the "betterment" (in social, economic, and physical terms) of the neighborhood in question. These structures for neighborhood governance constitute the Dutch way of trying to make (associational) democracy work (better) at the neighborhood level. This style of reform reflects the strong planning culture of the Randstad, which has contributed to more integrative and bureaucratically driven reforms. In the Randstad individual citizens seem to be kept passive by institutions that are generally perceived to be close and open to participation.

At a superficial level, the two cases would appear dramatically different in terms of the models of democracy inherent in the reforms and the agents driving toward change. In Los Angeles, there is more emphasis on protectionism and aggregative democracy, whereas the Randstad embodies greater emphasis on developmental democracy and integration. The Randstad is pursuing consolidation (integration of the various policy sectors) in order to avoid decomposition, while Los Angeles is attempting to avoid implosion (breaking up of the city) through decomposition (localizing governance). The latter difference is in keeping with the fact that in the Netherlands there is serious talk about parallel regionalization. Such discourse is completely lacking in the Los Angeles region.

Yet we see commonalities behind the differences. One is the limited role of formal politics in driving institutional change. While a formal political process (charter reform) initiated reform in Los Angeles, the driving force of implementation has been a neighborhood social movement given little support by the city. In the Randstad, namely, public administrators and neighborhood professionals design neighborhood reforms based on a situational logic. Another commonality is that neither of these reform movements appears to include all three arenas of democratic revitalization, namely, public administrators, citizens, and political officials. In both cases, elected officials are minor players, although they are somewhat more engaged in the Randstad than in Los Angeles. Los Angeles neighborhood council reform has been largely a middle-class citizen movement, with public administrators largely absent from the action. In the Randstad, although the rhetoric addresses the need for citizen governance, the major agents of neighborhood governance are public administrators, and citizens are treated in a selective, perhaps repressively tolerant, fashion.

Finally, both cases illustrate experimentalism in adapting to the diverse needs and characters of the neighborhood level, together with a drive toward institutional innovation that transcends the standard formulae of government. In the Randstad, the motto is "no new structures," and, instead, new, varied and flexible ways of working within neighborhood policy networks are advocated. While Los Angeles is taking a structural approach to reform, it is undertaking this reform in a spirit of bottom-up experimentation, allowing citizens to design council structures locally, with minimal regulation from the city. Both reform movements are attempting to respond to varying needs and preferences at the neighborhood level. In Los Angeles, the risk is a lack of democratic legitimacy and the development of parochial associations that serve to protect middle-class interests rather than empowering diverse neighborhood stakeholders. In the

Randstad, the risk is that the rhetoric of neighborhood governance masks attempts by local administrators to co-opt or manage residential populations.

Notes

1. Juliet Musso's research in Los Angeles was supported by the John Randolph Haynes and Dora Haynes Foundation and the James Irvine Foundation. Frank Hendriks's research was supported by the Netherlands Institute of Governance. We would like to thank Alicia Kitsuse for comments on early drafts of this chapter, the editors for comments on later versions, and Peter Bogason for bringing us all together.

2. Martina Navratilova: "Do you know the difference between involvement and commitment? Think of eggs and bacon. The chicken was involved. The pig was committed" (cited in Mike Gayle, 1999).

3. Utrecht also works with "area-aldermen." An alderman is traditionally responsible for a particular policy domain, but as an "area-alderman" she or he is also the contact person for a particular neighborhood. In the coming years, Utrecht plans to establish "area boards," which would make the Utrecht model look more like the Amsterdam/Rotterdam model.

4. The United States Bureau of the Census 2000 reports Los Angeles to be 46.5 percent Hispanic or Latino, 29.7 percent non-Hispanic White, 11 percent Black/African American, and 10 percent Asian. http://factfinder.census.gov/bf/_lang=en_vt_name= DEC_2000_PL_U_QTPL_geo_id=16000US0644000.html

5. The city has a mayoral office with weak powers and a city council composed of fifteen members, each of whom represents a gerrymandered district of approximately 260,000 residents. City council members often call the shots within their individual districts, particularly with regard to land use policies. City services are provided by thirty-two departments; oversight of city services is shared between the city council and more than 240 citizen commissioners who are appointed by the mayor.

6. This distinction of a "first language" and a "second language" is inspired by Bellah (1996) who distinguishes these two languages in American individualism in general.

7. Lijphart (1999) compares democratic systems at the macrolevel and he limits his explanation to two indirect democratic ideal types of democracy: consensus democracy (indirect and consensual; upright in our matrix) and Westminster or pendulum democracy (indirect and majoritarian; upleft in our matrix). In a conversation with one of us, Lijphart admitted that it may be useful to add the direct democratic ideal types to the conceptual framework when investigating democratic processes at micro or meso level.

Chapter 5

Democratic Consequences of Urban Governance—What Has Become of Representative Democracy?

Karina Sehested

In 1997, there was a celebration in the Danish city of Helsingør, which is famous for the castle Kronborg, the residence of Shakespeare's Hamlet. The celebration was about the opening of a new city mall on the edge of the old medieval city. The mall includes shops, residences, offices, and a multistory car park. The celebration, which included music and speeches, was a special event for many in Helsingør, and it marked the end of a dramatic political period in the city's history. For some it was a day of relief because they finally succeeded. For others it was a day of great disappointment because they lost. For seven years there had been a struggle going on in the city concerning the possibility of a city mall. Entrepreneurs, architects, lawyers, politicians, administrators, planners, interest groups, and many citizens had been involved in activities for or against the city mall, and numerous democratic means were used to influence the process. During this process, two policy networks were established—one to implement and one to prevent the city mall from being realized, and both of them became important for the result of the process. Due to the profound disagreement about the city mall, the process was very troublesome and sometimes dramatic for the persons involved. However, there was also disagreement about the concept of proper democratic behavior. The process revealed the clash of two very different expressions and perceptions of network-based democracy.

This case of the city mall in Helsingør is an excellent example with which to highlight important discussions about urban governance and its effect on urban democracy. In theory, governance through policy networks is a new form of steering and coordination. Public and private actors join resources in order to be able to deal with the very complex and differentiated problems and solutions in postmodern cities. The policy networks are relatively independent of a representative political center, the result being a fragmented political system with no center and no single actor in control of urban development. The fragmented political system indicates a problem for traditional representative democracy characterized by one elected political elite in control of all decisions in public matters. This chapter concerns this relationship between governance and democracy. The questions to be discussed in theory and practice involve how policy networks are established and operate in the city and how these policy networks affect urban democracy. Are they related to representative democracy at all? Or do new democratic forms arise from the governance processes?

The chapter first provides a theoretical overview of the governance perspective used in the empirical study of the city mall and a presentation of theoretical discussions about the consequences of governance for democracy. The second part of the chapter concerns the empirical study. The governance and policy network theories draw attention to the fact that governance processes and policy networks can develop very differently in practice, and in the second part of the chapter the specific forms of governance process and policy networks in Helsingør are discussed. In theories about the democratic consequences of governance and policy networks we find different interpretations of the consequences—some find that policy networks undermine democracy, others that policy networks can sustain democracy. We also find different democratic ideals and values used to evaluate the consequences. Whether governance is good or bad news for democracy cannot be answered in general; it depends on the democratic values one uses to make this judgment. The empirical part discusses whether the governance process in Helsingør sustained or undermined urban democracy, and how the governance process was related to representative democracy. In addition, this section illustrates how diverse democratic values were expressed in the process, and how this caused the actors to evaluate the democratic result of the process very differently.

Urban Governance as Policy Networks in the Shadow of Hierarchy

Discussions relating to governance concern ways of organizing and governing that exist in political processes. The idea of governance seems to have developed as a dominant theoretical framework for understanding the new form of governing in postmodern society and cities. In the study of the political process in Helsingør, the theoretical inspiration came from discussions of British governance, which interpret governance as being self-organized, inter-organizational policy networks (Rhodes 1997, 15). In the empirical study undertaken here, the first questions to be investigated were: how do these policy networks work and how do urban politics develop through these policy networks? But what do governance and policy networks mean?

The ideas of governance and policy networks have to be understood as standing in contrast to the notion of government and hierarchical relations espoused by traditional theory. Scharpf (1994, 41) argues that one has to look for policy networks in the shadow of hierarchy as being the most likely situation in practice. In that vein, Bogason (2001) argues that, in a Danish cultural context, it is likely that policy networks will be constrained by hierarchy, and that hierarchy can occur in different forms in a governance process. This approach was used in the study of policy networks in Helsingør, which investigated how policy networks worked in the shadow of hierarchy and how this shadow was expressed in the network process.

Government is typically described as a cohesive and integrated public sector with central political management, namely, the government being based on national parliamentary sovereignty and accountability through elections. The parliamentary chain of control is the center of the governmental process with elected politicians as the authoritarian decision makers and a neutral administration based on bureaucratic means to implement policies. Bureaucratic means are hierarchic relations between superiors and lower-level staff and units in which there is a clear division of work and responsibility between different actors and offices, specialized work functions, work based on expert knowledge and formalized work processes and information preparation. A precondition for government is a clear division of boundaries and responsibilities between politics and administration and between the public and the private sector (Bogason 2000, 13-18, Rhodes 1997, 181-84). In a Danish city this system places the city council and the elected local politicians in the central position. The highly professional and specialized administration is loyal to political decisions and implements policies using bureaucratic means. The citizens elect their politicians and follow the decisions made in the political center or in the administration. They do not actively participate in policy processes.

However, the argument is that this system is becoming outdated due to the development of a postmodern society, which is characterized by increased fragmentation, differentiation, and complexity in social and political life (Kooiman 1993b, 254, Rhodes 1997, 181-84). The consequence is the emergence of governance as a new logic of steering and policy networks as a new organization form. Governance indicates a new kind of sociopolitical logic characterized by a differentiated and multicentered political system with a mixture of private and public actors who participate directly in the decision-making process without any clear hierarchic relation between the many centers and actors. The actors recognize the interdependence between relatively autonomous parties based on the understanding that nobody possesses total knowledge, information, overview, or resources to solve collective problems. Governance becomes the result of interactive social-political management and the concern is, first and foremost, to find and develop a common understanding of problems and solutions among participants in political processes (Kooiman 1993a, 4-6).

Rhodes (1997, 37) defines a policy network as a cluster or a complex of organizations (public and private) joined together through their interdependencies and interchange of resources (such as money, information, know-how, and experience). Rules in the network are rooted in confidence and negotiated by the members and policy networks have significant autonomy in relation to government. Networks can develop in different forms (see, e.g., Mayntz and Marin 1991, Jordan and Schubert 1992). Rhodes argues that they can develop within a continuum from closed, exclusive, and stable policy communities to open, inclusive, and unstable issue networks (Rhodes 1997, 38-39). The closed, exclusive, and stable policy community consists of only a few public and private participants having very close contact over a longer period. They participate as equal partners, they trust each other, they share the same values, and they develop a common understanding of problems and solutions (Rhodes 1997, 42-44). At the other end of the continuum, we find the open, inclusive, and unstable issue network. There are a variety of participants and it is open to newcomers. The contact is unsteady and the participants do not agree on all matters. Conflicts are not unusual and some actors are more powerful than others (Rhodes 1997, 43-44).

In a Danish city like Helsingør, the consequence of governance would be a fragmented and multicentered political system with numerous open or closed policy networks related to different policy areas and political issues as arenas for urban policy making. The policy networks would have a large degree of autonomy in solving policy problems in the city, and the role of the city council is unclear. The city council could be either part of the policy networks or work side by side with them. The actors in the various policy networks could be politicians, administrators, interest groups, citizens, or private businesses depending on the political problem and the resources needed to solve the problem. However, it is likely that hierarchy would occur in some form and constrain the autonomy of policy networks. These governance ideas constituted the background for the study, and in the second part of this chapter they will be discussed in greater detail.

The theories indicate that policy networks and a governance process can develop differently in different cities having a variety of consequences for democracy. Theoretical conclusions about these consequences can be placed within two opposing interpretations of the relationship between policy networks and democracy. One is that policy networks undermine democracy. The other is that policy networks could sustain democracy.

Policy Networks Undermine Democracy

Theories about urban politics and democracy identify changes that are due to the rise of several political decision-making centers (e.g., policy networks) outside parliament, which involve a wide range of actors—most of them not elected. The result, for the state, is ungovernability and a loss of power in the representative bodies (see, e.g., Savitch and Thomas 1991, 246, Logan and Molotch 1987, 52-53). However, two different kinds of development are registered concerning ungovernability.

The hyperpluralists maintain that an extreme pluralism is emerging. The political decisions are made not in the elected political organs, but in the city's corridors of power where politicians, administrators, private businesses, citizens, and local pressure groups are involved in periodic negotiations over a share of power (Savitch and Thomas 1991, 246, Judge 1996, 26). The relationship between the actors may very well take the form of either policy communities or issue networks, and some researchers, such as Deleon (1991, 210-11), talk about urban regimes and antiregimes fighting for control of the city. It is no longer evident who represents the common interest of the city, and there is a constant fight between numerous policy networks relating to this right.

The neo-elitists disagree with this conclusion. They do not see a dispersion of power into different policy networks. On the contrary, they see a concentration of power in one or a few policy communities. Due to the ungovernability and the loss of power in representative bodies other actors enter the scene. These actors are usually private rentiers in coalitions with developers and city officials. They establish closed coalitions in the form of growth machines in order to exploit the exchange value of urban land. They all have a common interest in economic growth, are able to set the political agenda, and take control of power by using the argument that economic growth is beneficial for all urban citizens (Logan and Molotch, 52-53, Harding 1995, 42-44). By doing so, they claim to represent the common interest of the city.

So we are told two very different stories about what to expect as the result of urban governance and network processes in a city like Helsingør. Either extreme pluralist governance with various open and closed policy networks competing for control of the city or an elitist governance process with only one or a few closed policy communities in control of the city. Either way these theorists interpret the development as a problem for democracy. They find that policy networks in any form will undermine democracy. The reason for this conclusion is that they evaluate governance and policy networks from the perspective of representative democracy. They argue that the proper democratic institution for urban politics is a formal representative and elected body like a city council, and only this body can represent the common interest of a city. Against this background they argue for restraining and regulating policy networks and for keeping policy networks in line with representative democracy in order to reinstall the hierarchy and parliamentary control.

Having representative democracy as the preferred point of reference in an evaluation of governance and policy networks indicates an interpretation of democracy based on certain democratic values. These values can be labeled aggregative democratic values.

From the aggregative perspective, democracy is a means or procedure for the aggregation of different interests in politics. Democracy is also a means for the distribution and allocation of resources and power and for mediating societal conflicts (March and Olsen 1989, 118, Sørensen 1995, 29). Politics is a competition between conflicting citizens groups, and their interests have to be canalized into the governing system through the voting system (March and Olsen 1989, 120). Representation by delegation is a positive factor in democratic life. The citizens participate through elections and their participation has to be restricted because they are driven by self-interest. They are not competent decision makers. The elected, and enlightened, elite is the competent decision maker and represents the common interest. The elite secures stability and unity and protects the citizens (Sørensen 1995, 33).

This view of democracy explains why the theorists mentioned above see policy networks as bad news for democracy. Policy networks are examples of competing groups of organizations, people driven by self-interest trying to get more power for them than they have achieved through the voting system, and without having any concern for the common interest of a city. The elected politicians in city councils are those who are vested with the authority to make decisions on behalf of the people, and only they are able to represent and secure the common interest. They have to maintain a degree of distance from these policy networks and regulate and constrain them in order not to be influenced by them.

These democratic values are important in a study of governance and policy networks in European cities because the formal representative and parliamentary democracies in Europe build on these democratic values. Governance and policy networks develop in the context of representative democracy, and this is also true of the process in Helsingør were the formal representative democracy formally places the elected politicians in the city council as the main decision makers in the municipality. The interesting issue to investigate is how policy networks relate to or do not relate to the formal representative body. Viewed from the representative and aggregate perspective there is a great risk that this form of democracy will be undermined.

So far, the theories have contributed several useful considerations about the relationship between governance and democracy that can be investigated in the case study about the mall in Helsingør. The fragmented governance system can develop in a variety of directions and be dominated by different forms of networks. One possibility is a development toward an extreme pluralism in the governance processes with plenty of policy networks in different forms and with a variety of actors competing for control. Another possibility is a development toward an elitist governance process with only a few closed and stable policy networks taking control of the city. Viewed from the perspective of representative democracy, and stressing the aggregative elements and values of democracy, developments in either direction are bad news for democracy. The elected politicians and city councils are the proper decision makers and they represent the common interest. Policy networks only give way to strong citizens groups driven by self-interest to gain power on the behalf of the common interest and for that reason they have to be constrained.

However, in democratic theories we also find alternative interpretations of the relationship between policy networks and democracy that challenge this conclusion. In practice, most Western European democracies have developed a tradition for some form of democratic participation besides voting, without interpreting it as a problem for representative democracy. I will examine, in greater detail, these arguments concerning democracy and the related practices.

Policy Networks Could Sustain Democracy

As mentioned, representative democracy and the parliamentary chain of control dominates Western democratic institutions, but in different countries, and at different times, the idea of participation and citizens' influence in addition to voting has been balanced with the representative system in different ways. In Denmark, there has been a long tradition for participation through diverse channels of influence. Historically, the integration of large interests groups into the policy processes dominated democracy in the 1970s (corporative networks), and in the 1980s social movements became a new widespread channel for participation and influence (Eriksen 1995, 12). In the 1990s, new, more direct, forms of participation and influence have arisen, some of them inspired by New Public Management reforms. Examples of these are user boards of directors, advisory bodies, partnerships, public hearings, and citizen surveys (see Bogason's chapter in this book). In general, the tendency is toward more and different forms of participation coexisting with the formal representative and parliamentary democracy (Andersen et al. 1993, 223-27).

The reason for this development can be explained by the integrative view of democracy. This view is quite opposite to representative and aggregate views. The integrative perspective is not concerned with the aggregation and allocation of resources. It is concerned with the integration and socialization of citizens in order to achieve a common purpose and consensus in society. Taking this perspective will change the conclusions reached above about the effects of policy networks on democracy.

In the integrative perspective, democracy is a goal in itself and a lifestyle (March and Olsen 1989, 118). Participation and dialogue are the prior conditions for political decisions because it is through them that citizens become socialized by the norms and values of society (become democratic citizens) and because dialogue and participation legitimize the political decisions made by elected politicians. Politics is a matter of mediating conflicts through rational debate that generates consensus and common understanding (March and Olsen 1989, 126-27). The image of achieving the common good is central to this perspective and every citizen has a duty to serve for the common good. Representation is a practical necessity, but only as a mandate with limited autonomy for the elected politicians and strong popular control. Politicians are likely to be corrupted by power, and the competent citizens have to constrain and control them.

In this perspective we find quite the opposite understanding of the role of politicians and citizens from that presented in the aggregative perspective. Furthermore, the integrative perspective values participation in different forms, policy networks being one, because participation and dialogue provide political decisions made by representative politicians with legitimacy. In general, all citizens have a duty to be active and participate in political processes in order to reach the best decisions and develop a common understanding and consensus about the proper development of society. The relationship between elected politicians and citizens has to be very close in order for the politicians to make the right decisions. From this perspective, participation through a policy network could sustain democracy because these policy networks illustrate channels of influence and arenas for rational debate leading to common understandings and consensus.

This line of thinking and the development of more and different forms of participation in representative democracy have brought about the development of new theories of democracy which try to rethink the balance of representation and participation without having to take a stand for or against one or the other. Theories of deliberative democracy are one example. In deliberative democracy, the development toward governance and policy networks is interpreted as being part of a new and very complex and differentiated democratic system in a decentralized and fragmented society (Eriksen 1995, 13). The argument goes that this development should be sustained but in a manner which place pluralism and participation (and not elitism) as the fundamental value for democracy. Pluralism is preferred in order to prevent authoritarian tendencies in cities, but pluralism is redefined as continuous conflicts and struggles between interests, in, for example, different policy networks, with the possibility of obtaining only a temporary and contextual balance between opposite demands and interests. Integration is emphasized by pointing to the importance of not only one (the representative center) but a diversity of channels of democratic influence with policy networks being only one among others (Bogason 2000, 13-18, Torfing 1999, 257-258). In this perspective, governance and policy networks could be good news for democracy and have to be sustained, but this development has to build on certain democratic conditions concerned with deliberation.

Rational dialogue and reflection through direct participation is an essential part of the new deliberative democracy perceived as the precondition for the development of a sustainable and dynamic community, for achieving common understanding, and for securing support for social, civil, and political rights (Hansen 1999, 8 and 15-16, Eriksen 1995, 13). Deliberative theories build on the Habermasian ideal about rational reasoning in open communicative processes, which takes place in several public arenas in order to develop common interest and reach consensus about decisions (Eriksen and Weigaard 1999, 76). These communicative processes should be founded on certain communicative preconditions that allow the better argument to evolve in public discussions and in procedures—a discourse ethic—that secures a fair discussion (Habermas 1995, 33). The communicative preconditions and procedures keep the public dialogue free from power and strategic actions. The ideal is communicative action based on empathic and social rationality in opposition to the instrumental, cynical, and strategic rationality (Eriksen 1995, 15, Eriksen and Weigaard 1999, 76).

If the integrative and the deliberative perspectives are used to evaluate the development of governance and policy networks, we get a very different answer to the question of whether policy networks are good or bad news for democracy. It could be good news for democracy if a new understanding of democracy is developed, and if these policy networks develop under certain deliberative conditions. Democracy has to be exercised in intersubjective communicative processes both inside and outside the formal political bodies, and policy networks could very well be one of the arenas for these communicative processes. The elected politicians have to acquire their legitimacy through their ability to find the better argument (e.g., about the common interest) in the public dialogue. Public debate is the only way to create political opinions and in the end legitimize a political decision made by representative politicians. A properly democratic process of governance is characterized by integration, participation, and communicative processes based on confidence, consensus, and deliberation.

The conclusions reached so far concerning theory are that governance processes and policy networks are likely to be found in different forms in practice. The governance processes may vary from extreme plural processes with a variety of policy networks operating in different policy areas and relating to different political issues. The policy networks might take the form of closed exclusive stable policy networks or as open inclusive unstable networks. However, the governance processes and the policy networks might be functioning in the shadow of a hierarchy constraining the autonomy of the networks. Whether this development is good or bad news for democracy depends on the practice of the processes and on the democratic ideas and values used to evaluate the consequences. From an aggregative and representative democratic perspective, governance and policy networks might undermine democracy and policy networks have to be restrained and regulated by the representative center. From an integrative and deliberative democratic perspective, developments in governance and networks could sustain democracy by the increased participation and dialogue expressed in policy networks. However, the democratic processes have to follow certain procedures and a discursive ethic, which ensures a rational and fair democratic discussion.

The theoretical conclusions will be discussed further in the next part of the chapter concerning the empirical case study.[1] First, the city of Helsingør is introduced, and analyses of the governance process and the policy networks in the shadow of hierarchy in Helsingør follow. This leads to a discussion of the consequences for democracy and an evaluation of the process from different democratic perspectives.

Helsingør: A City in Need of Activity and a New Identity

In 1989, the idea of a new city mall in the center of the old city of Helsingør was introduced. The idea did not meet with great enthusiasm, and it soon became an issue of profound disagreement. This has to do with the history of the city.

Helsingør is the city that provides the scene for Shakespeare's *Hamlet*, and Kronborg castle is a major tourist attraction. The city is situated at the northeastern corner of Zealand and is a port on the narrow waters between Denmark and Sweden. It is the largest city in the municipality of Helsingør, which had 57,421 inhabitants in 1996. Trade and a large shipyard had been the economic basis for the city for almost a century, but in 1983 the shipyard closed as a result of economic problems. The city lost an essential part of its identity and unemployment and social problems became part of the city's major political problems during the 1980s, and they dominated the political agenda in 1989 when the idea of the city mall was presented.

The city has a very well preserved city center with half-timbered houses and narrow paved streets, which have survived from the Middle Ages. The city's old architecture is another important part of its identity. It is a very lively city center with people living in the old restored houses or operating its small shops, cafés, and restaurants that serve the many Swedes and other tourists who visit the city. The reason for the fine preservation is found in the city's planning policy developed during the 1970s, which was still the policy in 1989. The planning strategy was twofold. One was the preservation of the old city center with strict rules delimiting any change. The other was a strategy of decentralization, which had placed all large new building projects outside the city center. This planning policy and the common interest in the city's old architecture was the most important obstacle to the new city mall.

The city had for many years been characterized by centralized representative democracy with strong elements of corporatism. Social Democrats held the majority of city council seats for many decades, and they maintained a close cooperation with the leaders of interest organizations representing labor and industry (especially from the shipyard) but also trade. It would not be unfair to talk about a very closed and stable corporate regime as having governed the city for many years. This centralized and elitist situation had, over the years, caused many dramatic conflicts with the citizens about urban politics. When the shipyard closed in 1983, the foundation for this corporate regime fell apart and a more open and unstable political situation developed. In 1989, when the idea of the city mall was presented, the Social Democrats governed with support from a small socialist party, and the Conservatives were close to taking over power for the first time in decades. Several of the people involved in the former conflicts about urban politics in the city were also involved in the issue of the city mall.

This short historical overview provides the background for understanding Helsingør's problems. The closing down of the shipyard in 1983 caused high unemployment and social problems, and the city lost an essential part of its identity. The politicians tried to find alternative projects to provide the city with a new future but they did not succeed. The mayor had trouble in keeping his majority on the council and needed a successful project to showcase for the upcoming election. The city was in urgent need of a new economic impetus and a new identity and meaning. The old order had disappeared and a new one had to be established.

In this troubled urban situation two local people—an architect and a lawyer—fostered the idea of building a brand new city mall in Helsingør placed on a parking lot owned by local government at the very edge of the old city. The building project would include a large shopping mall, new dwellings, offices, and a multistory car park. The two men were local businessmen in need of new business. They had lived in the city for years and were active in its general development. They participated in local business life and they knew the political traditions in the city. They also knew important political actors, but they had not been part of the governing regime. They were aware that the idea of a new city mall in the old city center would be controversial and very difficult to promote in a city protected by the double planning strategy supported by most politicians, administrators, and citizens. It took seven years before their idea was implemented and there was much resistance and many problems occurred during the process. But they succeeded in the end. The reason they did so centered on the close cooperation of public and private actors in policy networks and with a certain tradition and interpretation of democracy that legitimized the whole process.

A Centralized, Elitist Governance Process and a Closed, Stable Policy Network

The two local businessmen who originated the proposal started the process by contacting the local government. They went right to the top because they knew that in this centralized governing system the urban manager and the mayor had to support the idea otherwise there would never be any city mall. This first contact between local private and public actors soon evolved into a closed, exclusive and stable city mall network. The director of a new planning department was integrated into the network soon after and these five men developed a relationship which can by characterized in terms of a policy community. During the process, a national building company and national investors got involved in the project but they never joined the local city mall network. They acted through one of the local businessmen because they realized that the local aspect was essential for the legitimacy of this closed and stable policy network. The city mall network illustrates how nonelected private businessmen are allowed to participate in an informal strong network relation with the highest representative of local government.

The five public and private actors worked together from the start and stayed in a very close, stable, and closed relationship during the whole process. They were dependent on each other's resources—the capital, the idea, and the public decision making authority—and they soon developed a relationship based on trust and a sense of mutual obligation to work hard to complete the building of the city mall. It was this policy network which carried the idea through despite resistance and many problems during the seven years. These actors possessed engagement and a strong belief in the idea and they kept on doggedly fighting for the idea. They always discussed and negotiated whatever happened in the process to be able to react properly to the situation.

This closed and stable city mall network became an instrument for effective decision making and implementation in the urban policy process. Due to its closeness and its stability it was able to counter numerous problems and strong opposition throughout the process. In fact there was never much attention paid to this cooperation between public and private actors in the city mall network. However, to understand its activity and success, one also has to examine its relations to other important political actors in the city. To obtain political support for their idea, the local private actors followed the informal rules and traditions of the existing corporate and centralized governing system. They not only made contact with the top representative of local government, but they also made sure to maintain close contact with the city council in general and with the representatives of the large interest groups. During the whole process the actors in the city mall network always followed what happened in city council closely, and they tried to influence and become an integrated part of the political activities in the council. By doing that, they accepted and sustained the central role of the city council in the city. Furthermore, they also started the process by making contacts with the large interest groups in the city so as to get their support. They knew they would get nowhere without the support from these traditionally important political actors. During the whole process they maintained close contact with the large interest groups to keep them informed and engaged in the project. They accepted and sustained the importance of the old corporate regime.

In order to convince these important political actors and the whole city to accept the idea, a discourse about the city mall was developed. The core element in this discourse was the argument that the city mall was beneficial for the entire city. The city mall discourse became a discourse coalition about problem solving in the troubled city and about creating a new identity. The city mall was not presented as the goal for the city but as a means to achieve other goals. Helsingør could again be the leading, trading city in northern Zealand, new employment and economic activity could be created, and a new form of trade could be established in the new city mall, they affirmed.

These arguments convinced the majority on the city council to support and vote for the city mall in the numerous discussions relating to the case over the seven years. The majority on the council constituted the political will in the case and was seen as the driving force for the process by all actors. By using these arguments, the city mall network, who constituted the majority on the city council, and the large interests groups in the city claimed to be acting on behalf on the common interest of the city.

The discourse coalition could develop due to the readiness for change in the city and the need for a new meaning to replace the old one. It grew stronger and more coherent as more arguments were presented for or against the city mall, and it soon created a certain limitation for the discussions about the city mall that was very difficult to break down for the opponents. It became very difficult for others to enter the arena of debate without offering an alternative solution to the problems of the city in presenting an alternative idea about how to develop the city for the common interest of all citizens.

Concluding about the governance process in Helsingør, it can be said that an elitist and centralized governance process was developed much like the one described by the neo-elitists researcher, but only related to one important political issue and not to the city as a whole. A closed and stable policy network made possible a strong coalition with the city council and the large interest groups in the city. The political activity in this coalition was legitimized by the problem-solving discourse coalition, which claimed to represent the common interest of the city. This way of making politics was not up for discussion in the first years of the process, the reason being that the city mall network worked in harmony with the tradition for corporate and aggregate democracy. The closed and stable form of the city mall network was well known in urban politics in Helsingør. The city mall network made contacts to, and alliances with, the former actors in the corporate regime who were still influential. They did what was appropriate in the city when a new political problem or issue entered the political agenda. It was politics as usual. What occurred in Helsingør was not a governance development in conflict with the former political system, but rather one in harmony with the former political tradition in the city. This might be one of the most important reasons for the success of the city mall project in spite of considerable resistance from citizens.

However, we also have to look at the activities of the opponents in this process to understand the governance process and why the city mall network and its allies were successful.

Policy Networks as an Instrument of Resistance in the City

In the beginning of the process in 1989, when the city mall network was established and the city mall discourse was under construction, there soon appeared several groups of actors who opposed the project. At first there were three existing political groups which had their own reasons to oppose the city mall. The small number of Socialist Party members on the city council and an urban planning department in the administration both worked against the idea because they thought it would destroy the old city center. In addition, a trade organization for a shopping mall outside the city worked against the idea because it would lose income. However, none of these groups joined resources (i.e., made a policy network) to stop the project. They worked in isolation against the project. This was due in part to the fact that they disagreed too much on other political matters to cooperate on this one.

It was not until 1994 that we saw the establishment of another policy network important in the process. This took place after the new planning documents (that cancelled the double planning strategy) were decided and the land (the parking lot) sold to the local private actors. However, the investors were still to be found. At this time, some local party members, a group of citizens, and some small shopkeepers from the old city center realized that the majority of the politicians actually meant to carry out the project, and it made them furious. They decided to try to make the politicians change their minds. To make this happen they established the opponent policy network.

The opponent network turned out to function as an open, inclusive, and unstable policy network much like an issue network presented in network theory. The participants changed according to the activities in the network, they only met sporadically, and anyone could join the network if they wanted. All the participants in this network had experience in active political work in the city. Some of them had been involved in former conflicts with the city council. In this policy network, they managed to cooperate in waging opposition and, as I will discuss below, they arranged a number of democratic activities to stop the city mall. But they did not succeed. The opponent network became an important instrument for resistance but not an effective instrument for influencing the process.

The reason for this is partly to be found in the lack of alliances between the different groups of opponents. The opponent network never joined resources with the exiting groups of opponents. The Socialist Party in the city council was loosely connected to and informed about what happened in the network, but they did not work together properly. Furthermore, the opponent network never tried to make coalitions with other influential political actors in the city. In fact, the opponent network deliberately chose to work outside "the system," as they called it, because they saw the system as the enemy. Looking at all the opponents of the city mall in Helsingør, none of them used the joint strategy of networking and the gathering of resources, which could have matched the strong coalition established by the city mall network. This lack of a strong coherent counter network made it easier for the city mall network to implement their idea. The same problem occurred in the construction of meaning against the city mall.

The arguments against the city mall from the opponents were several. One was that a new city mall would not be fair to the shopping mall outside the city. Another was that the new city mall would close down all the small shops in the city center. These arguments did not get a lot of attention in the process because they did not relate to the common interest of the city, and they were easy to exclude from the city mall discourse. A third argument was of greater importance. It claimed that the destruction of the old architecture in the city would ensue with construction of the new city mall. This was a very difficult argument for the city mall network to get around and the result was an integration of the issue of architecture in the city mall discourse. The argument was that a new style of architecture could blend with the old one if competent and local architects who cared about the old city were involved. The architecture issue was the only one from the opponents that concerned the common interest of the city and it became the only one which made a wider group of the citizens pay attention.

Furthermore, the opponents could not agree on a common understanding of problem solving or an alternative future for the city, and they never presented a strong alternative to the city mall discourse. Each of them had their own reasons to resist the city mall and they did not coordinate or unify their arguments. Mostly they defended the exiting conditions and their own business (self-interest), and that was a difficult discursive strategy to follow in a city dominated by numerous problems and in search of a new identity. It made it easier for the city mall discourse to exclude the opposing arguments.

To sum up in relation to the governance process, the case study in Helsingør revealed a centralized and elitist governance process based on a coalition between a closed and a stable policy network, the city council, and the large interests organization. This coalition claimed to represent the common interest of the city by solving several problems in the city, by creating a new identity and future. This specific form of the governance process worked in harmony with, and sustained the centralized and corporative tradition for, urban politics. That is an important explanation for the success of the city mall network. The process excluded opposing actors and meanings. Some of the opponents used the networking strategy to mobilize resistance and organize several democratic activities to stop the city mall, but none of them did so with success. The opponents never managed to make a strong counter alliance to match the city mall network's strong coalition and they never managed to form a strong alternative discourse to match discourse coalition about the city mall. These are also important explanations for the result of the process.

However, other explanations are important as well and they deal with the legitimacy of this centralized, elitist, and exclusive governance process. The question is: why was this process accepted by most of the central political actors, and how was it possible to overlook the resistance of the citizens? This has to do with the role of hierarchy in the governance process and with a certain perception of democracy dominating the governing coalition around the city mall project. First to be discussed is how hierarchy was expressed in the process.

The Expression of Hierarchy in the Centralized, Elitist Governance Process

As mentioned, there was little attention paid to the city mall network as an instrument for influencing the process. It has been explained as a consequence of tradition in the city where closed network relations constituted politics as usual. However, another important explanation for the acceptance of this form of governing was the representation of hierarchy in this closed and stable policy network, and in the process in general. In the case study, the phrase about policy networks in the shadow of hierarchy as stated in the theories became of great relevance. In fact, hierarchy was expressed as more than a shadow. Local government stayed in control of this governance process, and this was a very important factor for the legitimacy of the policy network and the process.

The hierarchy was expressed in different forms in the process. One was through the actors in the city mall network. Another lay in the principle of guidance in the policy network. And, finally, hierarchy was expressed in the relation between the city mall network and the city council.

Looking at the actors in the city mall network, it was those at the top of the formal hierarchy in local government who joined the policy network. Hierarchy in the form of the actors was therefore present in the policy network from the start. The political issue had a high priority in local government and the top managers and the mayor himself chose to be part of, and in control of, this network. This representation turned out to be essential for the wider acceptance of the functioning of the closed policy network.

However, the hierarchy was also expressed through the meaning of the proper guidance principles in the policy network. One principle was the political will of the city council, namely, the majority in the city council. The mayor represented this political will in the city mall network but in general the political will was used to legitimize the work of the policy network both inside and outside the network. All the actors in Helsingør saw the political will in the city council as the driving force for the whole process. The policy network saw itself as implementers of this political will, and as playing an active part in influencing this political will. This brought about the close relation to the city council. During the whole process there was political disagreement about the process in city council, and the city mall network had to work hard to try to maintain the majority for the city mall. The political will as a guiding principle was essential for the legitimacy of the network. Another principle was the bureaucratic rule-following represented, in particular, by the administrators in the network. From the start there was much attention paid to the project by the city council, the administration and the local press, and all this attention made the administrative executives anxious to strictly follow the bureaucratic rules—especially the planning laws. They wanted everything to go by the book, so nobody afterward could criticize the process for being unfair or illegal. The bureaucratic rule following is also an expression of hierarchy, and it became another legitimizing factor for the activities of the network.

A final form of hierarchy was expressed in the close relation established between the city mall network and the city council. As mentioned, all the actors in the city mall network worked hard to be an integrated part of, and create a very close relation to, the city council. It illustrates that the city mall network never became and did not want to become a relatively autonomous policy network, as governance theory would suggest. The reason was that the city council throughout the process was still regarded as the only legitimate center for decision making in the city. Policy networks served as a supplement for representative democracy but not a replacement. This is, of course, very important in the discussion about democracy, and I will return to the issue below.

To conclude this section, strong elements of government and hierarchy were found in the centralized and elitist governance process based on the closed and stable policy network. Hierarchy was expressed as more than just a shadow, as suggested in theory. Hierarchy did not take the form of formal regulation of the policy network and the city mall network never became a formal policy network. Hierarchy worked not only outside or beside this policy network. Instead, hierarchy was integrated into the policy network through the actors (the mayor and the administrative chief executives) and through the political will and the bureaucratic rulefollowing, as guidance principles in the city mall network. Hierarchy also was expressed in the close relation between the network and city council. The result was that local government stayed in control of this urban governance process and it became a legitimizing factor for the centralized and elitist governance process.

With this conclusion we move toward the answer to the question of what became of representative democracy in this process and to the question of whether policy networks undermined or sustained democracy in Helsingør. It is also through the answers to these questions that we find other important explanations on how this centralized and elitist governance process could succeed in the city.

An Aggregative Democratic View of the Centralized, Elitist Governance Process

The governance process and the policy networks in Helsingør did not undermine the city's representative democracy. Its role as the dominant form of democracy was never questioned by any of actors in the process. However, it was supplemented with different forms of participation—different channels of influence. In the case of the city mall, the corporative networks combined with the new policy networks became the dominant channels of influence. The policy networks were integrated in representative democracy. However, this integration took a certain form. The result was an aggregative and elitist form of a network democracy, and, as we know, this kind of a network democracy was not unknown in this city with a long tradition for corporate governance.

Representative democracy was the democratic point of reference in the case of the city mall, but different network relations were accepted in order to arrive at the best political decision and to implement political decisions made by the city council. The closed and stable form of the city mall network was well known from the former corporate regime politics. There was a tradition for an aggregate interpretation of democracy, and the study has shown that this form of democracy also dominated the case of the city mall. The city's representative elite was seen as the one to represent the common interest of the city. They had to govern at a distance to the citizens, who were motivated only by self-interest. Furthermore, the citizens had a chance to exercise their influence through the public hearings, which were held as required by the planning law. When they failed to present any objections during these hearings, they missed their chance to influence the process. This was seen as yet another example of the irresponsibility of citizens in matters of urban development. However, the definition of the elite expanded to include the politicians, the representatives of the large interest groups, and later on, in the case of the city mall, the local private actors. Together they claimed to represent the common interest of the city. The former aggregate and corporate version of democracy was developed into an aggregate and elitist network democracy.

This process could have colonized the political issue of the city mall in the city mall network and it would certainly have disqualified the process from being at all democratic. Nevertheless, this did not happen, and if we evaluate the process from an aggregative and representative perspective there were several elements in the centralized, elitist governance process that made it democratic. These elements also caused the city mall coalition to interpret the process as democratic. Most important, the central role of the city council served as the main reason for the entire process to be considered democratic. Furthermore, the political will in the city council had been developed in an open political discussion, which had taken place both inside and outside the city council. The process was characterized by a dramatic and long public debate in the city council and in the local press. The discussion of the city mall was always brought out of the closed, elitist city mall network, and into the city council where the whole group of representative politicians was integrated into the political debate. This also gave the opposition the chance to be involved in the debate and argue against the idea. Moreover, the local press could follow the discussions, which they certainly did very closely. This long and open public debate was, of course, an important democratic element in the centralized and elitist process of governance.

The combination of the centralized, elitist governance process with the central role of the city council developing the political will, and the long and open public debate made it possible for the actors in the city mall coalition to interpret the process as democratic in terms of the aggregative perspective. Throughout the whole process they upheld this interpretation of democracy and it caused the coalition to maintain a distance from the citizens and to propound the argument to legitimize the exclusion of citizens' protest when it finally came in 1994.

An Integrative and Deliberative Democratic View of the Centralized, Elitist Governance Process

All the actors in Helsingør wonder about why the citizens' resistance did not come earlier in the process, which started as late as 1994 when all the plans and the decisions were made and the land sold to the private actors. The Danish planning system demands several public hearings during a planning process to let the citizens' comment on the plans. This channel of influence did not work as a channel for citizens' resistance. As mentioned, nothing happened in the hearings and no comments were made except from the professional political actors, such as the interest groups. This lack of response from the citizens became one of the politicians' strongest arguments for neglecting the opposition later on. It was a big surprise when, as one of the actors in the city mall network expressed it, "all hell broke loose" in 1994. The citizens explained their late reaction in having trusted in the common sense of the politicians not to implement the project. However, when they realized that the politicians actually intended to build this city mall they became furious and acted. As we know the opponent network was established and this policy network became an instrument for organizing several democratic activities to change the political decision about the city mall. As one of the citizens said: "We used every democratic means we could think of." In 1994 the conflict about the city mall also turned into a conflict about the proper democratic behavior in a network democracy and especially about the proper relation between politicians and citizens. Now the aggregative and elitist perspective on democracy was challenged by an alternative perspective with strong elements of the integrative and deliberative ideas of democracy.

The opponent network used various classical and well-known democratic means of participation to resist to the proposal. Several of the participants had experience in using these channels because they had previously been involved in conflicts in the city. Four different forms of protest and participation were used. One was the use of citizens' meetings and public media to initiate public dialogue. They wrote letters to the local newspaper and arranged several public meetings, which were attended by hundreds of people. The meetings and the written protests became battlefields for very confrontational and aggressive forms of dialogue especially between the two policy networks. At every meeting the conflict increased and no common understanding was ever reached. The second took the form of establishing a new organization (a new trade organization) to defend the interests of the small shopkeepers in the city center. The opponent network made sure it received a lot of public attention as a manifestation against the city mall but the new organization only survived several months. The third form constituted official complaints about specific decisions and procedures in the process in order to get the decision out of the local public bodies and into a higher public body (the state) to stop the project. Some of the complaints were actually successful, but the higher authority decided not to take action because the land was already sold. By making formal complaints the opponent network used the system itself to fight a decision made by the system, as they expressed it. The fourth form involved a large petition against the city mall. The opponent network and many supporters in the city managed to collect 12,500 signatures against the city mall in a municipality of around 57,500 inhabitants. This was the form of protest and resistance that the citizens thought would be most successful due to the large number of signatures. But it did not work either.

These democratic activities illustrate a variety of democratic means with which to protest against a political decision: networking, public dialogue, forming organizations, making formal complaints, and petitioning. Combined they constituted a significant form of protest from a small group of competent citizens, but with wide support from other citizens in Helsingør, who joined the meetings, wrote letters to the newspaper, and signed the petition. This caused the opponent network to claim that they and not the city mall coalition represented the common interest of the city. These activities and the citizens' arguments expressed an integrative understanding of democracy.

The citizens did not expect their participation in the process to be limited to the formal procedures (the public hearings) in the planning process. They wanted to participate in forms of their own choice. Their saw themselves as competent and rational decision makers who had a duty to watch and control the work of the politicians and to act when the politicians failed to make sensible decisions for the city. They had to make sure that the decisions in the city council were based on the common interest, and this was only possible if there was a close relationship and debate between the citizens and the politicians—the elite. When decisions were not sensible, the citizens had to interfere and try to stop the politicians by using different democratic means. Otherwise, they would not be responsible citizens. Actually, they saw the politicians as people who could easily be corrupted and who could abuse their power due to self-interest. In the case of the city mall, they accused the politicians of being in the pocket of local businessmen and big investors. For the citizens it was appropriate democratic behavior to participate in every part of the process if they wanted, and, when they chose to act, the politicians had to listen and change their decision. Especially, when more than 12,000 citizens had the same opinion.

Evaluating the process from the integrative perspective of democracy made the citizens conclude that it was completely incomprehensible and undemocratic when the politicians ignored the resistance and maintained the decision about the city mall. They never understood how this could happen, and that the politicians could still be seen as democratic, which is how the politicians presented themselves. They did not accept the aggregative arguments about democracy just as the politicians and the city mall network never accepted the integrative and deliberative arguments. It was a confrontation of two opposite interpretations of how a representative democracy should develop toward a network democracy, which placed the politicians and citizens in two very different roles.

The process saw the rise of two opposite and competing interpretations of a democratic governance process. The two democratic perspectives of aggregation and integration/deliberation established two different bases for the evaluation of a proper democratic governance process. Consequently, both sides accused the other of not being democratic and they reached opposite answers to the question of whether the centralized and elitist governance process was democratic or not. From the aggregative perspective it was democratic due to several democratizing elements in the process. From the integrative and deliberative perspective it was not because it excluded the citizens' protests.

If in general, we evaluate the process from the integrative perspective, we certainly have to evaluate the centralized and elitist governance process as undemocratic and very far from moving toward a deliberative version of a network democracy. A common understanding of the city mall was never developed and neither was a common understanding of the proper democratic process in this case. Mistrust and lack of respect for the opposite side characterized the process, as did confrontations and conflicts. Both sides saw the process as a battlefield and used war metaphors when they talked about the process, for example, enemies, hand grenades, minefields, etc. There was no sign of empathic behavior between the opponents in the conflict and no sign of a communicative discourse ethic in the case of the city mall. Furthermore, nobody tried to mediate or develop any form of consensus in this process.

There is no doubt that the choice in Helsingør (made consciously or unconsciously) of the centralized, elitist governance process was not experienced as a positive and constructive political process for the actors involved. And it never created any common ownership to the decision about the city mall. Still today, the persons involved talk about this process as a bad experience that widened the distance between politicians and citizens. If one makes the political choice to develop governance processes like the one in Helsingør, one has to take these effects on urban democracy into account.

Conclusion

The chapter has presented a discussion about the relationship between urban governance and democracy both in theory and in practice in a Danish urban policy process. The purpose has been to highlight the democratic consequences of governance processes and policy networks. How did policy networks operate? How was hierarchy expressed in the process? How was representative democracy affected and did new democratic forms arise?

The chapter showed that governance and policy networks can develop in different forms in practice and this becomes important for the discussion of the democratic consequences. In the case of the city mall in Helsingør, the process was centralized and elitist, based on a closed and stable policy network (the city mall network) in coalition with the majority in the city council, and the representatives of the large interests groups in the city. This network coalition also developed a discourse coalition about the city mall, which entailed stressing problem solving in the city and a new identity and future for the city. Through this discourse they legitimized their actions by claiming to represent the common interest of the city. The policy process reflected the aggregate and corporate tradition in the city for engaging in politics, and by doing that the governance process developed in harmony and not in conflict with the former democratic system in the city. This was an important explanation for the successful realization of the city mall.

The city mall coalition was very exclusive of other actors and meanings in the city. At first, a few fragmented groups opposed the city mall but later on citizens and small shopkeepers used the networking strategy to form an open and unstable policy network, which was very effective in organizing numerous democratic activities to protest against the city mall. They legitimized their actions by defending the city's architectural heritage, and by doing so they also claimed to represent the common interest of the city. The opponent network and its activities became the most important threat to the implementation of the city mall. However, the opponents never managed to make a strong counter alliance or a strong alternative discourse coalition to match the one of the city mall network. This partly explains the failure of the protests.

Another explanation for the success of the closed, stable city mall network was the role of hierarchy in the process. The case study illustrated how hierarchical elements were integrated into the governance process and in the policy network. This was carried out in the form of the actors involved in the process (the top representatives of local government), through the guidance principles in the policy network (the political will of the city council and bureaucratic rule following), and through the close relationship between the policy network and the city council. The policy network never became autonomous to the elected political center and local government stayed in control of the governance process and the policy network. This became important for the legitimacy of the city mall network and its activities.

The centralized, elitist governance process did not undermine representative democracy. Rather it became part of it and can be interpreted as a development of representative democracy into an aggregative version of a network democracy. There was a long tradition for this kind of democracy in the city, and the chapter shows how the aggregate interpretation of democracy is expressed by the city mall coalition. This coalition upheld the argument that the competent representatives and the elites had to govern the city by maintaining a distance from the citizens because the citizens were mostly motivated by self-interest. In this particular case there were several factors which democratized the centralized and elitist governance process. One was the political will in the city council to build the city mall, which was the driving force for the process. Another was the long and open public debate about the city mall inside and outside the city council (especially in the local press). The combination of the centralized, elitist governance process with the central role played by the city council in the process and the long and open public debate made the actors in the city mall coalition evaluate the process as democratic from an aggregate perspective on democracy.

However, this conclusion was challenged in the process especially by the opponent policy network and its activities. They represented quite a different understanding of a representative democracy moving toward a network democracy based on integrative and deliberative arguments. They insisted on being integrated into the process and on having an influence on the political decisions as competent citizens. They felt obliged to stop the politicians and initiated, during a short period, a variety of democratic activities to change the decision about the city mall: networking, public dialogue, a new organization, formal complaints, and petitioning. Moreover, they expected these activities to make a difference. According to an integrative and deliberative perspective on democracy these activities should not have been neglected and this made the opponents regard the process as being undemocratic.

The chapter showed how two opposing and competing interpretations of a representative network democracy influenced the political process in Helsingør. The aggregative and the integrative/deliberative perspective turned out to constitute two competing bases for the evaluation of the governance process. From the aggregative perspective the process was democratic, from the integrative and deliberative it was certainly not. There was never any mediation between the two perspectives in the process. And the whole process was experienced as a war between the supporters and opponents of the city mall. Common ownership about the decision concerning the city mall was never constructed, and citizens' participation was never solicited in an atmosphere based on trust and confidence. Communication was not based on empathy and social rationality but on disrespect and on a cynical and strategic rationality.

Nobody in Helsingør has experienced this process as constructive and positive for urban democracy. They got the city mall, but the price paid was a high one for local democracy, engendering as it did all the dramatic conflicts in the city, and the disillusion among the citizens about the purpose of local democracy. Furthermore, the process created a wide gap between politicians and citizens that still influences local politics today. One has to consider these consequences if the choice is made to follow this centralized, elitist direction in urban governance based on the aggregate version of a network democracy.

Note

1. This is not the place for long methodological explanations. In brief, the empirical study has been conducted as a qualitative case study based on qualitative interviews and

written public documents, newspaper articles, reports, etc. The strategy for analysis was formed as a social constructivist bottom-up study of policy networks and policy processes in an institutional and discursive perspective (see Sehested 2002). The theoretical perspectives of networks (inspired by Rhodes 1997 and other network theorists), institutions (inspired by March and Olsen 1989), and discourses (inspired by Laclau and Mouffe 1985) were used as different perspectives with which to analyze events in Helsingør. Theories of governance and democracy were used to discuss general tendencies in the local context

Chapter 6

Entrepreneurship in Community Development and Local Governance

Lars Hulgård

Agents matter in modernization processes, and yet we lack specific knowledge about the influence and impact of important change agents, the social entrepreneurs. This is true of the entrepreneurial types of citizens who, either for limited periods or for a lifetime, commit themselves to the development of local communities and governance networks, or to projects aimed at crossing the borders of well-known professional and sectional lines. It also applies to professionals in the public administration who take chances and risks by their direct involvement in innovation in public institutions.

Who are they? What motivates them? What is the role of entrepreneurs in public policy innovation and community development? Such entrepreneurs are driven by two opposing types of motives: free enterprise and community. This may be difficult for social and political scientists to understand, but certainly not for the public entrepreneurs and social entrepreneurs themselves.

While rational choice-based revisions of classical economics understand entrepreneurship as merits of alert individuals seeking a business opportunity (Schneider et. al. 1995), research within the social sciences has begun to study new forms of entrepreneurship emphasizing community and governance (Wilson 1997; Healey 1997; Gittell and Vidal 1998; Evers 2001).

I argue that although community is an important concept in relation to public policy innovation, rational choice approaches have little to say about this. To overemphasize the individual entrepreneur's rational choices is to neglect that innovative actions are often embedded in forms of collectivity/community. "Private enterprise" carried out by "free individuals" who base their actions solely on individual calculations of costs and benefits hardly exists.

In the first part of this chapter, I discuss the issue of individual calculation versus community as explanatory factors for entrepreneurial activities with reference to contemporary studies of public entrepreneurship which have been conducted within the boundaries of a rational choice approach (Schneider et. al. 1995; Oliver 1996). My critique of rational choice is inspired by studies of civic entrepreneurship (Henton et. al. 1997), moral entrepreneurship (Hunter and Fessenden 1994), and the Weberian approach to cultural analysis.

Next, I present a number of cultural and sociological studies that emphasize community and social capital as key concepts in theories of entrepreneurship. The conceptual challenge is to link that which is already connected at the local level, namely, innovation and enterprise with community and local governance. All of these factors are crucial for understanding the role of entrepreneurs in community building and democratic governance. A similar binary focus is elaborated in several recent studies stressing that civic and social entrepreneurship combine two important traditions: entrepreneurship (the spirit of enterprise) and civic virtue (the spirit of community) (Henton et. al. 1997; Wilson 1997; Leadbeater 1997; Evers 2001).

This argument is further elaborated with reference to my empirical study of social entrepreneurship in California and Denmark. The study is based on interviews and secondary analysis of entrepreneurs engaged in community building in Silicon Valley (California), Coachella Valley (California), Randers (Denmark), and Vesterbro (Denmark). In this section of the chapter, I also draw upon my participation in a comparative European study on the emergence of social enterprises. Related to this study we have identified how such enterprises are blurring the frontiers between action for private benefit and action for the public good (Evers 2001). Social enterprises are activities that are simultaneously producing goods or services and engaged in local democratic governance.

The Rational Choice Approach to Public Entrepreneurship

Schneider, Teske, and Mintron (1995) and Oliver (1996) are anxious to argue that there is a lack of conceptual consensus concerning the importance of entrepreneurs involved with public policy and public administration. Oliver even mentions this lack five times in the first few pages of his article. He emphasizes that: "At this time, there is no consensus on the boundaries of the phenomenon. The existing literature also presents disparate views of the scope of entrepreneurial activities and functions in the process of innovation," (Oliver 1996, 5 and 9).

Oliver points to the fact that although there is a considerable consensus about the importance of entrepreneurs—they are even crucial in processes of social change—we know little about them. First, little is known about the supply of public entrepreneurs. Second, we are facing a "considerable disagreement among theorists as to what motivates entrepreneurial behavior in the public sector" (Oliver 1996, 8).

This lack of conceptual consensus concerning an important, easily recognizable, empirical phenomenon needs rectifying.

Public Entrepreneurs Are Profit-Seeking Individuals

Faced with the lack of a synthesis, Schneider, Teske, and Mintron (1995) build their definitions of the public entrepreneur on the work of the Austrian School of Economics. Using this approach, the authors interpret the focal point of recent economic literature on entrepreneurship as being "the emphasis on the 'discovery' of market opportunities by 'alert' individuals." (Schneider et al. 1995: 8). The reason for building a theory of public entrepreneurship on economics is the belief that "none of the social sciences has produced a fully formed theory of entrepreneurship . . . the economic approach is the most fruitful avenue to follow" (Schneider et. al. 1995, 12).

The authors stress the lack, and the necessity, of "truly rigorous theories" of entrepreneurship and in their search for a "rigorous" theory of public entrepreneurship in nonincremental processes of change, they rely upon the rational choice revision of classical economic explanations: "We believe that entrepreneurs actually respond to rational benefit/cost calculations in choosing their actions: that is, they are motivated by a desire for 'profits' or personal gain (pg. 6)...Fundamental to our study is the argument that entrepreneurs engage in rational benefit/cost analyses when deciding to pursue opportunities" (Schneider et. al. 1995, 12). Public entrepreneurs engage in innovative actions in order to earn profits. They are motivated by a desire for personal gain. Private action is action taken for the private good, but unlike the economic entrepreneurs, the public entrepreneur's motivation is not necessarily linked to an increase in personal wealth. Public entrepreneurs have other functions than those of reallocating opportunities on the private market. Usually, they have utility functions that facilitate their ability to influence public policy and their desire for power, prestige, and popularity.

According to rational choice theory, the costs and benefits to individual actors constitute the explanatory factors not only of public entrepreneurship but also entrepreneurship in general. When public entrepreneurs make the decision to allocate energies and scarce resources to public sector activities, they begin by comparing their possible gains with the expected costs involved in the implementation of the innovation. This comparison or calculation finally determines whether the entrepreneur decides to allocate resources and energies to innovative activities in the public sector.

The Schneider/Teske approach leaves us with one main explanatory factor: the public entrepreneurs' drive for profit, albeit not solely understood as economic profit. Although the rational calculation of costs and benefits made by individual actors now and then might serve as excellent "objectively verifiable regularities," this approach is much too narrow for the study of public and social entrepreneurship.

As I will show in the following presentation of results from my studies of social entrepreneurship in California and Denmark, the entrepreneurs demonstrated astonishingly little concern for the personal costs of getting involved in innovative activities. One was concerned about personal health, and another was motivated by the idea of "giving back to society because of my great luck in business," while most of them were simply inspired by the thought of empowering the community, either as a value in itself or as a precondition for competitiveness.

Critique of the Rational Choice Approach to Entrepreneurship

For the rational choice approach, however, such motifs as the sense of community or a wish to pay back carry only little explanatory value when they are applied to the study of entrepreneurship. Schneider, Teske, and Mintron (1995) dissociate themselves from cultural- and anthropological-oriented approaches to the study of entrepreneurship. After a short examination of cultural- and anthropological-oriented studies of social change as suggested by Weber, Berger, and others they conclude that such explanations cannot be tested empirically. Thus, they neglect the fact that the Weberian approach to social science is to a substantial degree empirically oriented, and that Weber's own cultural analysis of "protestant entrepreneurship" is widely known as a masterpiece in historical sociology (Lepsius 1990).

Instead, Schneider, Teske, and Mintron claim that approaches put forward by anthropologists, historians, psychologists, and sociologists emphasizing cultural, noneconomic factors are "doing little to facilitate rigorous empirical testing." Theories of entrepreneurship need to be "focusing on objectively verifiable regularities, such as the costs and benefits to entrepreneurship" (Schneider et al. 1995, 74).

Let us now turn to a fundamental question: is it possible or just acceptable to stay within the boundaries of theories originating in neoclassical economics, when we want to understand the role of public entrepreneurs in the policy process or social entrepreneurs in community building?

A restricted view of entrepreneurship will shed light only upon a very specific kind of action: those which fit into the cost-benefit universe. We still lack evidence supporting the assertion that entrepreneurs within public and civic spheres are simply reacting to individual opportunities based on cost-benefit analysis as stated by Schneider, Teske, and Mintron (1995).

The Problem of Identifying Public Entrepreneurs

Who are the entrepreneurs and how can we identify them? In their study, Schneider et al. identified public entrepreneurs by relying upon a survey of approximately 1,000 city clerks who were asked if, during recent years, there had been "any individual in their community whose policy proposals and political positions represented a dynamic change from existing procedures" (Schneider et. al. 1995, 89). Not surprisingly, 43 percent of the entrepreneurs identified by Schneider et al. in local communities were mayors, 26 percent were members of the city council, and 23 percent were city managers.

In total, 92 percent of the political entrepreneurs identified at the local level were "system insiders," but how can we be sure that the city clerks actually identified the entrepreneurs who changed the policy or maybe even changed the lanes of modernization? The result leaves us with 8 percent room for entrepreneurial individuals coming from outside the local policy system. The identification of 92 percent of the political entrepreneurs as coming from within the local political system might very well indicate a kind of self-reference, where a representative of the local government more than likely identifies good practice or innovative practice, but within the boundaries of the logic of appropriateness.

Asking the city clerks to identify local entrepreneurs is a plausible point of departure. However, the investigation cannot serve as the final result. I seriously doubt that entrepreneurs are identified that way by Schneider et al. Rather, the point is that this issue implies a bottom-up oriented research strategy including the backward mapping of what actually happened. Are the entrepreneurs at the local level primarily mayors or progressive city managers, who succeed in implementing the innovation in the public policy at the local level, or could it also be members of social movements and pressure groups who continuously raise questions of social, environmental, or fiscal character? Could it be a wealthy man working in a California food bank continuously claiming that wealthy cities should pick up responsibility for "the policy problem"? I believe so, and in the next section I will return to these questions on an empirical level.

Concerning the concept of "public entrepreneurs": The consequences of entrepreneurship are often innovations in the public sector. Nevertheless, this does not mean that the entrepreneurs initially need to be public servants or oriented exclusively toward the public sector. Often, entrepreneurs work outside the public sector when they start to be innovative. Often they are social entrepreneurs while the results of their actions are having profound consequences for the organization and modernization of the public sector.

Perhaps it is even more correct to talk about moral, social, or civic entrepreneurs working with innovations that have public consequences than it is to talk about public entrepreneurs. As emphasized by Kellner and Heuberger (1994, 164 ff.), innovations caused by moral entrepreneurs often have consequences for the entire nation, for example, civil rights, reproductive rights, non-smokers rights, animal rights, and, currently, the dawn of a welfare rights movement.

The Weberian Approach to Entrepreneurship

In contrast to the rational choice approach, I suggest that entrepreneurs often work as "servants" of interests other than their own immediate interests in profit, be they ideal motives (Max Weber 1904) or motives concerned with the importance of the collective (John Friedman 1992; Lee Staples 1995), or motives derived from the wish to pay back. When searching for ways of extending our understanding of entrepreneurs beyond the role of factors directly linked to costs and benefits, it is valuable to reconsider the Weberian notion that ideas and values matter in processes of modernization (Lepsius 1990, 31-44; Schluchter 1979, 39 ff.).

As stressed by Max Weber in his sociology of the world religions, perhaps the "benefits" of specific actions were often consequences of the environment/ context of the idea, while the value or the idea itself was the direct trigger of the action (Weber 1904; Lepsius 1990). According to this well-known perspective, ideas as well as interests can change the lanes of modernization. In his sociohistorical research into the relation between the Protestant ethic and capitalism, Weber showed how the Calvinist idea of predestination influenced the process of modernization in the West. The idea of predestination caused the religious entrepreneurs to work harder in order to "secure" their foreordination to salvation. The benefits derived from this work, one's calling, was linked to the environment rather than to "the idea" itself.

From Weber we get the notion of value orientation as triggers for action. From Durkheim we inherit the notion of a "conscience collective" and the idea of "the precontractual" as being prior to the autonomous individual calculating costs and benefits. For Durkheim the concept of the precontractual not only served as the "locus" of solidarity and social bonds, it also rested upon the idea that there are rules, norms, and forms of regulation which are prior to any given contract and independent of the contract. This emphasis on social solidarity or the possibility of mutual trust was Durkheim's answer to utilitarian and contract political theories. He understood precontractual trust in modern, organic society as being founded on an "ethical valuation of individual personality." This valuation of the individual, however, was not an acclamation of the utilitarian individual, but an acclamation of the "embedded" individual.

Let us now use the approach stressing value orientation (Weber) and the sense of community (Durkheim) as explanatory factors for current entrepreneurial activities. The argument is not so much to deny the importance of rational choice in specific situations as it is to emphasize the impact of values and community. Only when it is argued that "the economic approach is the most fruitful avenue to follow" (Schneider 1995) as a general theory of entrepreneurship, do I become very sceptical.

The Results from Four Case Studies

The following four cases all illuminate the role of community and value orientation as important explanatory factors for entrepreneurial activities. The first two cases are based upon research conducted in California between January and August 1998. They are based upon extensive use of secondary data and interviews with six leaders, whom I consider to be either civic or social entrepreneurs. The last two cases are based partly upon my study of the role of social entrepreneurs in community building in Denmark (Hulgård 1997; Bengtsson and Hulgård 2001) and partly upon my participation in a comparative European research project. The third case discusses the role of social entrepreneurs in two specific community development projects in Denmark, while the fourth case is a short presentation of the British Community Action Network (the CAN-network), a mutual learning and support network for social entrepreneurs in Great Britain.

Case 1: Social Entrepreneurship in Coachella Valley: The Entrepreneurial Motives Are Blurred

We begin with Mr. X from Coachella Valley in Southern California. When I first heard of Mr. X, I did not think of him as an entrepreneur—he seemed to be just another American millionaire spending time and money on charity. He was in fact a very wealthy man spending most of his time undertaking charity and cultural activities. However, as a social entrepreneur he was also spending a significant amount of time working for a local food bank:

> About five or six years ago they asked me to come in and do some work on their advertising, brochures, fund-raising and everything else, and I did. Then in 1994 they fell behind very seriously on their monthly agreement on rent. At that time I said, "look this place is gonna go under unless we do something about it." I made a deal with the management, I think at that time we owed them almost thirty thousand Dollars. I said look we are even going to go bankrupt. I will give you a check for twenty thousand Dollars.

> When I first started working there, we didn't even have electricity, so we had no lights, no heat, no air-conditioning of any kind, and you can imagine what it was like in the summer. So finally two years ago I put in an evaporative cooler. I am also working on the floor handling the food. Sometimes twenty hours a week. Most of the food would be in banana boxes—and we just constantly—and this is heavy work—take these boxes, empty them and go through everything. Clean it if it needs cleaning, like if a can of soda burst in a case. But all this dirt we work in—it is so terrible. We badly need to build a new building that is energy efficient. And I have promised to contribute one hundred thousand Dollars to a new building, and I know we can get free land.

Besides the work in the food bank this man has established, financed, and is running a local museum and several other cultural and educational activities. Is he a social entrepreneur, or is he just a very wealthy man doing charity work? He certainly creates, organizes, and finances social, cultural, and educational services which in some countries are considered to be public affairs. I believe he must be considered both a social and a public entrepreneur. He is a public entrepreneur as he generates solutions to policy problems, which in other institutional configurations are public responsibilities. However, from the perspective of rational choice and the strict and "rigorous" focus on individual costs and benefits his activities seem to be a bit strange. When establishing a museum and other major public services, he does not seek fame or fortune. We need to look in other directions in order to find plausible explanations.

So, I simply asked him: "Why don't you just send a check? That would be much easier emotionally."

> I like both. I feel it is necessary. Money is very important, but the man-hours are so vital. Because time is money. If I give them one hundred thousand Dollars—or whatever I give—to fund operations that are absolutely necessary like electricity or fuel for their vehicles or their rent. If they don't have to spend money to have people work there that is doubling my contribution. And as long as I have the time and health and can do something that I feel is beneficial—not wasting my talents on anything—then I am happy to do it. I know the people who I have worked with on voluntary work feel exactly the same way, they come from all walks of life. We are all there rubbing elbows together, and they could be in capital, in industry, or living in a trailer.
>
> And in my case it is also a payback, because I was incredible lucky in my business life. I was lucky to be in the right place at the right time. How can I explain that. I was very fortunate, and just feel that I want to do something for people to show my appreciation."
>
> The problem is not necessarily the homeless, hungry and starving people. It is the people who are making seven thousand Dollars a year, and they have three, four, and five children and there are a lot of people right here in the valley, living in their cars. We have the problem here that these people can go through these gaudy streets that we have, because these cities Rancho Mirage and Palm Desert have so much money to spend. And yet they only get five to ten thousand Dollars—I give more money to the food bank than Rancho Mirage and Palm Desert do, that is discouraging, but that is what happens.

This raised another question: "My impression is that we have a class of what you could call the nouveau rich. Often they lack this sense of responsibility you are talking about, for example, when you consider your initiatives to be a kind of payback?"

> The nouveau rich is the ugly American. We have them, they are here, and I have seen it happen so many times, where someone who gets wealthy quickly,

and a lot of that is happening on the market. It goes to their head, and it just seems to ruin all sense of reasoning and responsibility. But fortunately it is not a contagiously disease, and not everyone has it.

Mr. X earned his money from the invention of a new service, and from books he wrote related to this service. Later he sold his company at a rather young age. He is inspired by a vision of paying back some of the fortune earned in his business life, and he is inspired by a social indignation, a wish to get things done. In my opinion, such sentiments are based upon a "conscience collective" and a concern for social cohesion not recognized properly by public authorities.

To some degree, this is also the case among the civil entrepreneurs in Silicon Valley, although their primary thought is to use the art of networking to build resilient and competitive communities.

Case 2: Civic Entrepreneurship in "Joint Venture: Silicon Valley"

Douglas Henton (1997) uses the concept "civic entrepreneurs" for leaders from all spheres of society, government, market, and civil society when they gather in collaborative arenas. I met Douglas Henton in his firm, Collaborative Economics, in Palo Alto, California, in 1998. Henton is a coauthor of *Civic Entrepreneurs: How Grassroots Leaders Are Building Prosperous Communities*. (Henton, Melville, and Walesh 1997). I was interested in meeting Henton because of his experiences in creating arenas where leaders from civil society, private enterprises, and local governments meet in collaborative approaches to regional development. The goal is resilient and competitive communities. A civic entrepreneur is a change agent, a go-between who, not as a heroic individual, intermediates between various interests often in collaborative manners.

To Henton et. al. "civic entrepreneurs are catalysts who help communities go through a change process," and they are motivated by an interest in "making a difference in the world." Civic entrepreneurs share five common features, including that they: (1) see opportunity in the new (global) economy, (2) possess an entrepreneurial personality, (3) provide collaborative leadership to connect the economy and the community, (4) are motivated by broad, enlightened, long-term interests, and (5) work in teams, playing complementary roles (Henton et. al. 1997, 34).

During the interview about his work in building collaborative arenas for civic entrepreneurs primarily in Silicon Valley, I asked Douglas Henton why he always talks about civic entrepreneurs and not just entrepreneurs. Why is it important to emphasize that they are civic?

> It is a fundamental issue, and we try to make this point clear. There are three sectors, not two. Most people talk in terms of two sectors—private and public sector, and they act as if there is only business and government. But we believe that the most interesting and important work to be done is actually in the third

sector. That is not government, that is not business. So when a business person like the CEO (Lewis Platt) of Hewlett Packard, the largest company in Silicon Valley, who happens also to chair Joint Venture: Silicon Valley, gets involved in improving the educational system in Silicon Valley, he is doing that as a civic entrepreneur, not a business entrepreneur. He is doing that in the third sector. He is essentially taking his hat off saying, "I am the CEO of the largest company in the valley." Instead, he says, "as a member of this community I am going to spend a significant amount of time (as he has), in improving the educational system.

When the CEO of one of the world's largest corporations gets involved in community matters he suddenly becomes an important agent in changing attitudes in the valley. To Douglas Henton, he becomes a civic entrepreneur. I think this "designation" may be a bit of an exaggeration when applied to a major CEO who picks up responsibility for social and political cohesion in his business surroundings. A well-integrated community is, in the long run, undoubtedly serving the interests of big enterprises better than poorly integrated communities. Or as Robert Putnam states, "a well-connected individual in a poorly connected society is not as productive as a well-connected individual in a well-connected society. And even a poorly connected individual may derive some of the spill over benefits from living in a well-connected community" (Putnam 2000, 20).

This does not affect, however, the fact that the civic entrepreneurs in the Joint Venture played an important role in changing the attitudes among business leaders, leaders from local governments, and community leaders to a situation of mutual understanding. One and a half decades ago and well before "Joint Venture: Silicon Valley" the company's concern about community was limited. According to my interview with Tom Lewcock, former city manager in Sunnyvale, it was a widespread attitude among business leaders that "if the city (council) can not make this place work, then we are moving or at least establishing new branches in other areas." All five leaders I interviewed in relation to my research on civic entrepreneurship in Silicon Valley stressed that the attitude of mutual blame had changed in the valley.

To Lewcock, the Joint Venture is important because it consist of

> different sectors collaborating, networking and talking with each other as they have never done before. It has always been this sector here and that sector there, and this sector as an adversary of that one, without people understanding the common. Now you have people collaborating in such a fashion that rather than dealing with anecdotal information about who does what and why in the various sectors, there is a much deeper understanding. Networks are established, sometimes friendships are established, communication is much purer, more honest, and more accurate, and very often you tend to find that your assumptions about the private sector, or your assumptions about labor, or your assumptions about environmental interests are not exactly what you thought they were. People coming together where they can agree on a common agenda have a wonderful way of breaking through the traditional barriers that exist.

The making of collaborative arenas and civic entrepreneurship in Silicon Valley represents a similar approach to governance as the role of appreciative inquiry, and participatory democracy as it has been applied to public policy innovation (Spano 2001; Kristiansen and Hulgård 2002). Furthermore, it relates to governance as mediation and public policy facilitation discussed by Gary Marshall and Connie Ozawa (this book, chapter 8). They define mediation and public policy facilitation as mechanisms through which decisions requiring agreement among more than one party take place, and the overriding argument is that both individual and societal development can be furthered through mediation.

There is no doubt that the civic entrepreneurs forming the collaborative arena in Silicon Valley helped to change the attitudes among leaders from all three spheres, community, business, and government. As Henton stresses in the interview, the new form of collaborative relationship between business and government has prevented them from ending up "where we were seven years ago. At that time, they were fighting with each other, and we had a sort of cultural blame and a lot of things weren't getting done. It's just like anything else, you need a collaborate relationship."

In the case of "Joint Venture: Silicon Valley," the civic entrepreneurs acted as mediators between the government sector and the private firm. In an atmosphere where private firms resisted dealing with government, the hope was that the so-called civic entrepreneurs could enhance a climate of cooperation between the local community, private companies, and public authorities.

The civic entrepreneurs in Silicon Valley are working in a peculiar mix of facilitating the global economy and the local community. The title of the civic entrepreneur manifesto: "Grassroots Leaders for a New Economy," indicates this mixture of grassroots level and global economy. In this scenario, a well-functioning local community is "prosperous." Using the word "prosperous" as a synonym for "good community" indicates an approach that sees globalization and the making of community as a process of cooperation: The prosperous community is serving the new economy.

Summary of the Californian Cases and Introduction to the European

The Californian cases blur the beautiful conceptual sharpness built up to perfection in the rigors of the rational choice approach to entrepreneurial motives.

The rational choice approach requires "objectively verifiable factors" to explain motives and causes of entrepreneurial activities. This was indeed not the case with the wealthy social entrepreneur in Coachella Valley, and both cases show that there hardly exists a causal relationship between entrepreneurial activities and the individual calculation of costs and benefits.

Social entrepreneurship indicates a mix of community and enterprise similar to the civic entrepreneurs and their collaborative arena in Joint Venture: Silicon

Valley. But in the European cases of social entrepreneurship the mix of community and enterprise is different. In social entrepreneurship, the formation of an enterprise and the production of goods and services is a way of serving the community, and a way of experimenting with local governance. For civic entrepreneurs "community" is a means to facilitate the global economy, whereas social entrepreneurs are producing goods and services only insofar as such activities are expected to serve either the interests of the local community and the participants or some vulnerable parts of the population.

"Community" however is not a substantial category with a 'universal' pre-given meaning. Instead, it varies according to institutional configuration, which implies different patterns of institutional cooperation. The specific objectives, the participants, and the structures of cooperation are changeable according to the institutional characteristics of the entrepreneurial activities. In the Scandinavian societies, we experience a more direct involvement by public authorities in social enterprises than is the case in similar activities in other countries. However, despite differences there are a few overarching problems addressed by social and civic entrepreneurs no matter who they are or where they are working. These problems have to do with the need for community, social integration, and inclusion, and they usually involve the ambition to create new forms of local governance.

The third case to be presented in this chapter concerns social entrepreneurship in Denmark, especially as it is practiced in community development projects. The fourth case is a presentation of the British Community Action Network (the CAN-network), which sees itself as a network of social entrepreneurs.

Case 3: Social Entrepreneurship in the Danish Community

Though the characteristic of the Danish welfare system is a high degree of public involvement in financing and production of services, a new type of social entrepreneurship especially within community development has emerged under the influence of pilot and action programs (Bengtsson and Hulgård 2001). The "Wonder" in Randers and the "Side Street" project in Copenhagen, are two major Danish community development projects, and The Wonder, in particular, practices a multiorganizational approach to urban governance. Both are based on a resource mix between public and private funding. They are examples of new institutions that blur the demarcations between state, market, and civil society, and above all, it took the efforts of a social entrepreneur to realize the potentials.

The Wonder in Randers is a major multicultural and complex urban pilot project to improve employment prospects of marginalized communities in the Østergade district of Randers. The project is big, compared to Danish standards, and it is an important example of best practice in European urban regeneration. It is situated in the center of Randers, a traditional industrial city, which was relatively hard hit by the economic recession of the 1980s. It is located in two former industrial buildings connected with a roofed square. When fully developed, the Wonder covers an area of 5150m². It receives financial support from several sources: the municipality, the state, its own profits, and the European Union. The EU has provided the Wonder with a single grant of 2.25 million Euros from its funding for Urban Pilot Projects. Just as many other social enterprises, the Wonder has multiple objectives. However, its main objective is to visualize and enhance the cultural potential and resources of immigrants and refugee groups in the local community. It also focuses on improving the integration of immigrants into the labor market through extensive educational and training programs for immigrant groups, including entrepreneurship courses.

As with several other social and cultural development projects, the Wonder was founded by a woman, Lise Bisballe. A feature in a Danish magazine states that the Wonder would hardly exist without the fiery engagement of this social entrepreneur. In the magazine, she is portrayed as an *ildsjæl*, which directly translated into English means "fiery soul." In Denmark, "fiery soul" is a well-known word used to characterize civic and social entrepreneurs no matter from which sector they come.

The project began in the 1980s when Lise Bisballe, a trained weaver, established a workshop for female immigrants. Her goal was to improve the integration process through creative and entrepreneurial activities. Besides being a weaver, she was also engaged in urban development, and as such she soon became a promoter and spokeswoman for the Wonder. The ambition was to tell the Danes that refugees and immigrants have lots of resources and plenty to offer Danish society. These goals are still driving forces for Lise Bisballe, who now holds the position of "chief of development" for the entire enterprise. The fact that Lise Bisballe advanced to several positions from "just" being a concerned citizen, a "fiery soul," is a well-known phenomenon. Research on the impact of social innovation projects on social entrepreneurs show that being engaged in almost any kind of development and innovation activity is a direct rout to advancement in formal positions.

For the purpose of implementing the project, a new public-private management agency "the Wonder NGO," was created in 1998. Its main aim is to ensure the broad commitment and active involvement of the community, a crucial element in network governance. The organization's board of directors encompasses representatives from local private organizations in commerce, tourism, trade, and immigrant organizations. The city and county are represented by the mayor and deputy mayor. A comprehensive network—active at national and international levels—has already established and will continue to focus on exchanging experience and innovation in the Wonder. Today, the Wonder includes a regional center for arts and crafts, and a marketplace which will provide a multicultural meeting place. The marketplace enables artists, artisans, and entrepreneurs to make a living by marketing their products to tourists and other customers and thus act as a catalyst for further cultural activities and local tourism development (http://euro-urbanbestpractice.com/index.htm).

The "Side Street" was founded as a combined work training and community empowerment project in 1986. At that time, a social worker in Copenhagen working for a private nonprofit organization was feeling indignant at the sight that met him during his daily work in the, probably, most deprived area in the center of Copenhagen. The area had gone through a change from a working-class culture to a culture of poverty. The youngsters in the streets were unemployed, and the shops were closed. His idea was to combine the two things, and he created the "Side Street" with financial support from several private and public funds. His idea was to make a combined employment and community development project concerned with the empowerment of the participants and empowerment of the entire area. His vision was twofold: to open the shops, by making them into meaningful workplaces serving needs in the local area, and to change the private frustration and despair of the participants through an empowerment approach.

Today, seventeen years later, the project is not only still alive, it has expanded dramatically. There are eleven shops and workplaces related directly to the Side Street, and new projects have been established as spin-offs. The Copenhagen Recycling Company was established with close organizational relations to the Side Street in 1996. This company is cooperating with the largest refuse collection company in Copenhagen in connection with the training and education of sanitation workers. Another major project was the takeover of an old factory close to the Central Station. The factory is partly used by the recycling company and partly used for culture and sports activities. The main building has now been remodeled to a medium-sized sports and culture center with a handball hall, cafés, meeting rooms, and bathrooms. The purpose of this center is to serve as a cheaper and more approachable alternative to the new expensive "sports Mecca" recently built near by.

All these projects and new institutions are related to the Side Street, they are spin-offs of the social entrepreneur's original idea about connecting the unemployed youngsters with the closed shops in a combined community development and empowerment project.

What happened to the social worker who got the idea in 1986? Today he has advanced to a position as director of the entire organization (The Christian Student-Settlement), when, back in 1986, he was an "average" employee. If he at that time had engaged in a rational calculation of costs and benefits before deciding to pursue the opportunities, he would probably have chosen not to engage in the innovation project. As a social entrepreneur leading the project he had to work harder, the funding was insecure (it probably still is), since the local government in Copenhagen did not accept or support the project until years later.

For the rational choice approach, entrepreneurs engage in innovations only in order to earn entrepreneurial profits. The founder of the Side Street project did earn an entrepreneurial profit, because he now holds institutional power in his organization, in the local area, and in national discourses on social issues. That profit, however, was a consequence of the context rather than a consequence of his rational calculation of costs and benefits. What caused him to act? Well, we will never know in detail. But in a welfare rights project in the Kensington part of Philadelphia, I once observed that someone had written on a notice board: "Why do you do it?" "If I don't nobody else will." This statement illustrates precisely what causes many social entrepreneurs to act. It illustrates the theoretical ideas put forward by Patricia Wilson (1997), when she talks about the individual-in-community.

Case 4: Entrepreneurship in the British CAN-Network and European Social Enterprises

The "double-identity" of community building and enterprise is also the case in the British Community Action Network, a mutual learning and support network for social entrepreneurs (http://www.can-online.org.uk/). The aim of CAN is to increase the number of social entrepreneurs in the United Kingdom in order to strengthen (especially deprived) communities. CAN was founded by three people who already were identified as social entrepreneurs in a report by Charles Leadbeater (1997). Based on several case studies Leadbeater argues that social entrepreneurs are motivated by social goals rather than material profits. The report shows that social entrepreneurs are networking and bridging interests when they are helping people and local communities to "unlock potential" which has been neglected by the private and public sector.

The British Community Action Network for social entrepreneurs is based upon the founders' own experiences with social entrepreneurship. They see themselves as equivalents of business entrepreneurs, but they operate in the social economy: "They operate in the social, not-for-profit sector building 'something from nothing' and seeking new and innovative solutions to social problems. Their aim is to build 'social capital' and 'social profit' to improve the quality of life in some of the most 'difficult' and 'excluded' communities" (Community Action Network – CAN-Online).

Networking, connecting, mediating, and shaping collaborative arenas are some of the means used by CAN-Online, when going into action. That the Community Action Network has had an impact is beyond doubt. The scope of projects initiated by CAN, and the list of supporters are strong indicators of the impact. One project initiated by CAN is Asylum, an arts-based, community regeneration project in Wales. The town of Haverfordvest is a market town in a beautiful, but poor part of the United Kingdom. The objectives of Asylum are multi-dimensional, and they could almost be 'copies' of the objectives formulated by the Wonder. The aim of Asylum is: "to bring together key players in the local community to provide housing, jobs, training and other community services, along with facilities, such as a café, meeting areas, and, if possible, a performance space. At the center of the project will be a multi-media gallery displaying the work of the legendary Welsh artist Ralph Steadman." (http://www.can-online.org.uk/activity/regenerating/asylum.htm).

The similarities between Asylum and the Wonder are not coincidental, but consequences of their identities as being part of the same cross-national current which the current of social entrepreneurship that as a deliberate oxymoron unites worlds that usually are comprehended as belonging to separate spheres.

In a web-based article about Asylum, Julian Dobson reports that the model of social enterprise is moving out of the shadows of regeneration programs. It is now taking center stage. In the article, Dobson gives his own interpretation of one of the 'hits' in international social science: networking and mediation: "What has the artist Ralph Steadman[1] got in common with a mental hospital and an oil company? What's the link between a former Territorial Army center in Portsmouth and the Isle of Skye's first Internet café? And where does New Labour's favorite think tank fit in?" One of the leaders of CAN-Online Andrew Mawson gives an answer to this heterogeneous mix of people and interests. The idea is to build a plus sum culture where two plus two equals six.

However, "that won't happen if the local authorities sit over here, and the business community sit here, and the social sector sits here *People learn by doing, not talking.*"

This reflects the entire rationale of the Community Action Network: networking, mediating, establishing collaborative arenas. That this approach to community development has gained influence in Great Britain may be best indicated by some of the 'friends' of CAN-Online. Among them trade minister Patricia Hewitt, regeneration minister Hilary Armstrong and Prime Minister Tony Blair, who in a speech to the National Council of Voluntary Organizations spoke about the Community Action Network as an example of the wealth of initiatives being generated by the third sector. In the speech, he promised such initiatives to be priorities for the government, and he especially stressed the strategy of linking social entrepreneurs to share lessons and experiences.

Figure 6.1.

Adopting a Mission to Create and Sustain Social Value:
This is the core of what distinguishes social entrepreneurs from business entrepreneurs even from socially responsible businesses. For a social entrepreneur, the social mission is fundamental. This is a mission of social improvement that cannot be reduced to creating private benefits (financial return or consumption benefits) for individuals. Making a profit, creating wealth, or serving the desires of customers may be part of the model, but these are means to a social end, not the end in itself. Profit is not the gauge of value creation; nor is customer satisfaction; social impact is the gauge. Social entrepreneurs look for a long-term social return on investment. Social entrepreneurs want more than a quick hit; they want to create lasting improvements. They think about sustaining the impact.

Source: J. Gregory Dees, "The Meaning of Social Entrepreneurship"

Summary of the European Cases

The combination of entrepreneurship and community generated by European social enterprises seems to be part of an international trend in a variety of activities crossing boundaries of traditional divisions and images. Henton stressed that it is the combined effort of "the spirit of enterprise" and "the spirit of community" that can build prosperous communities. According to Patricia Wilson (1997) social capital, social entrepreneurship, and social enterprises are challenging the neoclassical imagination of the economic man calculating costs and benefits before choosing an action. Instead, the social entrepreneurs presumably all get their legitimacy from the idea of individual-in-community. Although there are substantial national differences in the way social entrepreneurship works the "accumulation" of social capital is a cross-national key factor.

In his summary of the experiences with European social enterprises, the German political scientist Adalbert Evers stresses that "a degree of entrepreneurial orientation (is an) imperative for each and every organization today, irrespective of its location in one or the other 'sector' (Evers 2001, 2). The point being that social entrepreneurship seems "to blur up a number of exactly those frontiers" which the analytical debates have created: the frontier between action for private benefit and action for the public good (Evers 2001, 1).

As we have seen in the presentation of the European cases, there are some interesting common features: first of all the combination of entrepreneurship with community and a goal of social sustainability. The resource-mix-structure is another general trend attacking the "three-sphere" model of social science, which maintain the sharp demarcation lines between state, economy, and civil society. Instead, it seems as if "reality has passed by the concept" of an independent voluntary sector, where influence and resources from neither market nor state plays a role (Evers 2001, 4).

Discussion: Social Capital as the Core of Social Entrepreneurship

Social entrepreneurs are involved in two types of activities that are usually seen as belonging to two very different spheres: community building and enterprise. They are building institutional capacity, and they are usually also involved in local governance. Simultaneously they are often producing goods or services, affairs that are usually carried out by private enterprises or public authorities. Perhaps social entrepreneurs are "oxymorons," insofar as they combine spheres that are often understood as contradictory. In that case, they are only oxymorons of our mind, since social entrepreneurs are already deeply engaged in building community and enterprises in one and the same time. They are building social capital and sustaining community through entrepreneurial means.

Looking at research into social entrepreneurship, one single concept continuously "pops up": social capital and usually the reference is to the work by Robert Putnam. "Social capital" happens to be another—but very similar—epistemological oxymoron that works perfectly in "the real world." Putnam's well-known thesis about the strange disappearance of civic engagement has been seriously questioned by many political scientists and social scientists (Cohen 1998; Skocpol 1996, 1997). However, the distinction between "bonding social capital" and "bridging social capital" is an especially promising conceptual distinction which can be used in research into social entrepreneurs' participation in community building and local governance (Gittell and Vidal 1998; Healey 1997; Wilson 1997).

The entrepreneurs I have interviewed in the United States and Denmark are only occasionally public entrepreneurs in the sense suggested by, for example, Schneider and others (1995) and Oliver (1997). Some call themselves civic entrepreneurs, and some I would judge to be social entrepreneurs. They share one concern: the concern for social sustainability and the concern for community. All of them are engaged in innovative activities.

In this chapter, I have argued that we need to look in directions other than costs and benefits to understand their actions. Explanations can hardly be found without looking at the embeddedness of social actions. This represents a sort of middle ground (structuration) theory between methodological individualism, which traces all social phenomena back to individual actions, preferences, and value orientation, and a more Durkheimian approach, which operates on a structural level emphasizing the role of a "conscience collective."

Cost-benefit analysis simply does not work, if we are to understand the actions of entrepreneurs engaged in community development and local governance. The Asylum in Wales, the Wonder in Randers, and the Side Street in Copenhagen are, besides their potential as social capital accumulators, all examples of deliberative democracy and public spheres generating ideas and input to the policy process (Habermas 1998, 304-08). They are, British political scientist John Keane's terms, "micro-public spheres." Keane suggests that a variety of local spaces today are counterparts to the coffeehouse, town-level meeting, and literary circle, in which early modern public spheres developed. Micro-public spheres are a vital feature of social movements, and they are "local spaces in which citizens enter into disputes about who does and who ought to get what, when and how" (Keane 1998, 170).

However, social entrepreneurs are more than 'just' activists in micro-public spheres generating ideas and input to be used by state institutions in "real politics." They are crucial partners in governance networks on the local level. As illustrated with the British "Community Action Network" they even tend to cross the limits of locality and become full-fledged partners in the making of postmodern democracy. At the center of the successful community we find social entrepreneurs, who mediate between segregated communities, fragmented places, and bonds and bridges of social capital.

Patricia Wilson even talks about social capital as a learning agenda for the twenty-first century. This agenda "mocks the leading tenet of mainstream economics—the idea of 'economic man,' the individual separate self-rationally calculating the costs and benefits of his every action on the basis of self-interest. The successful community is not a collection of atomistic individuals bumping into each other's self-interest, but rather is a network, a web of individuals-in-community" (Wilson 1997, 756).

Note

1. The British artist Ralph Steadman is well known especially to an American audience. In the 1970s, he joined Hunter S. Thompson on several "tour de forces" in American policy landscapes. Steadman was the illustrator of Thompson's famous books *Fear and Loathing in Las Vegas* and *Fear and Loathing on the Campaign Trail 72*, in which they together more or less invented the concept of gonzo journalism/new journalism."

Chapter 7

Democratic Governance and the Role of Public Administrators

Eva Sørensen

This chapter discusses the consequences for democracy of a series of changes in the role that public administrators play in the political system. The need for such a discussion is accentuated by the agreement among a number of social scientists that the political systems in the Western world are today more correctly described as systems of governance than as systems of government (Rhodes 1997; 2000; Pierre 2000; Mayntz 1999; Kooiman 1993; Kickert et al. 1997; Heinrich and Lynn 2000; Jessop 1998; Scharpf 1994; 1999; Bogason 2000; March and Olsen 1995). A system of *government* is based on the idea that there is a sovereign decisionmaker who governs by means of an institutionalized structure of hierarchical decision making and neutral implementation. In a system of *governance* there is no sovereign located on the top of a unitary, hierarchical political institution of government. The complexity, diversity, and dynamism of contemporary Western societies have led to the formation of a governance structure that is just as complex, diversified, and dynamic.

Internally, the political systems in many Western countries have become multicentered and fragmented. We have witnessed a simultaneous process of political and administrative decentralization and internationalization. Consequently, the contemporary political systems consist of many relatively autonomous levels of authoritative decision making. Furthermore, we have witnessed an introduction of New Public Management reforms that have increased the autonomy of public institutions and administrative units (Osborne and Gaebler 1993; Hood 1991). In this process traditional, hierarchical forms of authority such as law and bureaucratic rule have been supplemented, if not replaced, by more horizontal forms of regulation such as negotiations, agreements, contracts, and, not least, network formation.

Externally, we witness increased cooperation between public and private actors (Heinrich and Lynn 2000). One example of this is the establishment of partnerships between private firms and/or voluntary organization, and actors within the public sector. Another example is the establishment of various forms of public councils and boards with a number of private actors as their members. The result has been a blurring of the emergence of what has been denoted a "gray-zone" of societal governance, which does not respect the traditional claim for as sharp a dividing line between the public and the private sector (Greve 1998). In the gray-zone actors work together with little regard for formal structures and traditional divisions between the public and the private sector, and organizations are formed which mix organizational forms of state (rules and hierarchy), market (competition and economic incentives), and civil society (social norms and interpersonal bonds).

In the wake of these internal and external transformations, a variety of systems of governance have emerged in which governance is produced in and through networks among a range of actors with legitimate decision-making powers. For producers of societal governance—such as public administrators—two means of governance are available. First, governors have the possibility to participate as resourceful actors within various networks (Jessop 1999). Second, governors can govern indirectly through the formation of the conditions under which networks function. This can be done through the distribution of resources to network participants (Rhodes 1997), through the strategic formation of the incentive structures under which networks operate (Kooiman 1993), and/or through the production of narratives and discourses that enhance the formation of desired network identities (March and Olsen 1995).

This chapter seeks, first, to analyze the effects that the transformation from a system of government to a system of governance has on the role of the public administrator, and, second, to analyze the consequences of these effects on democracy. Hence, it is likely that the requirements of a system of governance do not square very well with the role that is ascribed to public administrators in traditional, representative democracies where politicians incarnate the will of the people. Accordingly, the democratic role of the public administrators is to act in accordance with the views of the politicians. In practice, this means that public administrators are expected to act in accordance with the laws, rules, and regulations that are decided by the politicians. In (the many) situations in which it is necessary to use administrative discretion they should act as they expect the politicians would want them to act. To put it briefly, in a representative democracy public administrators are expected to turn their attention "upward" toward the politicians. It is only relevant for them to turn their attention "downward" in the direction of the citizens in order to obtain the information necessary to apply the right laws and rules in a concrete situation. The views and ideas of the citizens are not regarded as relevant for the public administrators because the political role of the citizens in representative democracy is restricted to their participation on Election Day and in the public debate. Therefore, the traditional public administrator regards the citizen as an object of governance, for example, clients, and not as a co-producer of governance.

The change toward a system of governance that has taken place confronts this perception of what it means to be a public administrator in a radical way. Today, not only politicians and administrative superiors but also a whole range of other actors such as voluntary organizations, private firms and organizations, user boards, various semi-public councils, individual citizens, public professionals, and even the public administrators themselves, are involved in legitimate processes of societal decision making. It seems fair to presume that this state of affairs puts pressure on public administrators to turn their attention in more than one direction. They must continue to direct their attention "upward" to the politicians and the administrative superiors. However, at the same time they must direct their attention "downward" to individual citizens and to lower political and administrative levels in the multilayered political system and "outward" to the private actors in the gray zone of societal governance. I do not intend to suggest that the traditional public administrators did not have to turn their attention in more than one direction. As Michael Lipsky so vividly describes it in his famous book: *Street-Level Bureaucracy* (Lipsky 1980) traditional public administrators who are close to the clients feel that they have to direct their attention upward in order to meet demands from to the politicians and the executives, downward to meet demands for more and better services from their clients, and inward to meet the professional standards for good service provision that they have internalized as a part of their education. Lipsky show how street level bureaucrats develop a range of coping strategies and techniques that help them to handle this situation of cross pressure. However, Lipsky's study is not about democracy; rather, it is about dilemmas related to the promotion of quality and efficiency in service provision. This chapter is not about the role of public administrators in processes of service production. It is about the role that they play in processes of democratic decision making in an emerging system of governance. The two questions which I seek to answer in this chapter are: 1) what coping strategies do public administrators who act within in a governance structure use in order to be able to turn their attention upward as well as outward and downward, and 2) what consequences do the choices of different coping strategies have for democracy?

Since it is not possible to answer these questions in full within the limits of a chapter, I will confine myself to illustrating the relevance and importance of such an analysis. I will do so by describing and discussing the coping strategies of five local public administrators. They are all employed in a Danish municipality whose political system can largely be characterized as a system of governance. This proceeds as follows: First I describe the method used in the study. Second, I give a short description of the decision-making structure in the municipality where the five public administrators work. Third, I present the five administrators' coping strategies, and, finally, I discuss the problems and potentials for democracy that they bring about.

The Method

Five interviews were undertaken as a part of a large research project named "Democracy from below" which was financed by the Danish National Research Council. This research project was conducted in the period 1996-2000. It involved ten researchers who were all engaged in what could be seen as a Danish "Who governs?" revisited study (Dahl 1961). Hence, the aim of the study was to uncover the nature and processes of democratic decision making in a specific town (Bang, Hansen and Hoff 2000). The motivation for the study lay with the transformation of the Danish political system from a system of government to a system of governance, and this specific town was chosen because it was one of the "front runner" municipalities in this process.

All in all, approximately 125 qualitative interviews were made with politicians, administrators, grassroots organizations, citizens, businessmen and so forth. The study included a policy analysis of two policy processes—one in the area of culture and one in the area of sports (Sørensen and Torfing 2002). The interviews with the five administrators included in this chapter were made as a part of this policy analysis.

The fact that the interviews were made as a part of a much larger research project proved to be both a problem and an advantage. It is a problem that the questions asked were not directly related to the question of administrators' coping strategies. Had they been so, more detailed questions could have been asked. However, it is also an advantage. First, the fact that the main topic in the interviews where a concrete policy process and the role which the five public administrators played in them unearthed very fruitful implicit knowledge about their coping strategies and their view of democracy. Accordingly, I avoided the methodological problem of getting their politically correct opinion about democracy and their rationalized story about their coping strategies. Instead I deduced it form their stories about the policy processes. A second advantage of being part of a huge project is that it has produced considerable contextual knowledge about the organizational, cultural, and societal environment of the five administrators and about the concrete decision-making processes taking place at the time when the interviews with the five administrators were made. Third, the policy analysis has produced important knowledge about the impression that other actors have of the five administrators, and the impression they have of each other.

One might claim that the contextual knowledge policy analysis has given me about the coping strategies of the five public administrators makes it plausible to draw conclusions about their actual behavior. However, this is not my intention. The aim of the chapter is not to uncover coping behavior, but merely to draw a picture of the role perceptions and images of democracy that public administrators who are part of a system of local governance refer to. Such a picture might give an impression of the extent to which the traditional image of a public administrator is compatible with a system of governance and to what extent a new image is needed.

A Radical Model of Governance

It is now time to take a look at the specific institutional setting in which the five administrators are located. The Danish political system has always been rather decentralized, leaving considerable room for local autonomy for the municipalities. In the 1950s and 1960s this autonomy was reduced somewhat, but it was regained as a consequence of the reforms in the beginning of the 1970s. However, from the end of the 1980s onward, a strong and persistent wave of public sector reforms brought with it a radical reorganization of the relationship between the state and the municipalities. This wave not only gave the municipalities extended autonomy to experiment with new forms of organization. It also encouraged them to do so. A number of municipalities have used this new autonomy to make considerable organizational changes. The dominant features of these changes are as follows:

- An introduction of a system of political goal and framework regulation

- An institutionalization of a joint political-administrative leadership

- A decentralization of political and administrative competence to the individual public institutions

- An introduction of user boards in public institutions, and

- An emergence of a number of gray-zone organizations that take part in the political decision-making process as well as in the implementation of public policy

These five features are core components in the organizational structure in Skanderborg. It is a small provincial municipality in Jutland with approximately 20,000 inhabitants. The five public administrators I focus on in this chapter work in the municipality.

The process of organizational change in Skanderborg started in 1986 when a political system of goal and framework regulation was developed. According to this system, the role of the politicians was to define the overall political goals and financial framework for the municipality. They were to leave concrete decision making in the hands of the administrators and concentrate on defining the overall visions for the municipality. The role of the administrators and the local public institutions were defined as that of making all concrete decisions with reference to the political goals and financial framework. In 1989, the reform slogan "local leadership—central governance" was launched. The idea behind the slogan was to remove as many decisions and tasks as possible from the City Hall, and into the public institutions and gray-zone organizations and networks. This basic wish to decentralize as many public tasks as possible has been a leading principle for the reform process throughout the 1990s. Along with administrative and political decentralization there came an effort to establish user boards in all service producing public institutions in order to integrate users of public services more directly into the decision-making processes in the municipality. The last major organizational change took place in 1996 when the organizational structure within City Hall was altered, leading to a centralization of the political and administrative leadership. The number of political committees was radically reduced in order to concentrate political power in the hands of the mayor, the financial council, and the city council, at the same time, a new political-administrative body—the board of directors—was born. To sum up, the reform process has lead to both a simultaneous decentralization and a centralization of the internal decision-making structure in the municipality.

Simultaneous with this internal organizational development, there has been an intensification of the cooperation between the municipality and a broad variety of private actors such as voluntary organizations, business firms, and interest organizations. In some instances the cooperation remains informal while in others it has become more and more institutionalized through the formation of gray-zone organizations. The formation of gray-zone organizations has taken place in a number of policy fields, for instance, in the areas of culture, sports, and business where these organizations have formed three umbrella organizations: the culture umbrella Kultursamvirket, the sports umbrella Idrætssamvirket and the business umbrella, the Business Council. In the course of the 1990s these organizations have become integrated into the political and administrative processes within the municipality. Today, they all play a central role in the political processes both with regard to the formulation of political programs for the future, and with regard to more concrete decision making in their respective policy areas. Their close relation to the political system is illustrated by the considerable financial and administative support that they get from the municipality. The municipality pays for some of the day-to-day expenditures of the gray-zone organizations and the wages of the public administrators working for them.

All in all, the political system in the municipality of Skanderborg is moving away from a system of government and toward a system of governance. In this system of governance a multitude of actors from the public sector, the private sector, and from the gray zone between them cooperate in order to define and solve a variety of public tasks. The question is how this state of affairs influences the role of public administrators. In the following sections I present the coping strategies of five public administrators. Two of them are top executives on the board of directors while the remaining three are connected to different gray-zone organizations: one to the culture umbrella, another the sports umbrella, and the third to the business council. Their position in the municipal organization is illustrated in figure 7.1.

Figure 7.1. The Municipality of Skanderborg:

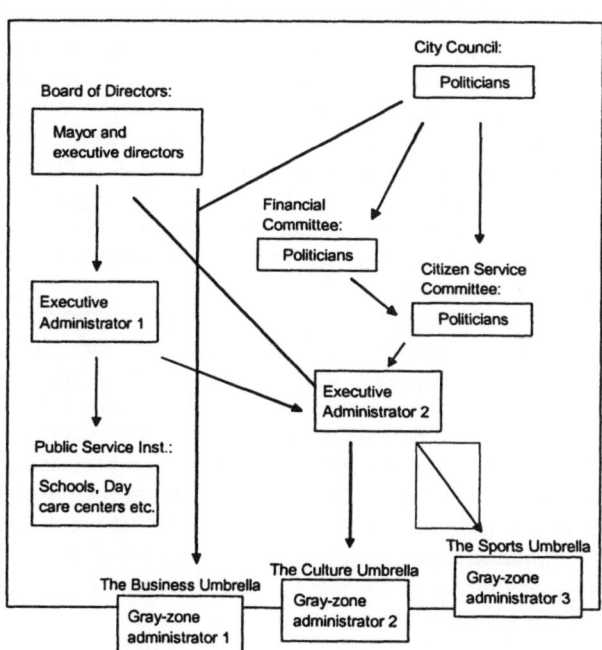

The Coping Strategies of Two Administrative Executives

As shown in figure 7.1 the two administrators are the highest ranking in the administrative chain of command. As such they are in close and frequent contact with the politicians, especially the mayor.

Executive Administrator No. 1: Code Name Sonia

Sonia is the highest ranked administrative executive in the municipality. She is like a big fish in a little pond in the new governance structure. She defines herself as an administrative "project maker" and one of her recent projects is the new governance structure, which to a considerable extent is her doing. Her project oriented approach to being a public administrator is reflected in her interpretation of what it means to be a good public administrator, who, in her opinion, is independent, full of initiative, and hard working. A good administrator is "an entrepreneur who strives to realize his or her goals and the goals of the municipality. As a leader I felt much more comfortable when I have to ask someone to slow down than if I have to push things ahead all the time." This interpretation of what it means to be a good public administrator is radically different from the traditional vision of the neutral rule-implementing bureaucrat. This is also true of her vision of what it means to be a good administrative leader. It is a leader "who lets things happen ... one who establishes the framework, and one who if necessary takes action." As might be expected by now she is not in favor of bureaucratic forms of administration. Her aim, she states, is to implement a nonhierarchical network structure within the administration in which it is easy and unproblematic for the individual administrator to move across formal organizational boundaries within the administration.

Sonia is fond of the new governance structure because it provides plenty of room for entrepreneurs, cross-organization networking, and framework governance. Furthermore, she appreciates the way the slogan "local leadership and central governance" balances the need for holistic political and administrative governance on the one hand and local political and administrative autonomy and flexibility on the other. Goal and framework regulation enhances the formulation of overall political and administrative goals and priorities that are an essential prerequisite for establishing a holistic orientation in the governing process. Increased autonomy to the individual institutions enhances the ability of the public sector to adjust to needs defined from below, that is, from citizens in general and from users of public services in particular.

In relation to the local public institutions she defines her role as an executive leader as a coordinator and as a discussant. This form of leadership is exercised in monthly meetings with the administrative leaders of all the public institutions. In the first years after the reforms had been implemented the discussions at the meetings were mostly about practical matters. In recent years, however, they have been about strategic issues concerning the future development of the specific policy area at hand.

Sonia spends considerable time on this contact to the local institutions. However, she does not regard it as her task to function as coordinator and discussant for the user boards. They are, she claims, not a part of the administration, and therefore outside her reign of authority. The user boards are "units in the political chain of political command." Therefore, she argues, the contact to them must go through the politicians: "I am very conscious of that, and if the user boards have any problems I make sure to organize a meeting with them where a number of politicians are present." This interpretation of the role of the user boards indicates that she, regardless of her enthusiastic support of network governance, has maintained a traditional view of politics and administration as separated entities in the governance process that should be kept apart. This impression is made evident when she explains that there is an informal rule according to which politicians are not allowed to contact a public administrator without consulting her first. This rule, Sonia explains, is meant "to protect the administrators who risk being placed in an awkward situation if they are contacted directly by a politician." In order to avoid this situation politicians are asked to go to her if they wish to contact the administration.

To sum up, Sonia regards the municipality as a network-oriented governance structure in which formal boundaries and traditional hierarchies have been removed. However, she does not regard the user boards and the politicians as a part of this structure of network governance. This is to a large extent due to the fact that she insists on an institutional separation of politics and administration. This separation, she claims, is even maintained in the board of directors where the three top executive administrators and the mayor are seated. She describes the board of directors as a forum for debate in which the participants reach an agreement about the views and visions that should guide the governance process in Skanderborg. Sonia compares the board of directors with a "lighthouse." She defines her own role on the board of directors as a discussant for the other administrative executives and for the mayor. She insists that this role is purely administrative even though it calls for a considerable amount of "political flair" to perform it.

Her insistence on a sharp borderline between administration and politics does not prevent her from arguing her case in debates with politicians—both on the city council and in the board of directors. An executive administrator can take active part in the debate, she argues, as long as it is ensured that the politicians finally decide. This perception of the relationship between administration and politics is visible in her description of the reform process. She does not perceive it as problematic that the administration has been an important driving force in the reform process because "the reforms were in the end decided by the politicians."

In general, Sonia defines her primary role as an administrative executive as that of being a discussant for all actors within the municipality from local institutions at the one end to the board of directors and the city council at the other. She insists that it is possible to perform this task without undermining the borderline between politics and administration. Her main attention is directed "downward" toward the administrative system of governance in order to balance the need for coordination and the need for autonomy in the governing process, whereas the attention that she directs "upward" toward the politicians is much more limited.

Executive Administrator No. 2: Code Name Bill

Just like Sonia, the second administrative executive, Bill, feels comfortable in the new system of governance. It gives him the opportunity to perform a "generalist" leadership role. The main objective of the generalist leader is to "coordinate the different areas of activity with reference to a holistic perspective on the governing of the municipality." Accordingly, Bill is a warm supporter of administrative delegation and of giving his staff a considerable amount of autonomy: "You get the most out of your employees if you have the guts to trust them and to give them a work area that they regard as their own." In some instances, he argues, it is necessary to interfere, but this can to a large extent be avoided if the administrative executive is ready to function as discussant when the employees need it: "In relation to my administrative staff my role is to function as discussant. I am much more a discussant than a formal authority." The role as discussant most often consists in helping the individual administrators in judging whether a specific solution to a problem is in accordance with the City Hall's line of thinking. They need to know "where one has to step carefully, what questions have to be presented to the politicians, what your view is on the matter, and if you have a suggestion or an idea as to where to go from here." Bill states that this task calls for a considerable amount of "political flair."

In contrast to Sonia, Bill believes that it is impossible to establish a sharp institutional borderline between politics and administration as intended in the new organizational model. This model defines the task of the politicians as that of defining the overall political goals and financial frameworks in the municipal-governing process. The task of the administrators is to make all concrete decisions. He claims that the dynamic relationship between politics and administration makes it impossible, once and for all, to draw a borderline between the two aspects of governance. In his opinion: "politics can grow out of anything." Therefore, a central objective for the executive administrator is to sense when an issue becomes political: "You must be able to 'stick your finger in the ground'" and sense what the politicians are going to do, and where potential conflicts are located. In Bill's view a public administrator is able only to do so if he or she does not, as many committed administrators tend to, have a specific objective of their own. He speaks in favor of administrative executives who do not concentrate on promoting their own ideas, and, instead, who concentrate on navigating their staff through the many dangerous political reefs in the seas of municipal governance in order to avoid conflicts between administrators and the politicians. To be able to navigate, the administrative executives must turn a considerable amount of attention "upward" to the politicians. Bill also mentions a less pragmatic and more normative reason for the executive administrators to be well informed about the views and visions of the politicians. He argues: "It is important to me is that those who are elected and thus represent the local interests have access to a neutral discussant, and it is important that someone ensures that the decisions which are made by the politicians are actually implemented."

Bill's negative view on committed administrators and his normative wish to help the politicians in the process of making and implementing political decisions is close to the traditional vision of the neutral public administrator. However, the apparent match between Bill's vision of the good executive administrator and the traditional vision of the role disappears when one takes into account his lack of interest in hierarchical rules and formal structures as a means of administrative governance. This is illustrated both by his discreet and unobtrusive way of exercising leadership and his pragmatic and situational relationship with formal rules. Even though he is trained as a lawyer his interest in the question of legality is limited. It is only taken into account if trouble and conflict is on its way. Legality and rule following is important when someone complains, otherwise not: "I don't see any reason to interfere unless somebody complains. We don't have to take action until that happens. Principles (read: rules) should not avoid people from using their common sense." The only form of rules that Bill seems to regard as important are rules concerning the internal distribution of powers among the administrative executives. It is vital for him to know: "where exactly my competence and responsibility to act is." Hence, his strategic move is to "find out who has the formal responsibility and if it is not me, well then it's not my headache."

All in all, Bill's image of what it means to be an executive administrator lies close to the traditional image of a public administrator. This especially pertains to his views on the relationship between politicians and administrators. However, in some respects his image of the executive administrator deviates from the traditional image. He does not believe in a permanent institutional separation of politics and administration. The most routine-oriented administrative tasks can become politicized overnight. This makes "political flair" an indispensable competence for an administrative executive. Furthermore, he tries to avoid the use of rules and command as a means of exercising authority over his staff. Instead he stresses his role as a discussant and adviser for a staff that enjoys considerable work autonomy.

Two Executive Administrators: A Comparison of Coping Strategies

There are both parallels and differences between Sonia's and Bill's coping strategies. Their shared perception of what it means to be an administrative executive is more in line with the vision of governance than with the vision of government described in the introduction. They both downgrade hierarchical authoritative leadership and speak in favor of a more integrative form of leadership that operates through the formation of a shared universe of meaning among those who take part in the governance process. This integrative governance is exercised through the shaping of a common understanding of the basic norms of the municipality, the problems it faces, and the possible solutions that are available. The role of the executive administrator's job in this integrative process of governance is to function as a discussant with, and a mediator between, the many actors who are involved in the governing processes.

However, there are also considerable differences between Sonia's and Bill's coping strategies. First, there are deviations in their perception of how active and promotive an administrative executive should be in relation to the politicians. Sonia argues that it is acceptable for an executive administrator to be highly active and outspoken in the policy process, whereas Bill speaks in favor of a more neutral, policy-implementing, administrative executive without a personal agenda. Second, their main attention is turned in opposite directions. Sonia is oriented "downward" toward her staff in order to coordinate the many activities in the network structure that the municipal political system has turned into. In contrast, Bill is oriented "upward." He regards it as crucial to keep well informed about the political climate among the pacesetting politicians. Third, Sonia does not regard the politicians as an integrated part of the network-oriented municipal governing structure. They should not take part in the complex processes of concrete decision making but stick to defining the overall political goals and the financial framework. Bill argues that everything can, at some point, become political, thus, it impossible to separate political tasks from administrative tasks. Accordingly, there is no reason to insist that politicians should not take part in network-oriented processes of governance.

The Coping Strategies of Three Gray-Zone Administrators

We now move our attention to the coping strategies of three gray-zone administrators. They are gray-zone administrators in the sense that their wages are paid by the municipality, while all or part of the administrative tasks they perform are defined and exercised within the framework of a private organization. However, there are considerable variations between them. First, one of the gray-zone administrators (no. 1) is only expected to use a small amount of her time in the gray-zone organization while the rest of her working hours are to be spent on more traditional administrative tasks. In comparison the two others (no. 2 and 3) are employed full time to work for the gray-zone organization. Second, their working environments differ. While the offices of nos. 1 and 2 are located in the City Hall, the office of no. 3 is located in the Business Council. As illustrated in figure 7.1, these institutional differences are important for the degree to which the gray-zone organizations and the gray-zone administrators can be understood as being a part of the municipality. The institutional ties to the municipality are strongest in the case of gray-zone administrator no. 1 and weakest in the case of no. 3. In the following sections, the issue at stake is how the three gray-zone administrators interpret and cope with the role of being a public administrator in a democracy, and whether the differences in the institutionalized ties to the municipality affect their choice of coping strategy.

Gray-Zone Administrator No. 1: Code Name Irene

Irene is working in the area of sports in the municipality. A total of 25 percent of her working hours are dedicated to serving as a secretary for the Sports Umbrella. Even though she works very closely with the Sports Umbrella there is no doubt in her mind that she "is the extended arm of the municipality." She defines the content of her job in terms of her understanding of what the municipality might expect from her: "my job it is to serve as some sort of consultant for the Sports Umbrella. I think that is what the municipality expects me to do." Her job as a consultant consists of a number of tasks, most important, being a secretary, but it also includes being an advisor for the Sports Umbrella, that is help to give the Sports Umbrella an impression of what are realistic and achievable goals in a given political and administrative situation. Finally, she feels that she is expected to play an active and initiating role as a network builder and network supporter within the sports area. This job entails making way for new activities among voluntary organizations and individual citizens within the field of sports.

Irene finds it difficult to cope with this role as network builder and network supporter. First, she does not like the autonomy she is granted in the performance of this task. It makes her feel alone and on her own in an unknown field of work. Second, in her search for a legitimate basis for her activities, she finds little help in the rules and laws that regulate the field of sports. There are no such rules and laws exactly "because we are in a gray-zone area" she explains. Third, it can be rather problematic to be placed between the municipality on one side and the voluntary organizations on the other: "you have to be able to make your own judgments. It is rather special at times. For instance I risk a situation in which I overrule myself. I can sit in the Sports Umbrella and suggest things that later when I work in the municipality I will have to turn down." On these occasions she always regards it as her task to choose sides with the municipality. In order to cope with this situation she and the Sports Umbrella have made an agreement that she leave the room "if something sensitive is discussed that the municipality should not know anything about."

It should now be clear that Irene finds her position as a gray-zone administrator difficult to handle. These difficulties are to a considerable extent initiated by her traditional image of what it means to be a public administrator. She feels most comfortable when her decisions are legitimated by either a law or a hierarchical system of rule. Most of her problems derive from the fact that this is seldom the case.

Gray-Zone Administrator No. 2: Code Name Karen

Karen, the municipal administrator in the field of culture, copes very differently with her job in the gray zone. In contrast to Irene, all her working hours are dedicated to working in the gray zone. Her job is to serve partly as a secretary and an adviser for the Culture Umbrella and partly as a network builder and network supporter in the field of culture in general. Karen is a true entrepreneur. She likes the autonomy and self-reliance of her job and her interest for formal rules is very limited. Her job identity is in many ways much more that of a grassroots worker than of a traditional public administrator: "Most of my work I do out there in the field. I often work at night. I meet with different groups of cultural grassroots [organizations] that are engaged in the production of cultural activities." She is unable to point to things that she would refuse to do. She is willing to give a helping hand wherever it is needed. She helps to carry chairs if time is scarce before a performance and she helps groups with applications for money to the municipality, to the Ministry of Culture, or to private funds.

Karen interprets her political mandate as that of promoting all sorts of cultural activities in Skanderborg. Her main aspiration is to establish a strong and wide network among all the cultural grassroots organizations in the municipality. This strategy is in her opinion the best way to make things happen: "as I see it my job is to make people pull forward together. Make them see that we can do something really big if we act together." For that reason she uses a lot of time: "gathering and connecting all the experience and knowledge there is in the many organizations and groups in the city." The Culture Umbrella is a central device in performing this task. Another of her tasks is to serve as a "link to and a spear head into the municipality for the groups and people who want something new to happen. I help to make things happen—a sort of midwife—in relation to new projects, and so forth." One final task is to help solving conflicts between the many individual grass roots and organizations in the area of culture. Karen seeks to reduce the level of conflict because conflicts put a stop to activities, and that is the last thing she wants to happen.

Karen has many fewer problems than Irene in coping with her role as a gray-zone administrator. The problems that she does experience do not, as was the case with Irene, derive from a misfit between reality and a traditional image of what it means to be a public administrator. Her coping problems concern the degree to which she is to regard herself as a grassroots or a public administrator: "I think that the grassroots see me as one of them, and I actually do so myself. I feel at home out there among the grassroots and I am actually crazy about it." However, she does try to maintain some level of professional distance in order to establish that she is actually a part of the municipal administration as well. She does so even though her experience tells her that it is not possible in practice to keep this distance. In order to cope with this dilemma, she explains, it is crucial for her to have a clear idea about when she risks "to step on the toes" of the municipality and when she "enters an area which could be a political minefield." In those situations she regards it as necessary to "maintain a low profile and say that you cannot participate because you know that it is in conflict with what is desired by the municipality."

The internal administrative network-oriented structure in the municipality is in many respects the best possible environment for her coping strategy. She has an administrative executive who is willing to serve as a discussant when she needs to reflect on her many tasks. Furthermore, she is given autonomy and room for the flexibility that she needs in order to work closely with the grass roots. In her view, traditional bureaucratic administrative structures of rule and command are incompatible with her function as a network builder, network supporter, and network participant. She states that it is necessary for her to be allowed "to cross all structural boundaries in the municipality." Just as she dislikes structural borderlines she is critical to the establishment of sharp institutional boundaries between politics and administration. Such a boundary is problematic for three reasons. First, she agrees with Bill that the political is potentially present everywhere. Politics and administration cannot be separated instrumentally. Second, she disagrees with Bill in arguing that it is only possible to make things happen if you—and that counts for the administrators as well—have your own agenda—something you strive for. Third, governing processes become much too rigid if politics and administration are kept apart: "I think that the governing processes in the City Hall would move much more smoothly if everybody relaxed a little more regarding the separation of political and administrative processes. But people don't for some strange reason. I think that some fear that sand will get into the machine if the politicians are allowed to go directly to the administrative staff." Karen states that she prospers very much from conversations with politicians who are interested in culture. In her view such conversations serve to improve the mutual understanding between administrators and politicians.

There is close to no congruence between Karen's and the traditional image of what it means to be a public administrator. A legal basis for administrative decision making and hierarchical structures of authority, which are considered as of central importance in a traditional perspective, play a remote role in her interpretation of what is important in her job. Actually, Karen does not focus her attention "upward" in the direction of the politicians and the administrative leaders to any great extent. In the instances where she does look upward her reason to do so is not to obtain legitimacy or permission to act. It is first and foremost in order to gain inspiration and a chance to share her reflections with others and to get an impression of the views and sentiments of the various actors in the municipal system in order to be able to avoid politically sensitive areas. Her main focus is "outward" in the direction of the individual grassroots, the many cultural grassroots organizations and the Culture Umbrella. She does not regard this "outward" focus as a democratic problem because she feels that she has a strong political support behind the overall goal which she was originally hired to promote, that is, the production of as many cultural activities as possible performed by voluntary actors within civil society.

Gray-Zone Administrator No. 3: Code Name Eric

The final gray-zone administrator is Eric. He is the administrative leader of the local Business Council. Like Karen he is employed as a full time gray-zone administrator, but while she has her office in the City Hall his is located in the Business Council. Both with regard to his institutional environment and his point of identification he takes a step further than Karen does into the gray zone and away from the municipality. Even though he represents the municipality in a number of cases his main identification is with the Business Council. Like Karen he tries to place himself in a double role: "we (the Business Council and himself) are the prolonged arms of business life and we are the prolonged arms of the City Hall. We are an autonomous unit that promotes both the interests of the municipality and the interests of the local firms."

Eric does not find it difficult to handle this double role, partly because of the extensive autonomy of the Business Council and partly because the Business Council does not have to do very much by itself. Hence, he defines the main task of the Business Council as that of establishing a network of "ambassadors" that includes politicians, administrators, businessmen, and private citizens who share the wish to do something for business: "We have been lucky to establish a productive interplay between a lot of resourceful actors. This is our contribution. It is not what we do that counts, but what we are able to put into motion in close cooperation with other actors." Similar to Karen, Eric regards this network-building and network-supporting role as his core objective. A final reason can be given for Eric's ability to cope with being located in the gray zone. Just like the dominant coalition in the municipality and most of the relevant network actors, he regards the interests of business life and the interests of the municipality to be identical. In Eric's view, the municipality cannot prosper without a strong and prosperous business life just as "business life cannot prosper if the societal conditions in the surrounding localities are not of a high quality. For this reason the Business Council takes part in close to everything which can help to improve these conditions." Due to the successful equation of the well-being of business life and the well-being of society, Eric, as is the case with the Business Council, has managed to appear not as a promoter of particular interests but as the promoter of the common good of society as such. This position has given the Business Council both a prominent and a legitimate position in the formulation of the municipal business policy and it has thereby made the question of where Eric's deepest loyalties are located irrelevant.

Regardless of the active and facilitating engagement of the Business Council in many areas of municipal policy making, Eric insists that the Business Council has not become involved in politics:

> I will not call it politics because I don't like that word. The concept is loaded with negativity. We try to function as initiators. We try to do what's right and signal our views and ideas. I don't take a political stand, but I do make a judgement of what would be the best thing to do in the light of the goals that we in the city have defined for ourselves. Our task in the Business Council is to influence the political decisions but not to make them.

As illustrated here, Eric is of the same opinion as Sonia who narrows down the political to the moment in which politicians choose a specific policy. The process before and after this decision-making moment should not be regarded as politics. Eric is happy that there is an official municipal business policy and that it has been formulated in close cooperation between the municipality and a large network of resourceful private actors. It gives the Business Council a double legitimacy: "When we go out and do something then it is in accordance with a policy that the municipality has decided but which more than a hundred people have taken part in formulating. Thus, I feel that we have been given a green light."

Eric's perception of what it means to be a gray-zone administrator is even further away from the traditional perception of what it means to be a public administrator than that held by Karen. While Karen perceives herself as an autonomous "lowest" level in a pyramid structure, Eric regards himself as the administrative leader of an independent organization that works in close interaction with the municipality as well as with other resourceful actors in the local community. He thinks horizontally in terms of network relations more than vertically in terms of hierarchies and this influences his perception of what democracy means. In his view democracy means cooperation and integration in and between networks and the municipality, more than democracy means that politicians make all decisions. Even though he is a strong defender of representative democracy, he does not regard the active role of the Business Council and other private actors in the policy processes as democratically problematic. This is due to his definition of network activism as nonpolitical. He paints the picture of the Business Council as a civil society organization that merely strives to influence politicians not to make authoritative decisions.

Three Gray-Zone Administrators: A Comparison of Coping Strategies

The description of the way the three gray-zone administrators cope with being public administrators illustrates that the traditional role perception has very little to offer: It does not help in guiding them through a jungle of complex, unclear and contradictory rules, laws, and structures of authority that is the rule of thumb in gray-zone organizations; it does not give any guidance regarding how to function as a network builder and network supporter in civil society; and it does not help them to answer the question: Who is the legitimate democratic authority for the gray-zone administrator? Is it the administrative leaders? Is it the politicians? Is it the networks within the administration? Is it the networks in and around the gray-zone organizations? The lack of answers to these questions leaves considerable room for maneuver for the individual gray-zone administrator. However, the three gray-zone administrators analyzed above do not handle this maneuvering with equal success. Irene has severe problems in coping with the unclear and complex situation she is placed in because she maintains the traditional vision of what it means to be a public administrator. First, she regards herself as a representative of the municipality. This approach seriously hampers her ability to function as a network builder and a network supporter. Second, her focus on legality and formal structures of authority gives little guidance and hampers creative thinking in the many situations in which rules and structures of authority are unclear, contradictory, or simply non-existent. Irene's coping strategy is defensive in the sense that she seeks to make sure that the activities she is involved in are, at least, not illegal. Her efforts to maintain a traditional image of what it means to be a public administrator most likely derive from the fact that she is educated, and has spent all of her professional carrier as a public administrator. This is her professional identity, and she finds it hard to leave it.

Karen and Eric chose a completely different and much more aggressive coping strategy. They don't regard the considerable autonomy they are granted as a problem. They see it as a necessary condition for the administrative work that they do. They downgrade their role as municipal representatives just as they focus less on rules, legality, and hierarchy as legitimate means of authorization. Instead, they give priority to being network builders and network supporters. The successful fulfillment of this job calls for the ability to act in an environment dominated by different and more diffuse forms of regulation, legitimization and authorization. These diffuse forms are produced in the governing process with the gray-zone administrator as one of the central producers of relevant forms of regulation, legitimization, and authorization. Regulation in the networks and between the networks and the municipality is often based on informal rules and norms, and interpersonal relations of trust, while legitimization and authorization is the dynamic outcome of the interplay between multitudes of more or less democratically authorized actors. In some instances, these actors constitute a network that produces negotiated agreements. In other instances they do not. In the first case, life is easy for the gray-zone administrator who merely has to interpret and act according to the negotiated agreement in order to obtain legitimacy and authorization. In the latter situation the task is more complicated since gray-zone administrators must either find a way to avoid potentially conflictual matters or take initiative to produce a network capable of reaching a negotiated agreement. The ability to perform the task of being a network builder and network supporter calls for a through knowledge of the informal norms and the central actors within the specific policy area in question. Accordingly there is no reason to believe that it is a mere coincidence that Karen is a former grassroots activist and that Eric is a former businessman. Both Karen and Eric have been successful in promoting the establishment of a strong network of actors in their policy area that includes not only a variety of private actors but also involves central political actors within the municipality. Accordingly, it has been very easy for them to gain legitimacy with reference to the negotiated agreements and shared visions produced in these networks. They have done so with reference to the existence of a large group of more or less integrated actors who form part of a network that includes private actors, administrators, and politicians.

The job of gaining legitimacy has been much harder for Irene. This is primarily because she has tried to gain legitimacy from a set of formal but inconsistent and contradictory rules and from executive leaders who expected her to act on her own. Second, it has been hard for her to obtain legitimacy because of the lack of a strong network among the actors in the field of sports.

Network Administrators and Democracy

It should now be clear that the situation in Skanderborg is a long way from the traditional administrative role pictured in the parliamentary chain of governance and the interpretations of what it means to be a public administrator in this study. It is possible to identify fragments of the traditional role perception in the coping strategies of all five administrators. Among other things, we find these fragments in their eagerness to ensure that their activities are supported or at least not in conflict with the views of the politicians. The fact that some of them insist that their active involvement in the policy process cannot be defined as political can be seen as yet another reminiscence of the traditional image of what it means to be a public administrator. However, for most of them the traditional fragments are integrated with individual role perceptions that derive from somewhere else.

What we face is a colorful multitude of administrative roles and coping strategies. They are all problematic seen from a democratic point of view. Irene's coping strategy is problematic because it does not work. It illustrates that it is, in fact, impossible to use the traditional role of being a public administrator in a governance context. The other strategies are problematic because they avoid considering the incompatibility between the traditional image of representative democracy and their individual interpretations of the role they ought to play in municipal decision-making processes. They are, in fact, successful exactly because they avoid facing what seems to be the most important question regarding the role of public administrators in a system of governance: Can democracy be institutionalized in a way that is more compatible with a political system characterized by governance than the parliamentary chain of governance has proven to be, and what role should public administrators play in it?

The coping strategies illuminate four questions that need to be answered in the effort to formulate an image of what it means to be a public administrator in a system of democratic governance. The questions are:

1) Is it or is it not functional for democracy to aim for a sharp institutional separation of politics and administration?

2) Should the administrative executives primarily direct their attention "upward" to the politicians or is it to the advantage of democracy that they focus "downward" to the administrative staff?

3) Is the widespread autonomy of gray-zone administrators compatible with democracy?

4) Is a gray-zone administrator with his or her own agenda a threat to or a gain for democracy?

The answer to these questions depends very much on the concept of democracy that is chosen. First I shall try to answer these questions with reference to an *aggregative concept of democracy*. Aggregative democracy is concerned with ensuring the position of the individual within a collective decision-making process. One goal is to ensure that the citizens have the same equal opportunities to influence the governance of society, and another is to ensure that citizens are treated equally by the system. A final goal is to make certain that the citizens are able to control and limit the activities performed by the political system in order to ensure some range of individual rights and liberty. Traditionally, the institutions of representative democracy have been seen as the best means of realizing these democratic values. Equal influence has been institutionalized through the principle of "one man one vote." Equal treatment and democratic control is obtained through the assurance that administrative activities are based on laws decided by elected representatives. Finally, individual liberty is obtained through the establishment of a sharp borderline between a public sphere of collective rule and a private sphere of individual liberty.

From an aggregative point of view, one immediately reaches the conclusion that a system of governance and the related administrative coping strategies represent a threat to democracy. With regard to the first question, the only legitimate decision maker in a democracy is the publicly elected politician. It is crucial that the division between politics and administration is maintained and that administrators, who are not elected, refrain from taking part in political decision making. Accordingly, the sympathy is greatest for the coping strategies that insist that politics and administration should be institutionally and functionally separated. However, apart from Irene, the administrators who call for a separation of politics from administration define politics very narrowly allowing administrators considerable room for decision making. Therefore, all the coping strategies—except for Irene's—represent a threat to aggregative democracy.

With regard to the second and third questions that derive from an aggregative definition of democracy, it is crucial that an administrative executive does as much as possible to ensure that the administrative staff acts in accordance with the intentions of the politicians. In Bill's case, he acts in accordance with this claim by putting much energy into investigating the views of the politician. However, at the same time, he does very little to control that the administrative staff acts in accordance with these wishes. The issue is, therefore, how far down into the administrative apparatus are the politicians' wishes are known and anticipated. At the same time, there is a considerable danger that his discrete and pragmatic form of leadership reduces the level of public control as well as the extent to which citizens are treated equally by the public administration. In contrast, Sonia's interest in focusing on the desires and wishes of the politicians is limited. Her main interest is directed toward the administrative staff. Thus she ensures a high level of executive control within the network administration, but the nature of this control is rather informal and unstructured and thus is in danger of challenging the principle of legal regulation of administration activities. To sum up, none of the two coping strategies performed by the administrative executives live up to the demands defined by an aggregative concept of democracy. Bill makes an effort to support political leadership, but he does little to ensure that it is sedimented in the lower levels of the administrative organization. Sonia gives priority to informal hierarchical administrative leadership, but she does little to ensure political leadership by means of legal regulation of the administration.

With regard to question four, an aggregative approach to democracy rejects the idea that public administrators who work autonomously have their own agenda, and that work in close cooperation with gray-zone organizations is compatible with democracy. Not only do they act according to goals that they have defined themselves. They also serve more than one master: the politicians, the gray-zone organization, and a complex network of public and private actors. This situation challenges the sovereign role of the politicians in the political system and endangers the equal distribution of influence among the citizens. If we look at Karen and Eric the problematic is evident. Their democratic legitimacy rests party on an abstract reference to the conditions under which they were employed by the politicians and partly on the existence of some sort of consensus in a diffuse network of actors that exists in and around the gray-zone organization that they administer.

To sum up, four out of five coping strategies must be regarded as non-democratic from an aggregative perception of democracy. If we measure the coping strategies from an integrative perspective of democracy, the conclusion we reach is radically different. Instead of focusing on formal equality and citizen control, the code words, in an effort to produce democratic governance are co-operation and participation. An integrative concept of democracy emphasizes the democratic value of processes that promote cooperation between and participation by as many citizens as possible. Cooperation and participation are expected to enhance a sense of community among the actors involved, an increased feeling of responsibility for society as a whole, and more well-informed and well-adjusted solutions.

Seen from an *integrative concept of democracy* there are many positive things to say about the five coping strategies. With regard to question one the sympathy is on the side of the coping strategies that give up the separation between politics and administration and, instead of marginalizing the politicians from the processes of governance, try to integrate them. Thus, the political process becomes more inclusive.

With regard to question two, an integrative perspective means that what is at stake for the administrative executives is neither to cling to the heels of the politicians nor to control the actions of the administrative staff. The main objective is to enhance the formulation of a mutual understanding among politicians and the administrative staff about what is at stake, what possible actions might be taken, and how and when it should be done. Such an integrative executive strategy makes it possible to combine extended autonomy to the administrative staff with democracy. The administrative staff is capable of navigating toward mutual goals because they are a part of the network that defined them.

With regard to question three, the situation for the gray-zone administrators is more problematic than for the administrative executives. The fact that they have two masters and, in some situations, are a part of two communities means that they do not necessarily regard themselves as a part of the municipal community. Hence, both Karen and Eric identify just as much with the municipality as with the gray-zone organization and the private actors who occupy it. The dilemma that now and then arises from this double identification can in some instances be reduced if there is a strong network between central actors in the municipality and in the gray zone. With reference to question four, the existence of such a network is especially necessary if the personal engagement of the gray-zone administrator is strong. Hence, such an engagement can be difficult to unfold within a municipal political-administrative network since it is normally characterized by slow integrative procedures and limited radicality. This might tempt them to place themselves at a distance to the municipality. This can be avoided if network participants make sure that the autonomy within the municipal setting is considerable. Accordingly, the autonomy of gray-zone administrators can represent a threat to integrative democracy if gray-zone administrators act on their own without a network or a community that legitimizes their actions. However, the entrepreneurial and autonomous gray-zone administrators also contribute to increasing the level of democratic decision making. Their position with one foot in the public sector and one foot in the private sector might serve the important function of increasing the mutual understanding between the political system and society that is crucial for a strong legitimate basis for the political system in a democracy.

To sum up, the evaluation of the effect that the five coping strategies have on democracy becomes more positive when we use an integrative concept of democracy than when we use an aggregative concept of democracy. In my view, both ways of measuring the democratic effects of the coping strategies stresses important issues. The aggregative perspective on democracy points to the necessity to investigate the way channels of influence other than the traditional channels of representative democracy affect the distribution of influence in society. However, instead of defining representative democracy as the only democratic form of influence, one should discuss how other channels of influence could be a supplement to representative democracy in a way that contributes to assuring of an equal distribution of influence among the citizens. The integrative perception of democracy points to the importance of public participation as a process that produces and facilitate, resources within civil society that can be harvested in the effort to define and solve societal problems.

Conclusion

The goal of this chapter has been to illustrate the necessity for a thorough debate of the role on public administrators seen in the light of a transformation in the political system in the Western world from a system of government to a system of governance. The coping strategies presented in this study illustrate that the traditional role model of public administrators defined within the democratic chain of government is ill-suited to solve the tasks that meet public administrators who are placed in a context of governance. Some public administrators cling to the old role, but they become frustrated because the distance from role to everyday demands is too big to bridge. Others drop this role model, and they gain inspiration from role models that have more to offer when it comes to solving the tasks they meet, although they derive from other institutional settings. Neither of these coping strategies is desirable if democracy is to be maintained in processes of public governance. What is called for is a deliberate effort to reorganize the democratic institutions of liberal democracy in a way that makes them compatible with a system of governance. Against this background, it will be possible to define a new democratic role model for public administrators. If we do not undertake this task we leave it entirely up to individual public administrators to find their way through the mess with uncertain consequences for democracy.

Chapter 8

Mediated Negotiation, a Deliberative Approach to Democratic Governance: Theoretical Linkages and Practical Examples

Gary S. Marshall and Connie P. Ozawa

A central purpose of this volume is to highlight more recent forms of democratic practice that influence the practice of public administration. In three countries studied—Denmark, the Netherlands, and the United States—the traditional forums for public decision making are in the midst of change. Historically, public decision making in the United States has been characterized by concerns for efficiency and effectiveness whereas in Denmark and the Netherlands public decision making it has been characterized by consensus and collaboration. Are there examples of more collaborative decision-making processes in the United States?

This chapter examines an established organizing process, known as mediated negotiation, that has become evident in planning, resource management, program development and delivery, and policy-making decisions in the United States. We, the authors, are university professors involved in the facilitation and evaluation of public sector consensus-building processes and this chapter draws on the public sector consensus-building literature as well as on our experience with cases at the local level. Our overriding argument is that the mediated negotiation setting is an effective container for the working through of public issues in a way that furthers both individual and societal development. From our perspective, the unit of analysis is relationship—the reflexive relationship one has with him/herself (the other) and the relationship that he/she has with the other members of the mediated negotiation environment.

Mediated negotiation practice, like most practice, is variable and difficult to regulate, dependent largely on microdecisions made by the mediator in response to behaviors by the participants. Our purpose is not to argue that mediated negotiation, in all its forms and applications, is democratic. Our purpose is to examine cases that we view as successful and to identify common elements or patterns in the processes that have a theoretical connection to notions of democracy. The intention of this effort is to sketch out guides for both the evaluation and the design of mediated negotiation processes, and, by so doing, contribute to the fields of public administration and planning.

The organization of our chapter is as follows. First, we provide a brief historical overview of the emergence of public policy mediation. Then, we clarify our definition of democracy, through reference to major writers on the topic. Next we elaborate on the connection between notions of democracy and consensus-building practice. Then we offer brief descriptions of two cases that we consider successful, providing examples of the types of evidence that indicate that mediated negotiation can be consistent with goals of democratic practice. In our conclusion we link these factors explicitly to our notion of democratic governance, and we suggest that these factors must be addressed affirmatively if democratic values are to be realized in public decision-making processes.

Background

Over the last third of the twentieth century, public decision making in the United States underwent considerable change. During the tumultuous 1960s, public demands for greater openness and accountability in decision making by the nation's leadership culminated in procedural requirements promoting public participation and protecting public access to government records that trickled down to the lowest levels. Over time and through the clarifying role of the courts in interpreting law, definition of this "public" evolved to include assumed beneficiaries or those bearing the burden of secondary effects of public decisions, as well as those directly affected. Such provisions for openness, however, have also been viewed as the cause of excessive legal challenges to decisions and substantial delay and cost.

While the disadvantages of broader access to information and participation were recognized, a return to closed-door decision making was unlikely. Harter's seminal *Georgetown Law Review* article, "Negotiated Rulemaking: A Cure for the Malaise," put forth an argument for a public decision-making process innovation that was emerging sporadically across the local landscapes in varied forms (Harter 1981). "Negotiated rulemaking" is a method of writing administrative rules through an open, structured negotiation directly involving a broad array of stakeholders including the regulators, the regulated, and other interested parties. Importantly, this negotiation process relies on the assistance of an outside party who serves as a mediator, shepherding the process along (Susskind and Cruikshank 1987). Whereas Harter's article targeted administrative rule-making, similar mediated negotiations were being used to augment many other instances of public decision making, ranging from site-specific permitting decisions and interjurisdictional land annexations to the development of policies and the allocation of scarce natural resources (Bingham 1984).

In most cases, these participatory processes are designed to supplement conventional decision making. "Stakeholder" groups serve as advisory committees inserted into an existing process, such as administrative rule-making or a comprehensive planning process. The outcome of the mediated negotiation legally constitutes a recommendation to the decisionmakers holding formal authority, such as the agency director or the planning commissioner. In a strict sense, because the official decisionmaker is not obligated to decide in a manner consistent with the recommendation, these processes appear to offer little that is new in terms of the democratic nature of decision making. The advisory status of the negotiated agreements, it may be argued, limits mediated negotiations to serve as a weak accoutrement to an existing system of representative democracy.

On the other hand, if the advice is accepted uncritically by the official decisionmakers, mediated negotiations may constitute another step removed from democratic decision making, in effect, delegating authority to a body who are not accountable to the public (Lowi 1969). Moreover, the intense experience of participation in mediated negotiation may create a division between members of the group and other members of the affected public. In very few cases are the participants elected by and represent any subset of the broader population. On the contrary, if participants are identified through a snowball method of word-of-mouth, the influence of existing social networks and relations of power may be accentuated (Carpenter and Kennedy 1984). Even when participants do represent loosely organized interests, such as neighborhoods, or collective interests, such as environmental resources protection, the extent to which such representatives maintain dynamic communications with their constituency may be highly variable. Viewed in this light, mediation supplements to conventional decision making appear to formalize elite influence within the context of representative democracy.

A third view suggests that mediated negotiation in fact challenges the hegemonic power of institutions and dominant elites. From this perspective, mediated negotiation is seen to fundamentally alter the substantive basis of the decision and the roles and relationships among the decisionmakers, public professionals, and the members of the public involved in the decision-making process. Specifically, the knowledge base for the decision is transformed as participants bring forward information from nontraditional sources. For example, industry groups may make available propriety data about technologies or production processes under scrutiny in a standard-setting rule-making process (Ozawa 1991) or community members may recall memories of favorite family fishing spots from years long past to help identify valuable natural resources in a land use planning process. Rather than various types of technical experts describing reality, the participants jointly create understanding drawing on diverse data sources and multiple methods of analysis. Local knowledge is constructively put to use (Fischer 2000). Alternatively, assumptions that are inevitably necessary for analytical models may be uncovered and subject to discussion, with the judgment of professionals challenged and sometimes overturned by the will of nonexpert participants. Power is tipped in favor of the advisory committee to the extent that the public rationale underlying committee recommendations are compelling and/or to the extent that the consensus-building process has reshaped the public understanding of the problem and alternatives for its resolution. Viewed in this manner, mediated negotiation offers a novel and promising turn toward democratic governance.

Interest in mediated negotiation in public decision making has come from many quarters. Somewhat similar to the support given community mediation programs in the 1970s, political support for public policy mediation can be seen to come from many points of the political spectrum. The Reagan administration funded pilot projects in regulatory negotiation at the Environmental Protection Agency. This interest emerged largely because, in the early 1980s, then EPA administrator William Ruckelshaus, a moderate conservative, worried that four out of five major rules promulgated by the agency were being challenged in court (Bryner 1995). Certainly some supporters were motivated for reasons similar to that of conservative Justice Warren Burger, who supported community mediation programs in the 1970s as a means to clear out an overburdened court docket in order to accommodate disputes among corporate and business players that were impeding the flow of capital. While some supporters might have regarded mediated negotiation similarly as a method for expediently dispensing with nuisance-type issues, Ruckelshaus and the EPA were concerned with resolving disputes in order to achieve some action toward environmental protection as well as to create a more predictable business climate. So, similar to the more liberal supporters of community-based mediation programs, who viewed this alternative as providing ordinary people "access to justice," paralysis in the court system was seen as hurting individuals by delaying environmental protection.

Finally, interest in mediated negotiation in public decision making arises from a concern about improving the political and technical basis for decisions. In the 1970s, the progressive left viewed community-based mediation programs as an opportunity to return justice into the hands of the people. The formality of the legal system represented the embodiment of privilege and prejudice, often sacrificing procedural justice for substantive justice and disempowering disputants through the intimidation of the system's rigid structure. Community mediation, in which the disputants speak for themselves and voluntarily enter into agreements to resolve their differences, it was believed, would achieve for more people a higher degree of self-determination. Moreover, when people most directly involved in a decision speak, relevant facts and conditions surrounding that decision are more likely to be appropriately interpreted and considered.

Whether mediated negotiation supplements to conventional public decision making are a step backward from or forward toward democratic governance is a question that warrants careful examination. This chapter explores this question by looking at the links between notions of democracy and specific conditions for mediated negotiation.

Democracy in Context

We turn now to the task of locating the democratic context within which we assume that mediated negotiation and public policy facilitation operate. The key tension that guides our narrative is the reassertion of a developmental/ participatory strain of public administration (King, Stivers et al.1998; Stivers 1990; Box 1998; Denhardt and Denhardt 2001). As White (1990) notes: "The essence of participation is a special texture or quality of relationship" (White 1990, 208) (italics added). In this context, we agree with White's subsequent assertion that "what is crucial is the dynamic of how people relate as they address issues of public action" (White 1990, 210) (italics added). Hence, this is the bias that we bring to our discussion of democratic theory. That is, we assert that public administrative action is strengthened when a context is created within which citizens are engaged in a relationship with others in the society such that they are self-reflective and have a reflexive relationship with others.

Participatory Democracy in the United States

Often, we in the public administration and planning fields argue that given the condition of politics, the "wicked problems" are avoided and typically resurface and are solved within the administrative setting (cf. Wolin 1960). And as noted above, what we also find is a great exigency for substantive participation. What we are asserting is a developmental view of democracy and governance. Such a perspective has a lineage that begins with the Greek polis, and moves through Marcelius of Padua, Rousseau, Marx and in the United States, the Anti-Federalists (McSwain 1985; Rohr 1986; and Held 1996). Political scientists such as Barber (1984), Sandel (1996), and Benhabib (1996), among others, have brought this discussion to the forefront. Benhabib in particular has championed the work of Hannah Arendt and Arendt's discussion of citizenship and human development. Finally, the work of two writers, Kensen and King (2000), have brought Arendt's work to the current debate with a particular focus on public space, which for these two authors is not a geographic limit but a frame for face-to-face interaction and effective participation. As we see, it participatory democracy suggests an "emphasis on the intrinsic value of political participation for the enhancement of decision making and the development of the citizenry" (Held 1996, 9).

The reassertion of the demand for participatory/developmental democratic practices is not without precedent. Rohr (1986) and McSwain (1985) both emphasized the importance of this participatory dynamic. Rohr, following the work of Storing (1981), emphasized the Anti-Federalist contribution to democracy in the United States. McSwain emphasized the Rousseauean tradition of collaboration and dialogue. The tie back to Rousseau is a critical one. As noted by Held:

> Rousseau saw individuals as ideally involved in the direct creation of the laws by which their lives are regulated, and he affirmed the notion of an active involved citizenry: all citizens should meet together to decide what is best for the community and enact the appropriate laws . . . In Rousseau's account . . . a political order offering opportunities for participation in the arrangement of public affairs should not just be a state but a type of society. (1996, 57)

As we know from political history the American form of government evolved not from the legacy of Rousseau but from the liberal tradition from Hobbes to Locke to Montesquieu to Madison. Nevertheless, the way in which democracy developed, particularly in the twentieth century, has resulted in a resurgent demand for citizen involvement in the governance process.

In the late nineteenth and early twentieth centuries, industrial society significantly altered the character of democracy. Industrialism in Western societies led to the rationalization of work and human relations with new forms of organization focusing upon the instrumental. The emphasis on instrumental rationality in all facets of society placed (and perhaps continues to place) significant limitations on the democratic tradition. For Weber, industrial democratic society was too expansive to entertain any notion of participatory democracy. Further, Weber argued that instrumental rationality could only address the means-end questions of societal development, not the normative questions. As Held notes: "Far from democracy being the basis for the potential development of all citizens, democracy [in modern industrial society] is best understood as a key mechanism to ensure effective political leadership" (Held 1996 172). What became operative was a technocratic society within which the average citizen was understood to be unable and perhaps incapable of doing little more than voting in or out of office a professional elite. This condition also had the effect of marginalizing or delimiting the human agency.

The resurgence of a more participatory approach is evident in the deliberative/discursive democracy movement (Benhabib 1996; Dryzek 1990, 2000; Elster 1998; Habermas 1996a), which is also a response to the delimiting of human agency. Deliberative democracy is concerned not only with who participates; it also emphasizes the quality of such democratic participation (Rubin 2001). Deliberative democracy melds the compromise, procedural fairness and protection of rights that are part and parcel of liberal democratic theory with the related participatory/developmental themes of self-understanding and cultural norms and values (Habermas 1996b). In addition, through the application of a discursive approach, "the success of deliberative politics depend[s] not on a collectively acting citizenry but on the institutionalization of the corresponding procedures and conditions of communication" (Habermas 1996b, 28). The emphasis on discourse is necessary not only within the separate sphere of civil society as championed by deliberative democracy theorists but also within those processes, such as mediated negotiation, which bridge the nexus between government (public administration) and civil society.

Mediated negotiation re-creates a missing element of the current condition of democracy. It is not a replacement for the political process, but a strategy embedded in the administrative setting that is increasingly used for making decisions on contentious issues or resolving a myriad of public sector disputes. White (1990) makes an interesting point when distinguishing between the political and administrative settings. He notes:

> There is, then, at least this sense in which the "politics-administration dichotomy" is true and real. Each provides a qualitatively (though at some deep and generic level they are related) different mode of moving forward the project of human development. Just as constitution writing is birth, so the is politics youth, and administration maturity, in the developmental cycle of societies. Dealing with the suffering and struggles of life is less costly and less wearing when we can contain these within the processes of administration. This does not make administration a higher form of social process than politics, however; rather it shows it to be a more settled aspect. (White 1990, 237)

This notion that administration is a "more settled aspect" of social process is significant because it suggests that effective participation can legitimately occur within the administrative setting. Our view is that mediated negotiation, with its unique language formats and potential for inclusiveness, constitutes an excellent form of participatory democratic practice. The mediation process requires that parties jointly work through a definition of the problem at hand as well as subsequently develop a joint solution. Participants typically emerge from the process with a stronger self-awareness as a well as an increased appreciation or regard for the other disputant(s).

For Dukes this appreciation of "the other" extends to societal impacts and includes:

- inspiring and nurturing, and sustaining a vital communal life: an engaged community

- invigorating the institutions and practices of governance: a responsive governance; and

- enhancing society's ability to solve problems and resolve conflicts: a capacity for problem solving and conflict resolution. (Dukes 1996 156)

This emphasis on the societal impact of mediated negotiation underscores the notion that mediators "nurture a process of public deliberation and learning, a process of civic discovery" (Forester 1999 173). An overriding point, then, is the citizens' engagement with institutions of governance as a necessary condition. Forester cautions, however, that consensus-building efforts can fall short of democratic ideals.

> Too much of the negotiation and consensus building literature, for example, remains economistic, more concerned with trading and exchange than with learning, more concerned with "interest-based bargaining" and "getting to yes" than with the broader public welfare and the practical and political significance of public deliberation. (Forester 1999 185)

While we agree with Forester about the shortcomings of exchange-based negotiations, we also cite a potential shortcoming of deliberative approaches, namely, failure to bring the discussion to a decision that results in action. What we seek is a re-presentation of mediated negotiation that includes deliberation and negotiation that goes beyond simply exchange-based bargaining and that results in actionable outcomes. We argue that such a "model" would constitute a contribution to democratic goals and a template for democratic practice.

Connections between Democratic Theory and Mediated Negotiation

If mediated negotiation is to be considered a form of democratic practice, then what are the essential features that must be evident, given the propensity for practice to vary? Based on our discussion of democratic theory above, and our admitted bias in favor of a definition that emphasizes individual human development as a constituent part of societal development, three aspects of mediated negotiation are particularly salient. These concern inclusiveness, the quality of participation, and relationships. Our focus here is on outcomes, on end states subsequent to the mediated negotiation process rather than on the details of the process itself, which we believe is discussed amply in other works (Carpenter and Kennedy 1988; Susskind, McKearnan and Thomas-Larmer 1999). We do not contend that this list is comprehensive, but offer it as the beginning of a conversation aimed toward developing a clearer sense of the attributes of public decision making with respect to democratic values and a framework for empirical research.

Our analysis is informed by our experience and knowledge with scores of public consensus-building efforts. Here we present two cases in which mediated negotiations were applied in planning and environmental management situations. These cases are not perfect examples of mediated negotiation by any stretch; our reflections are intended to illustrate an evaluative approach and to present suggestive, not conclusive, evidence for our argument. The first case concerns the development of a resource management plan and the second involves relicensing of a hydroelectric-producing dam. Whereas the first case was initiated by a local government agency, in the second case, a private firm employed a mediated process in the preparation of a permit application. As described elsewhere, mediated negotiation is a voluntary process, participation is by the consent of the primary stakeholders, and the process is facilitated by a professional who has no stake in the substantive issues under discussion. The format of the negotiations is usually relatively tightly structured, with agenda, ground rules, and agreement on shared objectives set forth early in the process (Carpenter and Kennedy 1988; Crowfoot and Wondolleck 1991; Susskind and Cruikshank 1987).

The Johnson Creek Resource Management Plan-Making Process

Johnson Creek is the focal point of a fifty-four square mile watershed lying fully within the urban and urbanizing extensions of the Portland, Oregon, metropolitan region. The creek itself meanders twenty-five miles from the foothills of the Cascade Mountains east of the city, to the Willamette River, crossing through woodlands, farmland, commercial and industrial areas, and some of Portland's oldest residential neighborhoods. The residential neighborhoods in the watershed's western sections developed in the 1930s, replacing agricultural uses in the creek's fertile floodplain.

Since then, flood control has been a major issue for the residents and various government agencies. The U.S. Army Corps of Engineers in 1958, Multnomah County in 1965, the U.S. Soil Conservation Service in 1969, and the Metropolitan Service District, also in 1969, each independently and unsuccessfully initiated attempts to resolve the flooding. In 1980, METRO, the regional planning authority, launched a major plan, but despite major public education campaigns, the proposal generated acrimonious opposition and failed to win voter approval for funding.

By the late 1980s, concerns about the watershed diversified. While residents who suffered from the creek's flooding continued to worry about flood control, the city was assigned responsibility for meeting new federal water quality standards in 1987, and local environmental groups began to mobilize around issues involving water habitat (for salmon in particular) and riparian habitat. Acknowledging the failure of previous top-down methods of major initiatives to manage this resource, the city of Portland's Bureau of Environmental Services (BES) in 1990 initiated a mediated negotiation process to develop a resource management plan. Five years and dozens of meetings later, a plan was accepted as a guiding document by the city of Portland and adopted as part of the neighboring city of Milwaukie's comprehensive plan.

Hoping to avoid objections raised in earlier management efforts concerning Johnson Creek, the city sought out a broad array of perspectives to form what became known as the Johnson Creek Corridor Committee. Participants included appropriate staff from relevant public agencies at the local and state level, resident representatives from each reach of the creek, as well as representatives from local environmental organizations. Committee members received documents generated by the technical consultants, meeting minutes, and so on, and they claimed a vote on committee decisions. All meetings, however, were open to the public. Although all documents that form the basis for agency recommendations are public by law, in fact, one must have a general sense of what is available before a request can be made. In this sense, a participatory vehicle such as the Johnson Creek Corridor Committee opens a wider window for members of the general public to view what information is generated, available, and considered in decision making.

The fact that the elected officials from two major jurisdictions accepted the plan as part of official city policy in open, public meetings is the only formal indication of the extent to which the general public approved of the work performed by this committee. While an admittedly imperfect measure, it is nonetheless a practical one. And the nod from the formal body is certainly a positive indication of the public response.

Another indicator of public acceptance and influence is the extent to which implementation of the plan has fared. In this regard, too, the signs are positive. The Lents neighborhood and Johnson Creek are the center of a number of major government initiatives, including a U.S. Department of Housing and Economic Development economic development effort. The city of Portland acquired a parcel of land in the floodway known as "Zenger Farm," which local groups are turning into a working farm hospitable to wildlife. The city has also converted some of the residential parcels it has acquired into a passive recreational park that includes a flood detention pond and wetland area. Most importantly, eleven of the Johnson Creek Coordinating Committee's seventeen original members organized the Johnson Creek Watershed Council, which is supported by funding from the state of Oregon. This watershed council is continuing to play a strong role in shaping land use and resource management decisions through involvement of its members on the advisory committees of local governments.

Whether the issues surrounding Johnson Creek and the Lents neighborhood were simply ripe for action or whether what began as a practical response to a political stalemate by a city employee, namely, the mediated negotiation, was responsible for catalyzing public activity in the area is, of course, difficult to determine. However, the continuing involvement of many JCCC members in local governance issues is a strong indication that these citizens involved in the plan-making effort felt acknowledged by their government and effective in their participation, since citizens are unlikely to continue to volunteer their time and energy if they feel ineffectual.

Clark Fork River Dam Licensing

The U.S. Federal Energy Regulatory Commission (FERC) issues fifty-year licenses to privately owned, hydroelectric facilities. The Avista Corporation owns and operates two power-generating dams on the Clark Fork River in Idaho and northern Montana. The company's dam operating licenses were up for renewal in the late 1990s. Rather than proceed through the conventional licensing process, which could be expected to be delayed years by citizen groups concerned about fish habitat issues and recently emboldened by actions pursuant to the federal Endangered Species Act, or to take advantage of a one-year nearly automatic provisional relicensing option offered by the U.S. Department of Energy (DOE), the company elected to undertake a collaborative application development process. With the assistance of a mediator hired by Avista but subject to the acceptance of all other participants, the mediated negotiation began in 1996 and ended with an agreement that won the company a new forty-five-year license and the community a strong sense of engagement in the management of the river's resources.

Of the thirty-nine original participating organizations, twenty-seven signed a final agreement. The signatories became the members of the ongoing management committee. Among those who did not sign were federal agencies, such as the Environmental Protection Agency (EPA), who had participated for informational purposes but had no formal authority or role in implementation of the agreement, state agencies with additional, formal licensing responsibilities, and local environmental groups who did not wish to play an ongoing role in the process and who believed their objectives were met with the commitment of larger environmental organizations.

Agreements achieved through consensus building are not expected to attain ideals set by any participants.[1] This case was no exception. The representative from the Montana Department of Environmental Quality, for example, expressed concern over the vagueness of the language in the agreement, particularly with respect to specific project goals (Simpson 2001, 22). Despite the misgivings participants may have had, however, the bottom line is that the collaborative process was widely perceived as "better than the old way of doing business" (Simpson 2001, 22). A representative of an environmental organization stated, "One thing we learned is that, if the issues are important enough, you just have to hang in there. Eventually you will make progress. Another thing we discovered is that, given the opportunity, even your fiercest adversary will teach you something positive." While the environmental group's fiercest adversary might be expected to be the dam operator, Avista's chief negotiator said, "We discovered right away that when you ask a conservation group to join in the process, and give them ownership in the outcome, they will be pragmatic and accountable participants" (Simpson 2001, 22). Clearly, the perceptions of the players were changed. Evidence of a change in relationships is suggested by another environmental organization spokesperson, who attested that, "They

[Avista] frequently call us to ask our opinion about different issues" (Simpson 2001, 21).

In the Clark Fork case, the public agency staff may not have taken back seats to management decisions addressing ecological impacts of the dams, but neither were they alone in the driver's seat.

Essential Features: Inclusiveness

An examination of democratic practice must begin with an assessment regarding the extent to which a process is inclusive. Who is present and who is not? What groups who wouldn't otherwise have been represented were present in our cases? Our measure of inclusiveness has three aspects: (1) all individuals or groups interested in the decision are invited to participate, (2) the range of participants is broader than in conventional decision-making alternatives, and (3) participants appropriately voice the interests and concerns of the groups they are presumed to represent.

In the Johnson Creek case, management of the creek had a long, difficult history. To avoid the objections raised in earlier efforts to address management issues concerning Johnson Creek, the city sought out a wide array of perspectives to form what became known as the Johnson Creek Corridor Committee (the Committee). As mentioned earlier, participants included staff from public agencies at the local and state level, resident representatives from several reaches of the creek, as well as representatives from local environmental organizations. According to the process designers, participants were selected on the basis of "whose cooperation was expected to be necessary to successfully implement a resource management plan as well as those whose objections would be likely to obstruct implementation" (Ozawa forthcoming, 5). These are criteria that are commonly cited in the consensus-building literature.

Certainly, the participation of government agency representatives in the management plan was not remarkable, although the directness of interagency coordination in this case is notable. The active engagement of environmental organizations is similarly perhaps not surprising. The particular individuals involved, especially the Friends of Johnson Creek group, had been active in an earlier battle to stop road construction in the creek environs. The high level of involvement of neighborhood representatives, however, especially those from the working-class Lents neighborhood that experienced severe flooding most often, marked a break from conventional decision making. In fact, although an active city-supported (but not controlled) neighborhood association existed, many residents in this area might be characterized as generally suspicious of government activities and doubtful of government promises. In Portland, such groups are less likely to maintain a consistent, vocal presence in proactive public discussions (Witt 2000). Consistent representation from this group can be seen as constituting a sign of a longer reach of participatory democracy than business as usual.

There were two stake-holding groups notably absent from the Committee discussions. These were the residents and agricultural interests in the upper reaches of the watershed and businesses in the lower reaches, in particular, an industrial firm located in the Lents area. In both cases, the facilitators had made special efforts to obtain engagement, going to the extent of convening meetings in homes in the upper reaches to attempt to generate interest among neighbors. Apparently, residents in the rural upper watershed were not inclined to become involved. The Lents firm had an incident of a Clean Water permit violation in its recent past, and apparently chose to stay clear of discussions concerning the creek.

In the Avista case, the long list of participants and the company's public face inviting participation are impressive. The negotiations included over 100 representatives from thirty-nine organizations, including Avista, federal and state government agencies (from Montana and Idaho), local and national environmental and recreational organizations, five Native American tribes, and landowners in the region. To identify interested parties initially, Avista had sent out notices in newspapers and passed along information through word of mouth to groups they believed would be concerned. All groups who expressed an interest in the process were invited to participate and Avista covered the travel expenses of most of those involved.

However, in the Avista case, as in Johnson Creek, not all parties likely to be affected by the decisions were in fact involved. Noticeably absent in this case were representatives of the utility rate payers, who would ultimately foot the bill of fish protection through rate increases (Simpson 2001). Although two state utility commissions, both of which do represent rate payers, observed the negotiations, neither signed on to the agreement. Whether or not the reason for lack of participation was because of the small impact on rates (as costs were amortized over forty-five years), this lack of participation perhaps suggests not a failure of inclusiveness, so much as it does the extend to which breadth of participation is practical.

In fact, participation of all affected individuals and groups is a decision-making ideal that is often difficult to attain. This shortcoming may not constitute a constraint imposed by the structure of the process or choice by the participants, but rather a reflection of a more profound political challenge, namely, the representation of unorganized interests. Imperfect inclusiveness, therefore, is not necessarily an indication of failure in mediated negotiation. Rather, the measure of success is the expansion of participation compared to conventional decision-making alternatives. On this count, both cases fared well.

Finally, Lowry et al. raise important questions about the appropriateness of representation of those participating. They ask to consider not only who participates but also:

> What does it mean to represent? Does it mean advocating the constituents' views as accurately as possible? Does it mean acting in what the representatives sees as the constituency's best interests? What accountability do those organiz-

ing the meeting have to those who participated? What accountability should there be between the representatives at such meetings and those they represent? (Lowry, et al. 1997 184)

In the Johnson Creek case, the degree to which the Committee maintained communications with the wider community can be measured only approximately by the extent to which the Committee attempted communications and the extent to which their ultimate recommendations were accepted through formal decision-making processes. In addition to the announcement of Committee meetings in the local newspaper, regular mailings to residents in the watershed, and the policy of open meetings, representatives from neighborhoods pursued several different strategies to keep their constituency informed of the process and to gather their reactions. The Lents neighborhood association representative sent out newsletter updates on Committee work and walked door-to-door to invite comments and ideas about upcoming agenda items. At key points during the process, this neighborhood association representative also invited the mediator and the city BES staff person to attend neighborhood association meetings to respond directly to resident queries. Representatives of neighborhoods in the upper reaches of the creek struggled to maintain dialogue with their constituency, reflecting the lack of organization of the neighborhoods and, perhaps, a weak sense of urgency regarding the issues since these residents were not flood victims.

Ultimately, in both the Johnson Creek case and the Avista licensing case, decisions emerging from the consensus-building process were sent back into the existing system of institutional decision making (the city councils and the U.S. Federal Energy Regulatory Commission). The supplementary nature of these processes ensures that accountability was not diminished in legal terms by the mediated negotiations.

Essential Features: Quality of Participation

Presence at a meeting does not ensure participation. The real question is whether all participants are given equal opportunity to participate. Are they all brought to a comparable level of substantive and process competency? Is there evidence of the recognition of legitimacy and value of different types of information and knowledge? And, do the participants feel that diverse perspectives were "heard"? Finally, is there evidence that all groups have influenced the final decision or product?

In environmental and resource management decisions, scientific and technical analyses are often thrust onto center stage as a pivot point for shaping the understanding of the "problem" as well as alternatives for resolution. As such, mastery of the technical elements can privilege certain participants and, in fact, constitute a hidden source of politics and values in the decision-making process (Ozawa 1991). Measures of effective participation must take into consideration how scientific and technical elements are discussed. In the Johnson Creek case, a private consultant was hired by the city to coordinate the massive technical studies that were contracted out to prestigious organizations such as the U.S. Geological Society (USGS). In a process akin to what mediators call "joint fact finding," the consultant led the Committee in discussions identifying data needs, methods of analysis, and findings. By his account, this consultant strived to maintain clarity in the communications between Committee members and the technical experts, attempting to ensure that the concerns of the group were well-addressed by the analyses. Several Committee members independently commented specifically on the conscientiousness and competency of the consultant in this regard, suggesting that members were not uncritically yielding to "what the experts say."

On a more comprehensive level, were the concerns of all participants given consideration? According to the participants themselves, the plan incorporates responses to each major interest and does so in an acceptable manner. The strongest criticism was that the funding mechanism for the largest project, a storm detention facility, was not identified and that even with the facility, flooding in the Lents neighborhood would not be eliminated. The plan dealt with this shortcoming by suggesting that flood-prone properties should be acquired for open space by the city of Portland from willing buyers at market rates adjusted to disregard the effect of flooding on land prices. In fact, fifteen parcels were purchased in the first two years after the plan was completed. Whether city employees would have been motivated to pursue this strategy, especially with this particular interpretation of "fairness," is uncertain. However, Lents neighborhood representatives clearly made strong impressions on other Committee members who supported this approach. In effect, these representatives had a substantive impact on the public reasoning behind subsequent public actions. As one scholar of deliberative democracy has stated, "Deliberation succeeds to the extent that participants in the joint activities recognize that they have contributed to and influenced the outcome even when they disagree with it" (Bohman 1996, 33). So while the Lents residents might have preferred a hard engineering solution to the flooding, it is evident that their views indeed affected subsequent public actions. (Indeed, many residents of the Lents neighborhood felt that they lost their battle and have subsequently relocated out of the area. If any group can be said to have gotten the "short end of the deal," it was perhaps this group.)

What is notable from the Avista case is the group's handling of scientific uncertainty. The five-year negotiation entailed considerable scrutiny of a litany of technical issues concerning natural systems and hydropower generating technologies. One of the difficult challenges in environmental management is overcoming the scientific uncertainties resulting from a lack of baseline information and understanding of the dynamics of natural systems and the inability to control the myriad of human-induced changes likely to impact the system in the future. Whereas the U.S. Fish and Wildlife Service (USFWS) was legally authorized to simply demand fish passage from Avista, doing so likely would be met by either stiff resistance and legal appeals by the corporation or an approach that may be technically inappropriate or ineffective. Current "best practices" in resource management recognize the limitations of scientific and technical understandings by incorporating a notion of "adaptive management," in which management decisions can evolve in response to additional information gathered over time. The adaptive management approach is especially significant in a public decision-making context because it does not require that one group's "science" overrule all others. Instead, it allows appropriately for ambiguity, which concurrently facilitates greater primacy of political interests and values (Ozawa 1991; Ozawa and Adler forthcoming). By agreeing to be part of the collaborative process, the U.S. Fish and Wildlife Service helped to shape a course of action more promising for fish. The agreement reached adopted an adaptive management approach, including as one of its key provisions the creation of a management committee to oversee implementation of the agreement in light of changing circumstances and a dispute resolution mechanism for handling subsequent conflicts.

Essential Features: Relationships

Finally, how did participants in the process relate to one another before, during, and after the process? If individual growth and a collective reasoning are to be obtained in a mediated negotiation, one would look for evidence that participants experienced a sense of connectedness to one another, a changed perception of the others, and some lasting sense of a need to maintain an ongoing relationship. Moreover, one would expect to find evidence that goes beyond words to action.

Participants in the Johnson Creek Corridor Committee developed strong respect for one another over the five years of meetings. In retrospective interviews, participants commented that the face-to-face nature and regular frequency of meetings provided a structure that cultivated tolerance and acceptance for what were at times volatile and emotional exchanges. According to participants, voices were raised and tempers flared at various points during the process. Although some would argue that the expression of passion is a constructive display of the intensity of one's concern, such outcries can be destructive. At such points, a skilled mediator can help to funnel the energies constructively by acknowledging the passion and smoothing the way for the group to move forward. As indications of a more lasting effect, Lents neighborhood and Johnson Creek are the focus of a number of major government initiatives at both the federal and the local levels since 1995. The attentiveness of the local and higher levels of government to the area can be viewed as an indication of the long awaited legitimization of the residents' concerns. Finally, perhaps most importantly, the Johnson Creek Watershed Council is recognized as an important player in regional resource management decisions. Currently, the watershed council has claimed a seat on a citizens advisory committee in a concept plan making process involving urbanizing lands in the upper watershed and have effectively advocated for increased resource protection relative to the competing demands of transportation connectivity.

Conclusion

Mediation-based public decision-making processes are forging agreements and producing actions in local communities across the United States. We have argued in this chapter that the potential for such processes to further the aims of democratic governance is contingent on particular features of the mediated negotiation, namely, the inclusiveness of participation, the quality of participation, and the relationships among the participants. The reasoning for these factors is straightforward: mediated negotiation without inclusiveness is elite decision making. Mediated negotiation without concern about the (e)quality of participation is deal making. Mediated negotiation without an observable change in relationships among participants is opportunism. Elite, opportunistic deal making falls far short of the democratic ideals of human and societal development.

Our intention was not to provide conclusive empirical evidence for our argument. Rather, it was to start a conversation about how to evaluate democratic practices and mediated negotiation in particular. We believe that focusing on relationships is one way to empirically observe democratic practice in action.

This focus on relationships is also a way of overcoming a particularly unwieldy methodological challenge, which is the analysis of the motivation for the agreements and behaviors. Skeptics will insist that agreements are reached because of the benefits of self-interested exchanges, not because of a commitment to any notion of the public good. Indeed, mediators, too, will distance themselves from claims about the transformative effect of the processes they facilitate. Susskind and Zion have addressed this question by pointing out the distinction between positional and integrative bargaining strategies, arguing that maximizing self-interest is not necessarily contradictory to democratic values if participants, who as negotiators, work to "create as much value as possible" and "distributing it in ways that help all stakeholders meet their highest priority interests" (Susskind and Zion 2001, 31). Integrative strategies require a level of deliberation that reaches to an understanding of others' interests. We argue that the recognition of others' interests is one step toward attaining the goals of democratic practice. However, we underscore the importance not only of what participants say about others but what they do subsequent to the mediated negotiation. Actions speak not only more loudly, but are heard more widely, than words.

Our two examples underscore the fact that both government and nongovernmental actors can successfully initiate mediated negotiation. This signals to us an important message about the possibilities of democracy within established administration and planning. It is that even within the so-called mature state of our current institutional and administrative structures, there remains the flexibility necessary to allow continued growth and development of basic, democratic values. The challenge for public administrators, planners, and mediators is to wisely protect and promote such opportunities when they arise.

Note

1. The concept of BATNA, or best alternative to a negotiated agreement, speaks to the practical measure of a good negotiated agreement, which is simply, one that is better than available alternatives (Fisher, Ury and Patton 1991).

Chapter 9

Interaction Research: Joining Persons, Theories, and Practices

Sandra Kensen and Pieter W. Tops

On the one hand, reforming local democratic governance is a local issue, but on the other hand, it is something many West European and American cities deal with. Both practitioners and scholars are interested in learning across cities. Some practitioners are just curious and want to know how reforms differ from their own. This may shed a new light on their own practices or it may inspire them. Both instances invoke a certain kind of learning. The interest of other practitioners is more pragmatic in a direct manner. Their motto is "let's not reinvent the wheel." They are searching for best practices and "how to"manuals. And there are also those who wish to gather information about general trends in society. This basic "factual" knowledge may lead to democratic governance reforms that are experienced as necessary. Scholars try to help practitioners to obtain these learning goals.

In the Netherlands, learning about democratic governance reforms across cities is organized in different ways. The Ministry of Home Affairs, for instance, houses an office for the dissemination of knowledge and experience concerning urban policies. In addition, a group of sociologists (who are affiliated to universities and research/advice centers) is well known and is often cited in local white papers on neighborhood approaches to policymaking (Duyvendak 2001; Engbersen and Sprinkhuizen 1998; Fortuin, Van der Graaf, and Van Vliet 2002; Tonkens 2000). Also, a number of consultancy and/or research firms have specialized in local democratic governance reforms. Finally, there are a number of "city networks" in the Netherlands that aim at fostering learning across cities.

As part of a group of six public administration scholars at the University of Tilburg, we participate in one of these city networks. Starting out with eight cities, we now have a bond with eleven cities. This city network, called Governmental Innovations and Neighbourhood Approaches of Policy Making, came into being in 1999. A "window of opportunity" (Kingdon 1984) occurred after the presentation of research findings in the city of Utrecht (Tops, Hendriks, Knippers, Spapens, and Verduin 1998). The city of Utrecht wanted to know whether other Dutch cities had similar experiences with reforms, and asked the researchers to find out. From this day onward, the city network, as well as the research and exchange activities within it, have developed in four unexpected ways: relationally, situationally, flexibly, and directionally (aiming at meaningful experiences).

Something else we found out along the way is that the city network is based on the idea that learning, also across cities, requires a strong personal commitment by both researchers and practitioners. Those who wish to learn, and in the city network there was no clear distinction between practitioners and researchers on this point, need to care enough to make the effort. These insights correspond well with those within the new experience and transformation economy (Pine and Gilmore 1999; Noordegraaf-Eelens 2002).

In this new economy of experience and transformation, raw materials, goods, and services no longer determine the price of a product. Instead, it is the personal value of the experience that counts. Successful entrepreneurship within the experience economy means transforming the clients (and being prepared, as researchers, to also become transformed in the process). The experience rendered is more than a memory; it is a memory that carries through into daily life. As a university department which thrives for a large part on contract research, and less on research grants and student inflow, we increasingly wish to develop experiences and memories together with our clients. These experiences, we hope, will then make a difference in their personal and professional lives. The research report and its contents as such no longer exclusively define our product. Our products have changed. They have become more differentiated. Our products are conversations, workshops, excursions, presentations, leaflets, and such. Their quality and success for providing good experiences hopefully reflect how well we are doing.

As is the case in each economy, to undertake an enterprise involves taking a risk. Noordegraaf-Eelens (2002) mentions the unpredictability of experiences. Apart from being illuminating or common, experiences may also be disappointing or harmful. In addition, experiences can be difficult to materialize. This makes them difficult to transfer or to evaluate.

In this chapter, we will focus on the kind of research that has developed within the city network. We will call this type of research interaction research in order to stress its relational, pragmatic, and dynamic aspects. We have learned that it requires a number of personal, institutional, scientific, and economic conditions. In this chapter we will discuss these conditions by describing and illustrating a number of fragments of the research. Each fragment is written in such a way that theory is intertwined with practice. This style represents our way of doing research.

This chapter is structured as follows. In section two, we will report on how we organized the city network research in general and we will discuss some of the difficulties we, as a team of researchers, encountered, as well as how we dealt with these difficulties. Therefore, this section discusses in particular the institutional and economic context in which interaction research could develop. In the next section, we will describe one of the research projects as a case in point of interaction research. In section four, we will relate interaction research to other research traditions, in particular, social constructionist research, narrative research, action research, and responsive research. In the final section, we will conclude by answering the question: What is required to conduct interaction research and what are the results of interaction research?

Organizing the Study

In theory, we are aware that everyone, including scholars, justifiably may mean different things when talking about a certain subject. During a study of the Dutch policy on social renewal, for instance, it became clear that, in order to make the policy work, the different actors involved needed to define the concept of social renewal themselves. This resulted in a diversity of meanings (Kensen 1999). An example of a theoretical concept which refers to different things is the concept of discourse (Kensen 2000). Scholars refer, among other things, to the social process of dialogue (Miller 2000), a particular choice of words (Howarth 1995), or an instrument of power (Fairclough 1995) when using the concept of discourse.

In the context of the city network, however, we experienced how difficult it is to deal with diversity in an active manner. In order to make joint action possible, differences need to be made useful somehow for the task at hand. The objective, indeed, is to produce something concrete together. Scholars, on the other hand, are used to "only" responding to one another with words or any other actions. Scholars often carry out their work individually, although they are part of several communities. However, within the city network, we wanted to obtain our results collaboratively as a group of six researchers and as a network of this group of researchers and numerous local governments. How did we try to organize this, how well did we do, and what were our results? These questions will be answered below.

Getting Started

At the request of the city of Utrecht, Hendriks and Tops, assisted by their colleague, Rodney Weterings, asked their contacts in other cities whether they, like the city of Utrecht, were interested in research into their neighborhood approach to policy making. The aim of conducting parallel research on these local efforts to reform democratic governance was to create conditions for exchanging knowledge and experiences across cities. Remarkably, Tops, Hendriks, and Weterings's search resulted in interesting no less than eight cities, including Utrecht, in such parallel research. Perhaps even more remarkable was the cities' readiness to each pay 50,000 Euros (excluding tax) for a year of research. The specifics and details of which would be specified at a later stage during talks and discussions with the researchers.

Normally, clients contact a research institute because they have a research question. The surprising thing happened with the city network that researchers asked clients, and these clients were asked to enter into a contract in a situation in which they had no direct need for research and no clear view of what the research would be about. The cities were willing to participate in this risky endeavor based on their relationships with Tops, Hendriks, and/or Weterings and because their experiences with their previous research was well acclaimed. In addition, the aim of the network, that is, to learn across cities by exchanging knowledge and experiences, was both concrete and abstract enough to be endorsed by the cities. Also, learning from others and reflecting upon one's own work in the process, is seen as positive, but proves to be difficult to accomplish in practice. Apart from having to deal with the (time) pressures of daily work and routines, one also needs to have a certain state of mind, for example, being ready to question and change one's plans. Therefore, the cities believed they could use some help with this.

Tops, Hendriks, Weterings, and three other researchers of the same department (Public Administration at Tilburg University) wished to commit themselves to the research task ahead for different reasons. Some of them considered the city network as one of several sources which could provide them with interesting empirical data for discussion and publication. Other researchers expected the city network to provide them with a meaningful research environment in which they could experiment with a new societal role for the academic researcher. However, at that time, which was toward the end of 1999, there was no awareness that these different approaches to the city network existed. A number of difficulties were encountered in relation to these differences, the most important of which are mentioned below.

In order to serve eight cities simultaneously, a basic research contract was produced by Hendriks and Tops. Although important formally, it soon became clear that this basic research contract was not of much help to the (other) researchers. Accompanied by Pieter Tops, each researcher had to find his/her own way in the city assigned to him/her. In each city, it took quite some time and effort to find out who the real contract commissioner was, and whether or not this was the same person as the daily contact person. To whom should a researcher turn for a discussion on the research design? Also, as soon as the money aspect had been dealt with, attention faded. It seemed as if it was now up to the researchers to do their thing. But it was clear that they needed the help of others to give shape and contents to the research project. The project would not work if there was no one who took an interest in the study. This showed the disadvantage of the way the city network had come into being, for example, without the need for an answer to a particular research question. However, it also revealed a positive side to this, namely, its openness and therefore the space we were allowed as researchers. In section three and four we will elaborate on the complexity of developing such a qualitative, open research strategy.

The Individual Researchers as a Team

What was obviously different from the start was the scale of the research (eight cities), the reverse contract negotiations, and, as a result, an open research question. Also new was the cooperation between so many researchers: six in total. We wanted to create an inspiring environment/primary work unit in which we could share all the interesting things we had found out in our different cities. Therefore, we had a meeting every other week from 1 p.m. to 5 p.m. The idea was that, if we saw each other often and long enough, we could become "a community." Later on we discovered that the ideas regarding the meaning of "community" differed substantially.

Since we were struggling with so many things, including our relationships with our contract commissioner/contact persons and our research questions (for they should be relevant to those engaged in the local developments), not many experiences were all that exciting, or delightful, or even fun. This was especially true at the beginning, although difficulties continued to arise and at later stages too. As a group of researchers we were going through the predictable stages of group development (Anderson 2002). Instead of sharing exciting new insights, we particularly needed to talk about our struggles. Consequently, the meetings were experienced like another burden, especially by those who considered the city network as only one of the tasks to be undertaken. This did not contribute to the team spirit. At the same time, the tacit assumptions of what we were doing and what we were experiencing were important to reflect upon so that we could find out what the effects of our research were. After quite a while we realized our tacit assumptions were the following. As researchers we took part in the production of knowledge, which corresponds with the social constructionist perspective on doing research.

Nevertheless, this realization process cost considerable energy and caused frustration. Most of the stories we told, in turn, reported our difficulties. They were complicated and so it took some time to explain the situation. However, the other researchers at the meeting could not follow these stories very well because they were not involved enough. Therefore, exchanging experiences was considered as taking up too much time and hardly invited any response. Our way of dealing with this was to spend most of our time discussing practical organizational matters, such as contract and financial matters, and the building of a web site and its maintenance. In short, the research meetings were not very successful. Even so, we continued to meet at regular intervals from the fall of 1999 until the summer of 2001. From the fall of 2001 onward, we met as a group only when one of us felt the need to. Between August 2001 and June 2002, we met four times as a group.

The research group as such could not provide the individual researchers with the support they needed. This void was filled by Pieter Tops who, since the start in 1999, had managed the city network. Pieter Tops, who is a full professor, supervised four senior researchers. Ironically, he has received no credits for supervising the city network, because until now this sort of work has not been and is still not included in the academic credit system. Tops could have achieved more by supervising Ph.D. students since this is more fitting in an academic tradition.

The city network was an even more risky business for the other researchers involved. In order to become a full professor it is more sensible to play it safe, and to write as many articles as one possibly can instead of building relationships with those who engage in making policies from a neighbourhood point of view, without being sure these relationships will pay off, that is, result in research projects relevant enough to share with the academic community. Not every researcher was able (given his position) or willing to take these risks. Again, the researchers did not relate to the city network in the same manner.

Another reason for relating to the city network differently was due to the openness of the research. On the one hand, each researcher had to find their own way in the cities assigned to them. Since many unknown factors were involved, each researcher needed to rely on their own knowledge and way of working in order to make something of the research, that is, to make it work. On the other hand, because of the openness, the research also allowed each researcher to specify, to a great extent, the study undertaken upon their interests, preferences, objectives, personal knowledge, and capabilities. A researcher was not totally free to do as they pleased: the content of the project had to be negotiated with at least the contract commissioner. Despite the differences related to the openness of the research there was one common factor. We shared the knowledge and interest in the practices of local governance with all its complexity, fuzziness, dynamics, chaos, and diversity.

Notwithstanding different approaches, generalizing forces were at work. Most of the attempts to treat all researchers the same or to require the same from everyone did not lead to very good relationships. For instance, we started to work on a book together. Each researcher was supposed to write a chapter for each city where they were conducting research. However, there was a big difference in the way the researchers conducted their research. Some of these research strategies were far more time-consuming than other strategies. Still, an average time frame was set, which did not work for everyone. This was frustrating for both the researchers who finished their chapter(s) in time and for those who could not. Although we did succeed in publishing our book, our current strategy on writing about our research is to leave it to each individual researcher to produce and publish texts at an appropriate time for the researcher.

The coining of the concept of interactive research turned out to be a constructive element. The concept of interaction research was originally conceived by F. Hendriks. It became an important binding factor within which the relationships between the researchers could develop (Tops 2002). As is the case with other concepts, the concept of interaction research was interpreted differently by each researcher. Below we will describe the different meanings which resulted from practicing interaction research.

For the six researchers of the city network, interaction research means the following:

> For one individual, interaction research means to invest in personal relationships on the basis of his own inspirations and aspirations: "Authentic relationships can only develop when you put something of yourself into them."
> For another the challenge of interaction research lies more in putting theory and methodology into practice: "It is one thing to talk and write about democratic discourse theory, but it is another to do it."
> Others put more emphasis on the role of the researcher: For one this role is special because of its diversity, ranging from making observations, giving advise and following processes to writing a report or having an interview that turns out to be a "therapeutic" conversation.
> A fourth stresses the importance of being on top of policy situations in which real life interactions occur.
> For yet another, interaction research shapes an opportunity to react directly and critically, but from an involved point of view: "I also feel partly responsible for the process under study." He creates one-to-one relationships with project leaders (professionals or public administrators) in order to discuss strategies and evaluate policy actions. This training dimension is also valued by others.
> The sixth adds to this the dimension of self-reflection. This researcher wishes to make public administration reflexive but not without reflecting upon his own role as well.

Interaction research: Joining persons, theories and practices

There are similarities as well as differences in the way the researchers understand interaction research. As interaction researchers we all wish to make a contribution to the governance of a city, and we may do so by following the ongoing interaction between actors, by becoming one of the actors ourselves, or by even becoming one of the intervening actors. However, we put this into practice differently. We mix our personality, with our favorite theories and special practical skills, such as writing, organizing learning activities, and/or doing presentations. The concept of interaction research stimulates us to play with the boundaries of academic research in a creative manner. Some of us play more than others, but in our own way, each of us is looking for ways to be good academics as well as good partners in societal discussions. In the next section, we will describe how this may work out in practice and what kind of results it may invoke.

Conclusion: Managing Diversity

A concept may mean several things. This diversity of meaning can be regarded as the strength of a concept, since the concept gives those involved the freedom to attach their own meaning to a concept, so a concept literally means something to them. Simultaneously the concept binds those involved, since everyone is talking about the same, or is working with the same, concept. However, some consider this possible diversity of meaning the weakness of a concept. Rather, they want a uniform meaning in order to make it easier to communicate and to manage. Also within our group of researchers, some needed time in order to accept the diversity of meanings given to the concept of interaction research. Currently we realize, in accordance with our own publications, that we should not want to solve our differences, but that we can use our differences as a point of departure for managing on the basis of diversity. We should not aim at changing ourselves, but rather at changing the way we manage our team.

Some believe there is no city network: everyone, including the researchers, is doing their own thing. To some extent, this is indeed the case, but the question is: Why should the city network be uniform without being ambiguous? In fact, we may conclude that the city network does work as a genuine network. Also the team of researchers is not so much a team but more a network of scholars. Managing a network means, above all, intensive communication back and forth between participants, in more than one way and at more than one determined moment.

Because we had to solve our differences as researchers, we now know what each of us is good at and what direction each of us wishes to develop further, and when we can make use of each other's (potential) talents, we will. We may do so, for instance, by asking a researcher to work together on (certain parts of) a research project. Speaking at least for ourselves (the authors), the city network trained us to become better at being interactive and therefore better researchers. Every day, we became better at organizing relationships, at building networks, at inviting those who we believe can play a positive role in a project, whether a practitioner or a researcher (sometimes from another institute), to work with us.

Those who want to organize research within the context of a city network need to make a tailor-made solution for every specific situation. This is necessary so that the experience is meaningful to the researcher. This requires thinking through each situation, and although it is hard to question standardized solutions, this will, in the majority of cases, lead to better and inspired work. Regular team meetings and the production of a co-authored book, are examples of how it should not be done. In the next two sections we will come back to this and elaborate on the process of developing tailor-made solutions (also in interaction with practitioners).

Below we will describe an example of a study in which the relational was taken as a point of departure for creating meaningful experiences for those involved (both researchers and practitioners). This research project was tailor-made for the specific situation at hand.

Interchanging Dynamics between Form and Content

One of the most telling examples of interaction research is "The Other" project in the city of Tilburg in the Netherlands. More than the other research projects, "The Other" project developed interestingly in unexpected ways. Somehow the relationships that evolved between researchers (in this case Pieter Tops and Sandra Kensen) and public administrators created a dynamic situation in which the contents and the form of the research project contributed to one another. The outcomes of this research project were therefore relevant and interesting from the point of view of both public policy and research methods.

After a series of smaller city network research projects, the manager of the department for district affairs of the Dutch city of Tilburg, who was also our contract commissioner, was keen to have a research project with more impact. In the summer of 2000, he asked us to assist him in taking a next step in approaching policy making from a district or neighborhood perspective.

Since the Department of District Affairs was set up in January 1997, much time had been devoted to getting to know the districts and their residents. In this process, professionals from third-sector organizations and residents had become much more involved in the policy-making process than before. As a result, the public administrators of the four district teams had become rather good at consulting citizens and cooperating with professional organizations. However, according to the manager for district affairs, these contacts were vague and not well structured. He, therefore, introduced the idea of working with themes. These themes could be inspired either by developments within the districts or by urban developments across cities.

Our research assignment entailed organizing a huge conference about a relevant theme. In consultation with the Department of District Affairs manager, one of his policy advisers, and one of his district managers (she led one of the four district teams of the department), we decided to address the theme of "The Other." "The Other" refers to a multicultural society in the broadest sense. So not only ethnic differences can make someone "The Other" in a specific situation, but also differences in habit, age, gender, occupation, and so on. The abstract title, "The Other," forced us in each and every situation to define exactly who we were talking about and what differences mattered. Until then, the public administrators department of district affairs was used to talking about "residents." But are all residents the same or do public administrators have a sort of average resident in mind? But what about those who differ from this image? How do public administrators approach individuals?

Fairly soon, the standard categories on which policy is based, such as "residents," "youth," "the elderly," "drug addicts," and "immigrants," were questioned, because one youngster is not like another, and policy is aimed at a certain type of youngster, so why not say so? In addition, what about those who "fit" into two or more categories? What to do, for instance, with a drug-addicted young man whose parents come originally from Morocco? Finally, which citizens do not fit into any category? Who are forgotten or overlooked? Should policy address these people too?

Questioning well-known policy categories raised a question that caused our three contact persons to worry. Because if local society is as colorful and diverse as it was suggested by the researchers, and people could not be put in one category or another, what should policy be based upon? Together with the three contact persons we then thought it a good idea to deal with this question at a conference.

An Unexpected Research Process

Our assignment was to organize a conference about the theme of "The Other." The conference should be open to the other cities within the network in order to provide learning across cities. The standard procedure of organizing a conference is: set a date, think about speakers, decide upon the objective of the conference, create suitable working methods in order to achieve this conference objective, and start advertising the conference. In order to define clearly the main question to be addressed at the conference, the policy adviser and district manager referred to earlier, helped to organize a number of interviews.

The first interview was a group interview with nine public administrators. These public administrators responded to residents' requests for quick and relatively small measures. These measures often entail physical changes in the street. So these were public administrators who spent most of their working time communicating with different residents. These residents, as the group interview learned, often asked for physical measures as a means to regulate social relationships with Other residents (residents who differ). Another lesson we learned was that these public administrators communicated in particular with residents within the unusual policy category of the "complainers" as they defined this themselves. To these public administrators, the category of the "silent," uncomplaining, residents were "The Other," and they wished they could spend more time communicating with them. Perhaps these "silent" residents had, instead of complaints, positive ideas they wanted to implement. However, this would require a different attitude from these public administrators. Instead of waiting for residents to come to them, they would have to go to residents themselves. No matter how difficult this may be, the advantages for citizens could be easier access to policy-making processes, the participation of residents in making neighborhood projects, and a better quality of participation, because of the chances for having true dialogue instead of consultation only.

The group interview with the nine public administrators thus taught us a number of things about the theme under investigation, but it was also informative for the others involved in the group interview. This included the policy adviser and the district manager who helped to organize the group interview. This group interview resulted in a regular meeting between these public administrators; the group interview had shown them they could learn from each other.

In the same manner as this first group interview, the next four interviews were not "just" preparations for something else, for example, a conference, but acquired a meaning of their own as well. These other four interviews were with four experts in the field of societal diversity[1]; originally they were considered as potential speakers at the conference. The original idea was to interview these experts in the presence of a public administrator and one of their professional partners in the district, such as a community worker or a police officer. The idea of taking two people along (two different people to each interview) derived from the manager of the Department of District Affairs (our contract commissioner) who wanted to have as many of his staff as possible to benefit from the city network and its activities. While preparing these four interviews, the original idea was altered. The researcher (in this case Sandra Kensen) made the appointments for the interviews, but the interview was prepared together with the public administrator and the professional partner. The public administrator and the professional partner (a community worker or police officer) asked the questions themselves. The researcher joined these two at the interview, chaired the meeting as far as this was necessary, discussed the interview afterward with the public administrator and the professional partner, and later documented it. The hours that were spent discussing the theme of "The Other" together and with the expert were as much a learning experience as the interview itself.

In this way organizing something *for* public administrators and their political leaders transcended to organizing something *together with* public administrators and their political leaders. Instead of providing knowledge that was simply consumed, the researcher's contribution was to challenge the practitioners to actively participate in the research. We all learned things about "The Other" together and many among whom the researchers themselves, changed during this learning process which increasingly consisted of experiencing "The Other" and reflecting upon one's own actions in relation to "The Other" instead of just talking about "The Other" in an abstract way.

And so it happened that the Department of District Affairs explored the theme of "The Other" itself. Apart from the five interviews previously described, a bus full of public administrators visited Rotterdam for an all day "city-safari" (which involved talking to ordinary, but also remarkable citizens). Two aldermen and the complete management team of the Department of District Affairs also participated in a workshop in which they interviewed one another as "The Other." As part of this workshop, for which we choose the metaphor of making a newspaper together, Pieter Tops presented "an oral editorial" and a guest speaker was invited to present "an oral column." On the basis of all these different research activities, an actual newspaper was produced together with a communication expert from the Department of District Affairs. During a rather informal meeting, we presented this newspaper to 200 employees of the department of district affairs. It included city-safari photos featuring some of the participating public administrators: they were the stars of their own research product!

Ripple Effects

After the research project had officially come to an end with the presentation of the newspaper, we were involved in two other projects. The project leaders wanted to apply the lessons they learned in " The Other" project to these projects and we assisted by helping them to shape their plans and process their results. One of these project leaders who is a public administrator worked as a sort of trainee at a third-sector institution (we should mention that during the traineeship she worked on nightshifts which is unusual for a public administrator who usually works from nine to five and writes reports). She first wanted to get to know the people before she wrote a white paper in order to address their problems. The second project leader, also a public administrator, wanted to develop a method to measure customer satisfaction. One of the methods was to ask colleagues to invite one of their customers to discuss, in a safe environment, the services supplied, the way they worked together, and whether these services were good and what could be improved. The above-mentioned projects were proof that "The Other" project did have an impact on the department's work and/or some of its staff.

Listing the Different Lessons Regarding "The Other" Project in the City of Tilburg

Interestingly, the more we experienced "The Other," the more we started to reflect upon the local government and the less upon "The Other." "The Other" was a means to reflect upon ourselves. How does "The Other" affect you? What does "The Other" tell you about you and your work? The research questions evolved into: With whom and how does a local government interact and, what does this mean for policy making? How can a local government interact differently with every citizen and, what could this mean for policy making and local democracy?

Therefore, research into "The Other" is a good example of the interchanging dynamics between form and content. The consequence is that another topic of research not only requires another research process but it is also served best by a process which is tailored to this topic and the situation in which it is investigated. Formulated in constructive or positive terms, this also means that the topic of research may inspire a researcher to develop new research methods.

Of course, these dynamics may also work the other way around. Researchers may feel that they participate in the respondent's dynamics. For instance, when the topic of research (this is contents) is the relationship between administrative departments or the reorganization of the local administration, the form of the study can easily become "administrative" as well. In general, this means paperwork, meetings, discussing finance, regulations, positions, procedures, and policy. The city network research in both the Dutch cities of The Hague and Amersfoort are examples of this.

Interaction research means, to a certain extent, democratic research. In the case of the research into "The Other," the two researchers and the three public administrators decided what to do and when. Together they built different networks to develop activities and to produce good learning experiences. Some of the activities were open to everyone (e.g., the public administrators of the Department of District Affairs and their political leaders), and also the trip to the Dutch city of Rotterdam and the closing meeting. Although five of the researchers determined the general theme, the research agenda was influenced by the different participants (seventy in total).

By definition, contract researchers do something for the contract commissioner. They supply certain goods and/or services in exchange for money. This is definitely a part of interaction research as we know it. "The Other" research project taught us that we can transform experiences. However, these come at a great expense. "The Other" research project took almost three times more research time to complete than budgeted. In reflection, we considered this as our personal as well as our professional investment in experimenting with interaction research. Had we been employees at a research firm, we could not have accounted for the extra hours we had put in. It was clear that our institutional context, the university, made this possible.

"The Other" project was evaluated very positively by the contract commissioner and the other participants involved. Its success was also due to their commitment, and whether they realize this or not. In any case, the success of "The Other" project led, among others, to a new research assignment in the city of Tilburg. In addition, both the researchers and the practitioners involved wished to share their good experiences with our other contacts within the city network. The researchers invited people from the other seven cities and organized a special meeting. This was not the conference which, in the summer of 2000, we thought we wanted to organize; that summit never took place. It was a small-scale meeting and part of it involved meeting others, and therefore ourselves in the city of Tilburg.

The Use of Research Traditions

In section three, we described how "The Other" research project developed in unexpected, but interesting ways, due to the interaction between researchers and public administrators on the one hand, and contents and form on the other. What we did not describe in section three were the theories we used, or the way in which we selected and applied them. Ordinarily, a researcher starts by discussing these matters, and perhaps describes part of the research process, for instance, in order to explain why adjustments were made. It is no coincidence we have turned this process around.

In the case of "The Other" research project, we did not present a fully-fledged theory about how to deal with diversity in society, even though we had developed one (Kensen 1999). Instead, we introduced our ideas and knowledge about the subject during dialogues with the other participants. It was because of this interaction between researchers and public administrators that we could implement certain theories in the first place. First of all we needed to find out what sort of questions the respondents were struggling with, to what extent our ideas helped them to either reformulate or answer their questions, and what would happen next. Only then would we find out what would be appropriate, useful, meaningful, and could be considered as additional knowledge for the issues at hand. In the course of the research, our scientific understanding of our theories also changed. For instance, we discovered it was not as easy as we had expected to approach an "Other," and to deal with otherness on a case-to-case basis. Therefore, we needed to start paying attention to this topic theoretically.

In this section we will turn explicitly to research traditions: which ones do we use, how do we use them, and what is special about this? We will discuss these questions in relation to a concrete research project because the relevance of theories or research traditions depends on the people involved, including the researcher. An interaction researcher draws heavily upon personal knowledge and skills, and is therefore also personally responsible for the usage and application of theory. This means that we will argue our choices both in the actual interaction and in writing. In other words, we will talk about ourselves and include ourselves in the research. Below we will discuss four research traditions in relation to the interaction research that we are conducting in Amsterdam at the moment. In Amsterdam we can implement the following research traditions: social constructionist research, narrative research, action research, and responsive evaluation. With the exception of the action research, we had worked with these research traditions in a more conventional way before. In Amsterdam we put our knowledge into practice, as researchers but also with the respondents.

Research Traditions We Live By (Lakoff and Johnson 1983)

Over the years a good research relationship had developed between one of the researchers and a mayor of a district council of Amsterdam. In the summer of 2000, the mayor was eager to join the city network, but because of financial and institutional reasons he was only prepared to do so if the other district councils of Amsterdam and/or parts of the city's administration were also prepared to participate. We therefore decided to join forces and contact possible partners. In February 2001, we talked to the director of the department of urban policy and learned that the ideas we had recently developed could be of importance to one of their policy problems. The policy problem in question is acknowledged nationwide.

In the Netherlands, urban policy takes areas as a point of departure. The idea is to approach living and working in such an area in a comprehensive manner. In other words, policy makers try to integrate economic policy, planning, and social policy all at the same time. Notwithstanding the progress that has been made over the last ten to twelve years, those involved still encounter many problems in connecting these policy fields in a satisfactory way (Kensen 2002a). We had a breakthrough in our understanding of the connection between policy fields during the first months of 2001. These ideas were based upon a social constructionist approach.

(Social) Constructionist Research

In recent social constructionist research, the focus has shifted from social constructs as such to their relational aspect because within social relationships social constructs develop and change (McNamee and Gergen 1999). The main question regarding constructionism has therefore become: How do actors relate to one another differently over time, what different meanings are produced in these dynamic relationships, and what are the consequences of these different meanings for the practices of those (indirectly) involved? However, this latest social constructionist approach is counterparted by a constructionist approach in which the "actors" are people, but also things, objects, machines, and so on (Jaeger 2001; Latour 1997). In this approach, the relationships are even more heterogeneous, but the basic idea is the same: human and non-human elements relate to one another differently and in relationships they produce different realities.

Translated to the policy issue at hand—how to integrate different policy fields—we suggested the following: look at the way citizens relate to the city, and vice versa, how the city relates to the citizens (Kensen 2002a). To be more precise, apart from relating to each other, citizens also relate to objects in the street, such as benches, fences, public squares, and traffic signs. In addition, these objects also have an effect on people. For instance, they can make them socially oriented or they can divide groups of people, or they prevent them from going somewhere. Seen from this perspective, the city is made up of social-physical networks, and it cannot be put simply into the categories of housing, public spaces, residents, and businesses.

Narrative Research and Action Research

As researchers we introduced two new concepts into the discourse of urban policy: social-physical networks and a relational method of thinking. The director of the Department of Urban Policy in the city of Amsterdam asked us to investigate to what extent these two concepts could be helpful to those making comprehensive urban policies. We applied insights from narrative research and action research in this project.

Narrative research examines the use of language as well as the effects of using language in a certain way (Blaakilde 1998). Action research focuses in particular on change (White 1999). An action researcher may suggest certain measures for change, and others and/or the researcher may implement these. The effects of the measures taken are described below. In Amsterdam the combination of narrative-action research consisted of conceptual renewal. According to Van Twist (1994), new concepts may invite new actions when given meaning by a certain number of people. In order to investigate whether the concepts of social-physical networks and thinking relationally could be of any use to those involved in urban policy, we first interviewed four councillors and five public administrators.

The interviews made three things clear. First, the respondents mentioned they confronted numerous problems when drawing up comprehensive policies, and, second, they mentioned various solutions on how to deal with these problems. Finally, they all thought that looking at these problems in another way could be fruitful. In other words, they wished to explore the advantages of looking at urban problems from a relational point of view.

This led us to organize a meeting of district councillors, public administrators and public administration scholars. Most of the respondents we interviewed earlier were present at this meeting and they had brought two or three of their colleagues along. From the beginning, our objective was to try to build up relationships with the respondents and, besides exchanging existing knowledge and past experiences, the aim was to also build up new knowledge and to experience something new together. That is why we limited the number of participants to thirty so that they would form a group. A "training day" seemed to be the appropriate form for this meeting.

Using the metaphor of "training day" inspired the further organization of the meeting. We published a reader so that the "students" could prepare the subject matter. The training day itself consisted first of lectures and then an exercise into looking at the city from a relational point of view. The participants were split into small groups and visited the city where they filmed their observations and street interviews. Afterward, each group showed their material to the whole group in a final plenary meeting.

During the training day, some of the things that became clear were that participants with different backgrounds, either in social affairs or planning, were interesting conversation partners to one another. From the interviews we learned that when gathered for a two-hour meeting in a conference room, participants from the planning and from the social affairs departments discussed the daily affairs of their own individual work. It appeared that during these meetings they were unable to help each other or ask critical questions or even tackle certain tasks together. However, by introducing two new concepts, and by linking these concepts together in a specific context concerning the city, they were able to discuss the previously mentioned topics. By walking through the city together, and being able to point at certain things and talk directly to the people in the street together about how they use or like to use, for example, benches or cycle paths, demonstrated the value of different perspectives in a very direct manner. In a sense, we made use of an insight from management theory: if a problem seems to be unsolvable then try to get around the problem and do not focus directly on the problem (Van Dongen et al 1996, 256). So, we did not discuss professional relationships as such, but we (first) discussed the contents of such relationships.

Seen from a narrative research approach, we learned that the underuse of skills, knowledge, and professional contacts was due, among others, to valuing words differently. For instance, for those engaged in social affairs, social processes are important products, and materials are means for making these processes possible. However, for those from the planning department, the opposite is true. They consider processes as means. What counts are the material products. When walking through the city together, everyone could see, for instance, certain things were used for a different purpose than what they were originally designed for. Therefore, if planning results in a certain usage of physical objects, then it is vital to engage users in the planning process by asking them questions such as: How do you (wish to) use this? With whom do you want to use this? What do you want to use this for? In addition, how the objects in the street or on a square are positioned and whether they invite or discourage a certain social usage. Therefore, if social affairs wish to obtain certain social objectives, they had better include the physical surroundings in their decision-making process. This entails other things besides considering the number of square meters needed for a project. For instance, they should first ask themselves and the users questions such as: What do these different age/gender groups want to do? Do they want to integrate their activities or do they want to do them separately, or both? The answers to these questions should be found in the design of spaces.

Based on the positive experiences gained during the "training day," the director of the department of Urban Policy and two district councils of Amsterdam, asked us to develop a number of new research activities. Among these, was the production of a short film and a booklet based on the training day. The idea was to make a presentation about the city to stimulate a discussion on social-physical cohesion with as many relevant parties as possible (Kensen 2002b and c).

Another research activity involved cooperating with two urban projects, one in each of the two district councils of Amsterdam. The research objective was to put into practice the experiences and knowledge on running urban projects which we gained during the training day. Apart from applying relational thinking, we knew we would come across many new issues regarding connecting policy fields. Therefore, we would have to develop our relational thinking as well. The basic idea was to take up these challenges together. As researchers we made clear that we did not have all the answers, but that we were willing to cooperate to find out what the answers were. This could only work if it was an authentic collaboration. The way in which the interaction research developed with both these projects was very similar to a responsive evaluation (Abma 1997; Guba and Lincoln 1985). Below we will describe only parts of one of the two projects.

Responsive Evaluation

An important characteristic of responsive evaluation is prolonged engagement in the research setting. According to Guba and Lincoln (1985), prolonged engagement is necessary, first, for a research design to emerge in collaboration with the respondents. This is a safeguard to conduct relevant research for those involved. Guba and Lincoln describe the task of the researcher as moving in-between data collection, data analysis, writing, discussing these writings, and rewriting drafts of the research design.

From an interaction research point of view, we would say that the researcher first has to build relationships with enough respondents in different positions. It is within these relationships that meanings are communicated and understood and the research design can emerge. This was also the case in one of the districts in which we conducted research.

The council there was planning a new leisure center for youngsters. This project involved a combination of a new social program for youngsters and a new building to organize the activities in. According to the manager of the Department for Social Affairs, our contract commissioner, it was therefore a suitable project to try to integrate social and physical aspects from a relational point of view. The project leader was a public administrator from the Department for Social Affairs, who was also our contact person on a daily basis. The project leader had hired an external consultant, with a background in pedagogy, to implement the plan. All three respondents were female, and they played an important role in setting up the research. However, since our research task was to help integrate social aspects with physical ones, we also contacted public administrators from three other departments: district maintenance, housing, and communication. Within five months we took part in a number of meetings and had several interviews/discussions with six public administrators and the external consultant after which the research design began to emerge. As a group we discussed the final draft of the research design.

In the meantime, we had begun to organize the first research activities. These activities involved not only talking about the new leisure center but also jointly paying a visit to the site where it was planned to see it for ourselves and to talk informally to the users, including parents, youth workers, and the people living nearby the site, about it. A group of twenty district councillors, public administrators, and professionals from third-sector organizations were invited for this activity. Also the idea was that the researchers had to build and maintain relationships with these respondents.

According to Guba and Lincoln (1989), respondents may have different claims, concerns, and issues regarding a certain public matter. These claims, concerns and issues are filled with different values. A central research question to Guba and Lincoln is: What should we do with these different values, both within the research and within the situation itself? Responsive evaluators have mainly chosen one of two options: an evaluator either constructs an agenda for negotiation or constructs a conceptual framework with which the different readings of a situation can be connected to each other (Erlandson, Harris, Skipper and Allen 1993). In both instances, the aim is to instigate a fruitful dialogue among the respondents. Responsive evaluators differ in the extent to which they guide and/or take part in this dialogue.

In the case described above, many different claims, concerns, and issues were put forward by twenty people with different backgrounds who experienced a particular site in the city of Amsterdam to look at the way in which social-physical networks function. As researchers, we did not want to "solve" the differences among these twenty respondents. Therefore, we asked each of them to write a small report. We distributed these reports among the participants and held a two-hour meeting in which everyone gave their opinion about the reports. In addition, everyone discussed what ought to be done with the reports results for the project in question. Based on this meeting, followup activities were prepared.

With each new person a new meaning has to be negotiated and re-negotiated. We assume that knowledge is created through communication and that this is an ongoing process: time and time again (other) people have to use their language (which can only exist in a community) to interpret what is going on and to express what they mean. In this social interaction process, meanings slip and slide and are therefore changed. Also these changes need to be discussed with the respondents. All in all, many hours are spent communicating and being with the respondents. This makes it possible, however, to get an understanding of the mechanisms or patterns that function within the research setting. A good example is the following case.

As described above, the project under investigation was led by a public administrator from social affairs and the external consultant she had hired to implement the plan. It took the researchers and two public administrators (one from housing and one from communication) nine months to get "connected" to these two professionals. The project leader and the consultant had consulted us all a couple of times, in particular to coordinate actions, but they had done so bilaterally. Therefore, the other parties involved did not know what contribution had been made or what the two women had done with the information they obtained from us. It was clear it was their project and they were going to do it their way. They felt responsible to make it work. But because we did talk and they did join some of the research activities, it took us quite a while to find out that their idea of collaboration was to obtain their information from other sources. There was no question of working together.

The researchers and the two other public administrators had complained to each other about how they were not involved and how frustrating it was. As a result, neither the researchers nor the public administrators felt like giving the project leader and her consultant any information anymore. It was during a conversation with the project leader and her manager (who is the head of the social affairs department and who is also the contract commissioner of the research) that we found out how they approached the situation. The conversation between the researchers and the project leader was repeated in front of the manager. This is another example of the value of face-to-face meetings and conversations for relevant knowledge production and dissemination.

As the above example shows, it is very difficult to discover certain routines, even when the persons involved are directly confronted with them, and it is even more difficult to break lose from them when you want to. The next thing we tried to do was to set up a new group comprising the public administrators, the external consultant, and the researchers. E-mails were circulated: no more bilateral communication. However, the question still remains: What kind of conversation can we have as a group? What positions should be taken? Should we remain only advisers, but this time as a group, or would it be possible to develop cooperative relationships?

Conclusions: Taking on Several Roles as an Interaction Researcher

We played with language and narrative form without hesitation. We felt we were able to do so because we conducted research from a social constructionist point of view. A construction process always assumes an active input from participants. Only the degree to which participants contribute to this construction process can vary. Analytically, three positions can be distinguished. One can follow, participate, and/or intervene. (The last two may have resemblances with different variations of action research [White 1999]). In the case of the city network, we combined all three. Depending upon the time and situation, we either did one thing or another.

Following Interactions of Others

When following the interactions of others, a researcher mainly listens and watches. In short, the researcher observes, and may do so from every possible theoretical point of view. However, in order to perform this role, a researcher also needs to relate to the people he or she interviews or watches in action. By being in a room together with others, if only as a spectator, expresses a certain relationship. In addition, a researcher needs to act too. They need to ask permission to attend a certain meeting. And those present at the meeting expect the researcher to comment somehow on their meeting at a certain point, either in writing or orally. Finally, understanding and interpreting what is being said and done are activities as well. In short, from a social constructionist point of view, a researcher cannot escape from becoming part of the interactions of those being studied, no matter how low their profile is. In this context, the following question is relevant: To what extent is it justified to exclude ourselves from of our analysis?

Participating in Interactions

Participating in ongoing interactions means "talking back," not later at a certain point at a special meeting, but in interaction—here and now. Researchers then explicitly join the social construction of realities they are simultaneously analyzing. The sort of input can be theoretical, practical or knowledge based on (former research) experiences. Apart from being an observer and an author, a researcher is also a respondent, and therefore the data consists partly of their own notes, comments, utterances, and so on, communicated in interaction with the other respondents. Also, the way in which the other respondents respond to the findings, interpretations, and additions of the researcher are part of their dataset. In this way, the distinction between researchers and respondents disappears to a certain extent, although the researcher's position and contribution is still distinct from the other ones.

One of the advantages of participating in interactions is the chance you get to learn immediately how your contribution is understood and valued. This gives you the possibility of adjusting your approach. However, it also makes the research more uncertain. This may be considered as a disadvantage, although the researchers do not experience it as such. Also, as a researcher you can communicate what you learn from the respondents. Learning becomes an authentic mutual process this way. In addition, giving feedback is something that goes two ways. Not only are the actions of the others examined but also those of the researcher. This exposes a vulnerability of the researchers and their research. We find this vulnerability a strength because it opens up people. However, others may not appreciate this.

Intervening in Interactions

Finally, an interaction researcher may try to intervene in the ongoing social interaction process which they are also studying. The objective may be to improve the interaction process, namely, to work toward a process in which (very) different types of people may speak out, are heard, and are shown respect. These process criteria may help in discussing the quality of the interaction process and ways to improve it.

Ways in which the interaction process may be improved include to set a good example as a researcher. For instance, asking for a second dialogue partner, one from the other department, when the objective is, among others, to improve working relationships between the two departments. Another intervention strategy may be to point out perspectives and to involve people who were not involved before. Furthermore, a researcher may organize and chair special meetings. The researcher can play with words, formulate things differently, and see whether this conceptual renewal invites other actions. The researcher may raise questions for reflection. He can make meanings explicit and/or symbolize them in different ways. And so on.

Intervening in interactions is the most risky research approach of all, since interventions may be either successful or unsuccessful. As for other managers who intervene in processes, one must wait and see how people respond to these interventions. The dynamic of social interaction processes cannot be predicted or controlled. There is always a surprise element involved. Several questions may therefore be raised in connection with intervening in interaction processes as a researcher.

When is it a good time to intervene? When is it appropriate to intervene? Are we allowed to intervene in processes only when we are explicitly asked to do so? Or may we intervene when we ourselves believe this is better for the interaction process? And how do we intervene? Perhaps it is sometimes wise not to say anything?

As when following interactions and participating in them our interventions in social interaction processes and the way people respond to them, are research data to be reflected upon. In the case of intervention we can leave experienced knowledge behind. Whereas in the case of following and participating in social interactions, it is merely a case of leaving written knowledge behind.

Final Conclusion: Interaction Research, Its Requirements, and Its Findings

This chapter described and illustrated a number of fragments of the interaction research that we have been conducting since 1999. We will conclude this chapter by answering the question: What is required to conduct interaction research and what are the results of interaction research? Four classes of requirements can be distinguished: institutional, scientific, personal, and economic.

Institutionally, interaction research requires colleagues from the same department who support and conduct this kind of research themselves. Interaction research is too complex and perhaps too unorthodox to be carried out individually. The next requirement is to manage the relationships between these colleagues. We learned the hard way. It requires intensive communication in various ways and at various times. In addition, interaction research has variations. Accepting differences among colleagues is another requirement. It should not be taken for granted that a colleague's work will be found interesting to the same degree as another colleague's.

Given the experimental character of interaction research, since each situation requires its own approach and process, the institutional setting should be such that there is time to try things out, to constantly reflect upon the research, and to learn about the latest developments within theory. In an academic setting these things are easier to organize than in businesslike situations.

Interaction research requires from the researcher personally an open research approach; interaction research develops as relationships are built with many respondents and a number of colleagues. Furthermore, interaction research means spending many long hours in the research setting and working with many people. This is very demanding and quite different than being left "in peace" as a researcher, to observe, to listen and to study.

It is important for the success of interaction research that respondents and the contract commissioner all work together on the research as a team. And it is important that the researchers get paid for conducting interaction research. The reason for putting a price tag to interaction research is to ensure that the respondents take a stake in the research. This is important, since interaction research, and its study of ongoing processes, aims at creating moments of learning that carry through into daily (working) life.

Interaction research is an undertaking which is carried out in close cooperation with—in our case—local democracy. It can give local governance the following: good questions, assistance in developing answers, training possibilities for staff and citizens, relevant meetings among people who have struggled with the same issues, awareness of certain hard but possibly better to change routines, and research findings by way of presentations, newspaper articles, videos, booklets, and co-authored volumes. To us, interaction research presents us with an inspirational context so that we are able to take part in society and continue our personal and academic learning processes.

Note

1. These experts were (1) a social psychologist who ran a huge social experiment in the multicultural city of Rotterdam, entitled "city etiquette"; (2) a chairman of a district council in Amsterdam in whose district at least eighty nationalities live together and "they do not make a fuss about that," according to him; (3) a popular local celebrity from the Dutch city of Tilburg: a former Catholic priest (1930) who supports the "leftovers" of society, as he calls them, by delivering them bread at night, by sometimes paying their regular housing expenses, or by helping them to fill in forms; and (4) a female entertainer who was born in Turkey, but now regards herself as an authentic Amsterdammer.

Chapter 10

Democratic Epistemology

Hugh T. Miller

Research methodology is not usually regarded as a political process, much less a politically democratic one. The standard scenario for empirical research in the social sciences is that researchers (and their supporters and financers) determine the agenda for inquiry—something having to do with some social or political phenomena—and the role of the subjects is to be data points.

Suppose, instead, that democratic research were conducted democratically. Imagine the research subject to be an active participant, having a say over the purpose of the research project just as the others do. One can imagine that different kinds of knowledge, functioning to benefit different kinds of people, would be built up under the subject-as-participant scenario.

In this chapter, I will investigate the subtle but substantial difference between (1) democratic research and (2) research on democracy. The latter project tends to view citizens as subjects or data points in a research project while the former assumes that citizens are active participants in their own public-oriented projects.

Empirical data gathering is one of the traditional activities of research; it has always involved sense perception, possibly aided by testing instruments. The protocols of this sort of research are designed to enable the researcher to record her observations—seen, smelled, heard, felt, tasted, or somehow experienced. Social scientists, especially those in the behaviorist school, have endeavored to limit their theoretical claims to observable phenomena, in this way honoring the disciplining function of empirical data. Theories potentially could be falsified through empirical research. More recently, the gathering of data in vivo, without the explicit guidance of theoretical propositions, has gained acceptance in anthropology especially, generating thick descriptions and narrative interpretations. (In public administration, see White 1999, Jaja and Miller 2003.) Whether testing propositions or gathering data in vivo, observation in the social sciences involves listening in a way that is foreign to the natural sciences. We listen when we ask people questions and hear their responses. Merely observing action provides scarce access to the meaning of those actions, so we listen to explanations and people's accounts of things to see patterns and learn meanings.

The Contestable Priority of Objectivity

In normal social science, the listening is to be done methodically so as to ensure objectivity. Under these protocols, method is the leading light and takes priority over the researcher's personal interaction with the subject. Lately, however, "the" scientific method has lost its mystique and its monopoly as regards justifying belief. A highly structured methods protocol may well be consistent with "research on democracy," but "democratic research" (research conducted democratically) would not necessarily accommodate the a priori standards that typify highly structured research protocols (for example, the closed-ended survey research questionnaire). There are other ways of conducting research that do not require the agenda to be so strictly one-sided. Listening, in democratic research, must be open to the experience of the subject, and method would not be allowed to take precedence over the expression of that experience. The research relationship can be thought of as an interpersonal interaction that takes place in a social context. Subjects interpret their situations, and act appropriately in concert with that interpretation. For the research subject, his understanding shapes his perception of appropriate action. For the researcher, understanding the subject's interpretation enables an understanding of his actions.

Researchers listen not only to research subjects; they also listen to other researchers. This conversation among researchers takes place in journals, in scholarly books, at conferences, and so on. When social researchers report their findings, they quite often are reporting their own interpretations of their subjects' interpretations. If this is the case—that research reports are interpretations—knowledge is not as stable as it would be under the presumption that researchers report facts, descriptions, and explanations gathered under the protocols of scientific research methods. The (normal science) anxiety is that if facts, descriptions, and explanations were subject to interpretation, "science" would be purely subjective. This anxiety about preserving objectivity strikes me as a sociocultural phenomenon—as if "objectivity" were crucial to some religious myth structure, and now that myth structure is threatened by new paradigms. Researchers, after all, are engaged in a conversation with colleagues about some set of concerns that has its own history and background. A community of inquirers has developed around some common interests; their conversation is sustained through interpretive commentary that is shared among the community. Scientific truth—since Kuhn (1970)—is itself contextual, historical, and revisable. The production of truth is a sociological phenomenon. The crucial challenge to normal science is the claim—built up by thinkers such as Nietzsche, Wittgenstein, Dewey, and Rorty—that all truth is perspectival. Specific communities of inquirers build up truth according to their projects (Miller and Fox 2001, Miller 2002). In epistemology, the effort to purify foundational science so that it can go about the noble task of producing universal truth is finished, kaput. The universal survives only in the realm of the abstract.

Therefore, the proposition that any narrative would be "the" accurate interpretation of the world is one that invites debate. If a particular interpretation is not accurate, might an alternate interpretation be accurate? Any substitute interpretation is subject to the same contestation, of course. Monday's truth claims are trumped by different ones on Tuesday, and so it goes throughout the week. The upshot is that our research efforts have built-in limitations because we lack the culturally independent "truth test" for assessing claims. Yet this ambiguity and uncertainty with respect to truth claims keeps the epistemic community vital and alive through the possibility of contestation. With Rorty (1998), we might as well give up the hope for the omnipotent, noncontingent, ahistorical ally, a futile hope that threads from Platonic forms to divine authority and through rational moral philosophy. These noncontingent abstractions are forms of idealism.

As a form of epistemological idealism, objectivity is the perspective claimed by many and held by none. A radical departure from the myth of objectivity would also be a radical departure from normal science. In studying social phenomena, we do not access "objective reality." This is not at all problematic as many suppose because we can uphold the same norm of inquiry by adjusting it somewhat. We can pursue increasingly less partial views by apprehending increasingly diverse perspectives on the matter at hand. This never yields the whole truth—the partial views never quite add up to the whole view—but it is a workable way of striving to go beyond one's own biases (Miller 2002). Science, however it is practiced, can go on doing what it has been doing. In the social sciences (whatever practices that term refers to), one can gain (imperfect) access to others' interpretations of their experiences and actions, and little more. And one can add one's own interpretations. It has ever been thus. Our research interpretations might be incisive as the piercing sunlight, enlightening everything and everyone in the room. Or the research interpretation may simply muddy the puddle. Either way, the researcher's interpretation changes the meaning of events somehow. For example, even when I as a researcher quote a research subject verbatim, my tone of voice may be different; the emphasis may be on a different word in the sentence; the context that I am speaking in is different from the subject's original context. Moreover, in my interpretation I sort and search for patterns in the subject's responses—patterns that have meaning for me but not necessarily the subject. Inevitably, the researcher interprets differently than the subject would. Gadamer's (1996) "double hermeneutic" identifies this sort of problem. Social science is a matter of interpreting interpretations, which is to say interpreting and advancing social constructions. And then the interpretations cycle themselves back into the mix as interventions. Objective reality is nowhere in the cycle. There is no need to feel trapped or inhibited by this feature of social investigation. As Rorty (1999, 85-86) put it, "Once we give up the idea that the point of discourse is to represent reality accurately, we will have no interest in distinguishing social constructs from other things. We shall confine ourselves to debating the utility of alternative constructs."

With respect to democratic research, certain problems arise because "democratic research" would be one of those alternative constructs whose utility is being debated. In democratic research, the researcher does not set the agenda unilaterally. We are instead imagining a democratic research situation in which the researcher and so-called subject acknowledge one another as mutual investigators. This approach provides a sense in which the subject is also the investigator (and a sense in which the investigator, too, is being studied). In the protocols of action research, for example, the researcher's "interpretation of interpretations" is brought back to the so-called subjects—perhaps we should call them participants—for still more reinterpretation. Eventually, interpretations that retain their vitality over time settle into social practice. If this is democratic research, perhaps we have been doing it all along without knowing it.

Agency and Efficacy: Changing Social Practices

An interpretation can settle into established practice once it begins to resonate as an appropriate way of looking at things. Well before the knowledge claim has been settled (which is to say, accepted as true within the community that investigates a problem and provides the problem with a context), it exists as one possible interpretation. The interpretation wends its way into the situation. Or perhaps the situation seeks out a satisfying interpretation. Either way, a new understanding has the potential to change social practices. As an interpretation or a claim becomes a settled matter, it can change social activity—via participants' understandings and reinterpretations of the situation. These understandings and interpretations shape the next steps to be taken and the next questions to be asked. Interpretations interact with the situation, and survive when participants accommodate their actions and practices to them. This is how an interpretation becomes an intervention.

The term intervention suggests that democratic research may entail action as well as understanding. Narrative meanings often cohere around themes of agency and efficacy—or lack thereof. Achieving change, resisting change, getting things done, resisting bad ideas—these are the dramatic moments of story telling. These are also political moments—when the status quo prevails or not; when movement is to the right or to the left; or up or down. Part of the drama is that not everyone can be an efficacious agent simultaneously. But we can imagine some parameters involved in something called democratic research. The researcher's agency and efficacy, probably expressed through the research project, cannot, it would seem, automatically override the subject's agency in democratic research ethics. In normal research on democracy, on the other hand, the ownership of the agenda is not democratically distributed. Agency and efficacy, like power and wealth, seem never to be equally distributed.

Nor is the ability of theories (or frames of meaning, ways of understanding, worldviews, or ideologies) to propagate themselves equally distributed. Some elite theorists have posited that the worldview of elites will always dominate because it has insinuated itself into the institutional superstructure of society. Others have posited theories of ethnic, cultural, and class conflict that problematize democratic aspirations. Some theories, like Maslow's hierarchy of needs, prosper because they dovetail in with agreeable metaphors of cultural and personal development. Some theories spread more readily than others; some are generalizable; some endure over time. But theoretical statements have problems more immanent. If a theory's aspiration is to be universally relevant, it will always fall short. After Hume, we harbor doubts that phenomena can be generalized at all, even though some concepts seem to travel across cultural and temporal boundaries better than others.

Let us reconsider, then, the kinds of theories and action we want to put into circulation. In research into democracy, the familiar theories (stories) about oppression and exclusion, and the struggle for emancipation and inclusion, are told and retold. There are many other narrative themes; democracy itself is one of the grand narratives of Western society, and very many lesser narratives support it. The narratives of actual people (that is, the demos), we are sometimes shocked to discover, may affirm stories excluding the immigrants, or ethnic minorities, or women, or people from other religions. A democratically generated agenda might not reiterate a democratic narrative. In this light, democratic research may not be self-reinforcing.

In the social sciences, the point of research is not merely to understand the world. Even if that were the intention, too much else is involved. Research, imbued as it is with interpretation, changes history by changing the way people understand their actions and their potential actions. A researcher's interpretation can change the way the situation is understood. A changed understanding leads to a changed view of what an appropriate action would be. The old epistemological aspiration for value-neutral research is not possible. Worse for the notion of impartiality, the researcher is a political actor (Flyvbjerg 2001). Politics changes as new interpretations are offered, or old interpretations are refuted.

Absent value-neutrality, what values does the researcher express? I do not exactly know the answer to this, but I suspect that if we all discussed it for a while, we might be able to generate a list of fine values, acceptable for researchers to hold and cherish. These fine values would then take precedence over the values that are endogenous to the situation under investigation. We would teach our graduate students how to go about this, how to behave consistent with these values in the conduct of inquiry. But in the field, politics returns: "these" fine values (of the researcher) want priority over "those" fine values (of the researched).

Democracy as a social science research topic is as interesting as any other social science research topic, but this does not mean that researchers will subordinate their fine research values to the demos, or to the research participants randomly culled from the demos. Researchers can and do investigate democratic and antidemocratic phenomena through the usual protocols, for example, quantitative and qualitative empirical methods. Theory, I suspect, will remain a useful term for organizing these data into a coherent story.

Theory as Story

Theory has come down from the blue-sky heights of universal truth and now situates itself alongside other grand and less grand narratives that reside closer to the red concrete, that is, closer to grounded everyday practices and actions. Theory is but a coherently organized story that gives meaning to some phenomena. Like all interpretations, it is subject to revision. This is not to minimize theory, narrative, or any interpretation of reality or experience. This should not be read as disappointment. Theory, like any understanding of the world, configures one's judgment of appropriate action. This is to say that we all act in ways that are consistent with our understanding of the situation. In a sense, then, theory is action under contemplation (Miller and King 1998, Miller 1997).

Interpretations do not settle disputes so much as create them. By this I mean that interpretations engage one another through social interaction. Interpretations challenge one another, enlighten one another, expose the other to different ways of looking at things, or accentuate some aspect of a situation while downplaying others. In this way interpretations shape not only inquiry but also the experience of life. A new or different interpretation is a new or different way of understanding one's world and one's perception of appropriate actions in it.

Narrative, theory, and action may not be such separate categories in democratic research as they might be in more traditional conceptions of research, where theory is viewed as something quite distinct from story telling. In the pragmatic research I have in mind, inquiry is interpretation, which is understanding, which is narrative, which frames appropriate action, which is what makes history and culture move. Note that truth (understood as universal generalizations) is not necessarily present in this sequence of understanding and communication and action. The epistemology of truth is rapidly losing its caché.

For some, this return to terra firma creates a problem of legitimation. As reality dissociates from objectivity, the research hypothesis is no longer accorded predictive value and this provides an anxious moment for realists and many physicists. The once-revered hypothesis counts mostly as an indicator of whose question gets asked. Knowing which questions get asked is, in turn, an indicator of what counts as knowledge. At every step, however, every claim is contestable. Where is the proof that my proof is true? Politics returns. This is the lament of epistemologists.

Haack (1997, 67) deploys a considerable amount of ink complaining about the anti-foundationalist, pragmatist philosopher Richard Rorty. "Rorty tells us he does "not have much use for notions like . . . 'objective truth'; to call a statement true 'is just to give it a rhetorical pat on the back.'" She continues her complaint against Rorty:

> "How does having knowledge differ from making poems and telling stories?" he asks rhetorically. . . . The only thing exemplary about science is that it is a model of "human solidarity." . . . Rorty's radical claims about truth, representation, etc., are radically false . . . [Contra Rorty,] "true" is not a word that truly applies to all or only statements about which we agree; and calling a statement "true" certainly doesn't mean that we agree about it. (Haack 1998, 64)

Rorty, for his part, rejects the correspondence theory of truth; his critique of representationalist epistemology is fully developed in his landmark *Philosophy and the Mirror of Nature* (1979). Rorty argues that images and metaphors too frequently come to be accepted as literal truth. Scientists are inclined to picture science as a grand mirror containing numerous representations that can be studied. Naturally, questions then arise about the accuracy of any author's representations. Centuries-long contestations ensue. This obsession is not proprietary to the natural sciences. Many of us in the social sciences, too, try desperately to demonstrate that our images actually reflect the real world.

Correspondence theorists hope that they can develop sentences that accurately correspond to reality. The problem is, the known facts about the real world always seem to take the form of word-shaped remarks. As word-shaped objects, facts lack the constancy and incorrigibility that is required of them in normal science. Those who subscribe to the correspondence theory are constantly in a tussle over which vocabularies (e.g., Marx's) work better than others (e.g., Weber's) because they represent reality more accurately.

Rorty (1998), expressing doubt about the appearance-reality distinction, states, "We have no idea what 'in itself' is supposed to mean in the phrase 'reality in itself.' So we suggest that the appearance-reality distinction be dropped in favor of a distinction between less useful and more useful ways of talking" (p. 1). Truth talk is not especially useful speech. Notions such as "intrinsic reality" and "correspondence to reality" are equally unproductive. Because truth is an absolute notion, phrases like "true for you but not for me," "was true then but is not true now," or "true in my culture but not in yours" seem relativistic when held to a standard of absolutism. A phrase that would avoid the paradox of relative truth would be something like "justified belief." A belief can be justified in one culture, but not in another, and the point is easily made because there is no implicit claim about universal, absolute facticity.

Pragmatic Research

Therein lies the opening for democratic research. Once we lose our concern about whether it is "the world" that makes sentences true or "us" that makes sentences true we are freed of the burden of speculating on what is "out there" in "objective reality." Instead, we can look to one another. As Dewey (1927, 184) put it, "Democracy will come into its own, for democracy is a name for a life of free and enriching communion. . . . It will have its consummation when free social inquiry is indissolubly wedded to the art of full and moving communication."

In the best circumstances for the demos, researchers actively engage the world of their research subjects in order to better their lives and conditions. But the question for democracy is "Who are the change agents?" Will some guardian class of researchers serve to liberate their research subjects? Meanwhile, for better or worse, researchers will have imposed their fine values on the lived experience of those being researched. Research on democracy potentially serves as one more way the researcher (as an elite) may come to colonize lived experience.

Imagine an alternative. Research conducted democratically would be willing to share power. When conducting democratic research, the researcher may not get to have it his way but may instead have to adapt to community norms. Consider these three propositions regarding what it means to conduct research democratically:

- Democracy means not having to obey commands, standards, criteria that are imposed from some exogenous authority system. As a corollary, democracy means not having to submit to the researcher's a priori agenda.

- Expressions about lived experience, rather than theory testing methodology, are the basis for any epistemology, or any research project that calls itself democratic. Theory testing—an inherently imposed agenda—means that one interpretation (and its corollary set of questions) wants to take precedence over all others. On the other hand, the narratives that are gathered together in democratic research would access descriptions and accounts of historical practices, current impasses, and intentions and aspirations.

- Some cultures hold values that are anathema to the researcher's own values—which is to say, democratic research in some contexts may be repulsive. This may lead researchers to take into account how far they want to go in the democratic empowerment project. Do researchers who aspire to democracy want to let go of the research agenda?

The community of social scientists who pay attention to social phenomena has developed norms of inquiry over the years. Democratic research radically de-privileges those norms. This de-privileging comes at a cost: The researcher who refuses to prioritize the fine values of research over the fine values of the demos must be willing to risk her status vis-à-vis others in the research community.

Pragmatic research can be thought of as joint activity with consequences. Both researcher and research subject have a share in producing it. In this way research has a role in creating a common interest. The dissociation of reality from objectivity does not register as a problematic if inquiry is regarded as a social activity. A research community is not the kind of society that seeks to dominate its constituents, but it is nonetheless constituted by relationships.

The Distribution of Freedoms and Authorities

A researcher engaged with a research subject interacts in that particular relation differently from the way that she would as a researcher participating at a conference with colleagues. The powers, protections, and responsibilities are different, but the researcher belongs in both relationships. In either association, collegial or with respect to a research subject, the researcher cannot be outside of the relationship in which she presents herself. The individual and the social constitute one another in either set of relationships. The problem within all social formations is to develop and then reconstruct ways and norms of appropriateness. The researcher need not "free" herself from the norms of the relationship for the sake of neutrality, objectivity, or impartiality. Similarly, in democratic research the research subject/participant need not liberate himself from the oppression of the research protocol. Rather, there is simply the everyday problem of readjusting social relationships so that everyone feels adequately liberated. Looked at this way, the practice of democratic research inquires "into the consequences of some particular distribution, under given conditions, of specific freedoms and authorities, and . . . what altered distribution would yield more desirable consequences" (Dewey 1927, 193).

Of preeminent importance are questions of cultural geography, historical moment, and situational context. A distributive judgment appropriate for one context may ill fit another. Dewey (1927) was keenly interested in the distribution of "social integrations." This distribution of status, authority, and freedoms changes as society evolves. When talents are wasted and institutions are felt to be repressive because modes of association that are inappropriate have become dominant, it is time to bring about a redistribution of social integrations. In Dewey's words, "Life has been impoverished, not by a predominance of 'society' in general over individuality, but by a domination of one form of association, the family, clan, church, economic institutions, over other actual and possible forms" (p 194).

Whether the activities of some need to be regulated so that others may enjoy a deeper and fuller experience is a judgment that requires knowledge of their experiences. It also requires imagination about the consequences of continuing with the status quo as well as some alternative distribution of social relations. The opposite of democratic research, in Dewey's conception, is lack of imagination and lack of efficacy with respect to the distribution of social integrations.

There is no detached, ahistorical abstraction in this focus on the distribution of social relations. The research subjects belong not to the objective world but, instead, dwell among us researchers, as participants in relationship with us. We cannot disqualify them from the discourse by making the illegitimate move of disconnecting them from relationship. Actions are influenced throughout the life of the research project by cultural predispositions, the researchers, and the subject's. Culture is both transmitted and created in relationship. Actions take place vis-à-vis culture, both in protest of established norms and in conformity to them.

In democratic research, the program, the purpose, the telos, is not determined in advance. Events are not brought into view for an assessment of how obedient phenomena are to theory. Rather there is an investigation into historical patterns, and what needs to be done and how to do it. There is an investigation of historical sequences that got us to the historical "now" and an appreciation that culture is malleable to some extent. There is an imaginative openness with respect to what we should do next. So if there were a challenge to normal science presented by democratic research it would be this: Concepts and theories and narratives are but tools of inquiry; they are not allowed to lord over it.

The social formation known as "social science" should not confuse itself with knowledge; it is not. Social science is an institution that matters, but the social formation known as social science has no claim on universal truth or objective reality. What, then, is the relation between a democratic researcher and a democratic public? Is it one wherein the intellectually qualified researcher makes decisions for the nonexpert public? This is not out of the question, but the question would not necessarily arise under the alternative mode of research that I am calling democratic research. Think of experts and nonexperts as two separate subcultures. Subcultures (even epistemic communities) may nurture practices that are incommensurable with the practices and beliefs of other subcultures. One cannot know ahead of time what any group or participant should do without investigating those same practices and norms in some problematic context. Indeed, discussion, consultation, and persuasion aimed at some social problematic are what constitute democratic research.

Discourse as Method?

Debate and the potential for modification of views must remain alive in social relations that locate themselves in the social geography of democracy. In short, what is needed is improvement in the methods and conditions of discourse. The process of inquiry is integral to that task. If it happens that an elite group, namely, the researchers, discover and publicize their findings, it is necessary only that these same researchers have the ability "to judge of the bearing of the knowledge supplied by others upon common concerns" (Dewey 1927, 209). Research for Dewey has a performative expectation; knowledge is "for" common concerns. Expertise may be distributed unequally no matter the sphere or domain, and stratified structures are often allowed to retain their legitimacy by performing societal tasks. (I am not claiming that expertise is all-important here. Regarding future policy consequences, there is more guesswork than knowledge, both on the part of the public and on the part of experts from the social sciences, about the actual social consequences of following policy alternative A or policy alternative B.)

Once the research is fulfilled, there remains this: the potential reintegration of social relations and the redistribution of specific freedoms and authorities. Researchers and participants alike have a stake in deciding which alternative distribution might yield more desirable consequences. Much is at stake here. The potential disintegration of local communities follows from a lack of relationship and from cultural gaps too wide to traverse. Impersonal bonds, built on the basis of market exchange and legal-rational instrumentalism, haunt and displace relationships built on embodied, locally shared experience.

These sorts of concerns are frequently dismissed as nostalgia for a democratic solidarity that never existed. This point is well taken; democratic participation sometimes seems like a dreamy, romantic idea. A second source of resistance is that standardization, the market system, and legal-rational institutions generate sufficient liberty, creativity, and social equality necessary for the realization of our collective and individual potential. Good as they sometimes are, these standardizable generalities miss something of utmost importance: the nonuniversal particularity of my (and your) everyday life. The moment of the particular problematic is precisely when intellectual methods meet practical procedures. They both collide and fuse. Abstract linguistic symbols interact with the affectively charged, in-the-moment conversation about some immanent problematic.

In the social sciences, the research subject is a participant who speaks and develops a strategy that may even run counter to the researcher's. The kind of change with which the research is confronted is not neutral, distant, objectifying, or indifferent. Rather, the change is behavioral, strategic, political, and agonistic. Lyotard (1979) discussed where this might be heading:

> Postmodern science—by concerning itself with such things as undecidables, the limits of precise control, conflicts characterized by incomplete information, "fracta," catastrophes, and pragmatic paradoxes—is theorizing its own evolution as discontinuous, catastrophic, nonrectifiable, and paradoxical. It is changing the meaning of the word knowledge, while expressing how such a change can take place. It is producing not the known, but the unknown. (60)

Postmodern, pragmatic, democratic research adds up to a search for (or at least an acceptance of) ambiguity in the sense that there is no "right" answer to be arrived at through discursive methods. This knowledge-building activity is to be distinguished from realism, in which the inquiry investigates stable constants presumed to exist outside of our own web of beliefs, desires, and symbolic representations. In realism, there is a sense in which an object of inquiry has a content of its own. There is a thing-in-itself whose essential nature is to be discovered. In pragmatic research there are phenomena that someone can interpret and discuss. The form of democratic research known as pragmatism will address itself to questions like "What are you talking about?" "What is it that you want to find out?" Legitimation comes from these local communities, from their own discourses. These local inquirers are not so interested in finding the theory that represents reality accurately; they are trying to figure out which construction of reality works better given the contingences of local context. Social inquiry then can be appreciated as a matter of reweaving beliefs about the appropriate distribution of social integration, freedoms, and authorities.

Chapter 11

Extra-Formal Democracy: A Reflection

Hugh T. Miller

Formal democracy is the kind of democracy indicated by electoral processes. The regularity of elections is the prominent marker of whether a political entity is counted as democratic or not.

There are other less systemic conceptualizations of democracy, such as the direct democracy of smaller social groupings, mediated negotiation surrounding environmental policy controversies, or social entrepreneurship as a democratic inspiration. Direct democracy, as mythologized in images of ancient Greek city-states and bucolic New England town meetings, continues to serve as a focal point for the gathering of transformational values such as political inclusiveness and social betterment. This direct democratic tradition has informed much of the movement in public administration that would include democratization among its professional commitments. As Cooper (1984) suggested some time ago, public administration under democratic norms might prefer to share "power with" its fellow citizens rather than exercise "power over" its externalized clients.

The direct democracy tradition has combined with the increased awareness of the necessity, actuality, and perhaps even the desirability of administrative discretion in public policy implementation to inform a challenge to formalism in public policy formation and implementation.

Will the Discretionary Bureaucrat Be a Democrat?

When the issue of politics is raised in the context of public administration, the conversation has in the past bogged down in long-standing political science/political theory debates about the legitimacy of the state, the role of public administration in a liberal society, and the problems of administrative discretion. Despite the astute and highly regarded investigations of policy implementation by Pressman and Wildavsky (1984), despite the research of Michael Lipsky (1980) on street-level bureaucracy, and despite the more recent "new public management" justifications for managerial discretion, a political theory on the use of discretion by public administrators remains underdeveloped. The use of discretion by public administrators seems dubious to numerous formalistic political theorists (for example, Lowi 1993).

Can discretionary public administration—a logical precondition for successful citizen participation—succeed in securing the blessings of liberty? Abuse of discretion is the key suspicion that many Americans and Europeans have of their bureaucrats. Their fears are often justified; bureaucrats, especially those involved in police, military, or security functions, sometimes do pose a threat to liberty. Yet, in other contexts, discretion for them is necessary in order to further the aims of democratic participation. At best, discretionary public administration serves democracy and the values that go with it; at worst, discretionary public administration serves tyranny and corruption. It has been said before, and is worth repeating here, that disrespect of liberty is a display of ignorance about the art of governance in a world of diverse cultures (Foucault 1991).

Pragmatic Liberalism

Public administration needs political theory, one that is grounded in pragmatism as well as liberalism and pluralism—but not so concerned with formalism. A pragmatic liberalism would not be overly concerned to prevent politics from occurring in nonformal locations. The art of governance is no longer about legitimizing the state, or about state sovereignty, or framing a constitution, or promoting ideologies. The art of governance means developing the capacity and competence to deal with problems that arise from the population.

In this view—pragmatic liberalism—government is transformed from an object belonging to the sovereign (e.g., God; the king; the people, the republic, the constitution) to an art and craft composed of practices and procedures invoked in pragmatic situations. The politics of "who should rule us?" is thereby displaced by the politics of "what should we do next?"

There are several seemingly disparate movements that tend in this direction. One is the new managerialism, including new public management and reinventing government. In this school of thought there is an eagerness to solve the problems of the population efficiently. A second is the discourse movement within public administration theory. The urging that public administrators reach out beyond the boundaries of their traditional submissive and subservient roles to actively work on solving public problems continues on a vector first conceptualized by Harmon (1971) as the "proactive administrator." Postmodernism, communitarianism, and deliberative-communicative schools of thought create additional momentum toward a pragmatic politics.

Hendriks and Musso, in their comparative study (one site in the Netherlands, the other in Los Angeles) described in chapter 4, found a remarkable commonality between the two sites they studied: the limited reliance on formal politics to accomplish institutional change. In particular, a neighborhood social movement, which was not given much support by the city, energized the change in Los Angeles. In the Randstad in the Netherlands, public administrators teamed up with neighborhood professionals to design situation-specific neighborhood reforms. While the public administrators were formal players, the role they played was facilitative of public deliberation (rather than expert at some specific technical task). Elected officials in both cases were relatively minor players. The major players in the Los Angeles neighborhood council movement have been middle-class citizens. In the Randstad, the major change agents were public administrators. Fed up with debilitating structures, they sought new ways of working with neighborhood networks. Both the Randstad and the Los Angeles examples seem to indicate some headway in reconceptualizing the art of governance.

Public administration competence and capacity (to solve particular problems) are crucial in these debates. In the Randstad, the rhetoric of deliberative democracy may eventually serve the attempts by administrators to co-opt local populations and/or control them. A permanent climate of conciliation and bargaining between the discretionary bureaucrat and the empowered citizen-client would be thereby achieved. As coercive methods of social order recede, participative iterations of governmental rationality gain ascendance. The upshot of this extension of bureaucratic rationality is the permanent politicization of policy implementation. Critics of bureaucracy will be wary of this sort of bureaucratic flexibility. However, many public administration theorists would not share that critical pessimism. For them, bureaucratic formalism and rigidity, which prevents democratic responsiveness, is the more present danger.

Democratic formalism derives from the politics of early modernity, when the state needed a way of legitimating itself; a different legitimation strategy is needed nowadays, and perhaps deliberative democracy will serve as the ad hoc, situational, pragmatic legitimation strategy. Does public administration need to legitimate its existence through direct participation schemes? Or is it more worthwhile to get important work done efficiently and effectively? Either way, public administration is open to three charges, namely, that it (1) is a servant of power; (2) is a power in its own right; and (3) needs power to accomplish its projects. And in the Los Angeles case, public administration is open to a completely different question: Where were you when neighborhood governance was taking place?

These concerns about public administration—its legitimacy and its power—may be receding in importance. A project-oriented politics is not especially concerned about who stands in for legitimate authority. For one thing, legitimacy of any politics is always a contestable political question. But more important, the pragmatic political question is about the ends and means of doing a thing—or not. Legitimating these projects, rather than institutional structures, is as far as we need to go. This less-formal mode of democracy legitimates itself through its aims and practices. Formal democracy relies on voting and representation. Lever pulling or computer-assisted ballot marking done in the privacy of a voting booth are not considered to be robust, deliberative democratic practices.

Formal Democracy as Problematic

The preference to work within a direct-democracy tradition stems from dissatisfaction with status quo institutions, on both substantive grounds and process grounds. Pateman (1970) argued that a democratic society requires that its people have a democratic character, and that a participatory environment can help to develop this character and the sense of political efficacy among the citizenry. While the formalistic, electoral-representative democratic theory she criticized relies on the noninvolvement of the people for its social stability, in her view one learns to participate by participating—and with an intensity more profound than periodically marking a ballot in the secrecy of a polling booth. In the Port Huron Statement, the Students for a Democratic Society (1962) sought to create a social system whereby the individual would share in those social decisions determining the quality and direction of his or her life. Hence, participation should be a part of everyday life, a way to stave off alienation and enhance civic and personal development. But the argument for better quality participation goes further than personal efficacy.

For Pateman (1970), formal democracy, on the face of it, does not serve the interests of the poor. The system seems to succeed mostly at perpetuating itself. Voters express preferences via periodic elections in a rational way, it is assumed. Select individuals then act in place of ordinary citizens. The implicit claim is that everyone's interests are looked after, and so private life is conducted separately from politics—until the next election. Yet poverty, discrimination, homelessness, social unrest, and other symptoms (social, economic, and environmental) give evidence that everyone's interests are not looked after.

Further, assessing the success of any individual's vote is quite difficult. Candidates and parties are marketed, using advertising and public relations techniques. Campaign promises go unredeemed. Special interests with resources are better organized, as evidenced by large corporate contracts, subsidies, and postponed enforcement of watered-down regulations, altered to accommodate campaign contributors and powerful interests. Substantive results for the electorate are difficult to trace back to the electoral mechanism.

Therefore, electoral representation is a formal matter and does not imply that the interests of the people are looked after. Among socialists, it has long been felt that electoral democracy was not enough. Exemplary is this quote from V. I. Lenin:

> Under socialism much of "primitive" democracy will inevitably be revived, since, for the first time in the history of civilized society the mass of the population will rise to taking an independent part, not only in voting and elections, but also in the everyday administration of the state. Under socialism all will govern in turn and will soon become accustomed to no one governing. (Lenin 1924/1976, 20)

After Lenin died in 1924, Joseph Stalin took over the reigns of the Soviet Communist Party, and this democratic-humanistic aspiration (and rhetoric) went by the wayside—at least in the old Soviet Union. Some deliberative theorists may be horrified at the suggestion that there is any kind of link between their work and Lenin's thought. Indeed, in practice, Lenin embraced Taylorism, an efficiency-oriented form of hierarchical managerialism that generated supervisory mechanisms such as time-and-motion studies. Contemporary theorists may further reject any implied link between socialism and deliberative democracy; yet, the lineage to socialist thought (not necessarily Lenin's) perhaps should be acknowledged. The quotation above is full of import for deliberative democrats because it articulates the view that democracy should be seen as an everyday activity. Primitive Athenian-style democracy serves as background assumption for many contemporary deliberative and communitarian inquiries, in particular, those studies that regard democracy as an everyday social practice and not merely a principle.

For example in chapter 2, Scott, Adams, and Wechsler described deliberative democracy as careful thought and discussion about issues and decisions. As a process of social inquiry, learning, and persuasion, it is inherently a communicative process. Deliberative democracy can also be a transformational process, given a norm of openness among the participants to new ideas and attitudes. The possibility for increasing community capacity for practical judgment is also in evidence. As Scott, Adams, and Weschler point out, both tolerance and inclusiveness are important virtues for deliberative governance. For all the hopefulness about democratic social change, they also assert that there is no a priori expectation that (1) anyone will change his or her perspective or that (2) participation is a worthy humanistic aspiration in and of itself (though other democratic humanists would disagree with some aspects of that assessment). Yet, there is very little that is conclusive about deliberative democratic research. Its definitional features remain undetermined. Its cultural appropriateness, meaningfulness, and authenticity are open to question. Hence, Scott, Adams, and Weschler call for formal, empirical research (implying that the theoretical work that has taken place thus far is inadequate, as are case studies).

The "causes and effects" that Scott, Adams, and Weschler seek recalls for us the positivism-as-usual mode of social research. But Miller's chapter on democratic epistemology (chapter 10) does not assume it is necessarily the case that the researcher's agenda is simultaneously a democratic agenda. Empirical cause-and-effect studies tend to situate the observer at an objective distance from the object of inquiry, whereas many new approaches to democratic research admit the researcher into the world being studied. The chapters from Kensen and Tops and from Marshall and Ozawa indicate that a quite different approach is beginning to take shape—a new focus on actual democratic practices.

In chapter 9 Kensen and Tops report that social research in the Netherlands can be very practical and applied. For them, research was a team effort and required commitment not only from the researchers but also from the practitioners who were part of the studies. Research was not expected to be objective in the positivistic sense, but transformative and experiential. The interaction research they wrote about withholds the commitment to neutrality and instead commits itself to collegiality and experimentation, along with open-ended learning on the part of all who are involved. Research thus tries to be part of society, rather than apart from society.

Sticky questions such as "who funds the research?" and "who is included/excluded?" are not resolved in interaction research. But because of the democratic aspirations of this sort of research, some questions stand out. How inclusive does the research have to be in order to be considered democratic? Does a discussion require a face-to-face encounter to be counted as democratic deliberation? How many discussion meeting are required? That depends on situational and contextual factors, of course. Any attempt to answer these sorts of questions underscores the difficulty of making generalizable cause-and-effect claims about deliberative democracy, or of setting criteria for its evaluation. Must deliberative democracy rescue civic culture from its morass and failure in order to be deemed successful? If not, what are the lesser aspirations for it? The alternative research approaches leave unanswered, and seem less concerned about, most of the questions that Scott, Adams, and Weschler posed.

Deliberative democracy is a romantic notion; perhaps it is a form of wishful thinking. As Michels put it, in explicating his iron law of oligarchy, "Democracy is a treasure which no one will ever discover by deliberate search. But in continuing our search, in laboring indefatigably to discover the undiscoverable, we shall perform a work which will have fertile results in the democratic sense" (Michels 1962/1984, 41). While the formula for democracy may remain elusive, the aspiration for it has endured, usually in tension with hierarchy.

Democracy and Hierarchy

Writing in about 1919 or 1920, Antonio Gramsci picked up on the idea of the soviet, which is a reference to the factory council model of industrial-economic democracy (Gramsci 1969). The intrinsic value of participation as a personal growth experience is not retained in Gramsci's work. Indirect participation in political decision making was more to his liking, because of the need to integrate and plan. Gramsci also advocated decentralization so as to maximize flexibility and freedom among the collection of local factory councils. This model vaguely endorses hierarchical bureaucracy; decentralization is not extended to far as to accommodate direct participation. Gramsci—like most contemporary public administration theorists—prioritized the necessity of implementing the programs and plans of the legitimate authority, which in his writings was the soviet.

Implementation of programs, plans, and policies—this is what public administrators do, above all else (before the deliberative democrats had their say, that is). If one is a public administrator, one is likely to be concerned about getting the work done. This means keeping the system going, be it the sewer and water system, the trash collection system, the traffic system or mass transportation system, the social welfare system, the educational system, the law enforcement system, and so on. The systems that public administrators are called upon to maintain and improve arise from the needs of the population.[1] Does direct participation help administrators maintain and improve these systems? Participation about the daily operation of the sewer and water system seems like a waste for everyone. On the other hand, the system may not be working the way people want it to work if, say, tap water is no longer perceived as potable. Open, participative practices may inspire ineffective systems to become more responsive to the needs of the population.

Parsing public administration responsibilities into the categories "amenable to participation" and "not amenable to participation" is not a task that would be easily accomplished. Perhaps all social systems could be reengineered to accommodate participation. But mandated participation devolves into system maintenance and "going through the motions." So much of it (for example, those meaningless American-style public hearings that take place to satisfy legal requirements) seems pro forma. Moreover, relatively few public administrators are process facilitators of the sort that Marshall and Ozawa described in chapter 8. Public administrators typically are hired because of their expertise in one area or another. Seldom is "citizen participation" the sought-after skill in the United States—"customer service" is the closest analogy. However, Denmark and the Netherlands show evidence that this sort of skill for public administrators is increasingly appreciated and valued.

Classic organization theory does not rule out the citizen participation skills, but these were not present at the ascendance of modern bureaucracy and such skills remain mostly out-of-role for bureaucrats. "The decisive reason for the advance of bureaucratic organization has always been the technical superiority over any other form of organization" (Weber 1946, 214). Typically, the work gets done via hierarchical pyramid-style social formations. It may be no comfort to democratic intellectuals that "the dictatorship of the official and not that of the worker is on the march," as Weber (1946, 50) phrased his response to Marx. Advocates of direct participation face a dispiriting array of challenges.

The comprehensiveness of bureaucratization is in its rationalization, in its mechanistic depersonalization, in its system-maintaining routine. The type of person who survives the necessary role requirements tends to be narrowly professional and public certified via advanced degrees or credentials. Practices such as heroism, human spontaneity, and inventiveness are exercised with caution. System coherence long ago preempted participative democracy as the top priority. Yet, Bogason, in chapter 3, asserts that, amidst the complex network and governance systems in place today, local governments are compelled to take upon a new role—that of intermediary among actors in a fragmented political, social, and institutional environment. Hierarchical means of control are not up to this task, Bogason contends.

Hierarchy under Siege

The institutional shift Bogason described, which took place in Denmark, changed local government from a nationally uniform system centralized at town hall to fragmented, multichannel localism, characterized by new venues for citizen participation, aptly termed the ad hoc democracy of activists. Not voters (who are now beginning to look more like spectators), but users, perhaps from third-sector organizations, take advantage of the newfound openings in the governance process. Among these activists is the type that Hulgård, in chapter 6, called the local entrepreneur.

As Sørensen's research implied, public administrators sticking to the traditional hierarchical chain of command are not suited to perform the tasks necessary for deliberative democracy at the micro level. By investigating the coping strategies of five local public administrators, as reported in chapter 7, Sørensen attempted to say something about what a transformation from government to governance would have on the role of the public administrator, and on democracy itself. The message from Sørensen is that institutional change—away from the hierarchical model—would well serve those public administrators who wish to make their way through the uncertainties of micro-level democratic processes on a vector toward participative democratic governance.

When public administrators exercise the discretion that most of us believe is indeed exercised (see Lipsky 1984), what happens as a result may or may not be democratic. The public administrator operating within the role constraints of traditionally bureaucratic hierarchy operates within a zone of authorized conduct. Sørensen observed that public administrators must adapt their traditional role prescription when faced with a new environment of decentralized governance networks. But she also noted that their coping strategies are problematic for democracy. Hence, both (a) retaining the status quo role of the public administrator and (b) changing the role requirements are, in practice, problematic for participative democracy. The old roles are not conducive to participative deliberation, and the new role prescriptions can generate debilitating uncertainty.

Despite new ways of looking at democracy, such as network governance, the demise of traditional representative democracy should not be overstated. In Sehested's chapter 5 there was evidence that—even in a political context characterized by profound disagreement to the point of the development of an important instrument for resistance she called an opponent policy network—the elected representatives were more equal than others in the political process. Moreover, these elected individuals were given the deference of the planners in the planning department. The role prescriptions for public administrators operating within the representative-democratic system may be incompatible with a more proactive decision-process role indicated by the various forms of extra-formal democracy studied in the various research projects reported in this book.

The coping strategy of three public administrators in Sørensen's research seemed to be avoidance of the issue. Bogason, with an eye out for a change from the "bureaucratic controllers" mode to the role of intermediary for the community at large, returns our attention to the old question of institutional separation of politics and administration. Hovering in the background, this question of political action generates ambiguity and uncertainty for public administrators trying to figure out what to do next. Nor is it obvious which way to look for more and better democracy: upward toward politicians or downward to street-level bureaucrats and their citizens/clients? And if one relies for democracy on the public administrator, now empowered with discretion, would such reliance be repaid? There is probably not a generalizable answer to that question.

Discretion and Facilitation

There is reason to believe in the possibility that bureaucratic discretion can be shared with the client/citizen/customer/co-producer in a "power with" as opposed to "power over" relationship (Cooper 1984), but this is only the beginning of politics. The politics of power sharing came into full view in Helsingør, Denmark, as reported by Sehested in chapter 5. Local public administrators and planners were willing to work with opponents of the downtown pedestrian mall; and others were willing to work with the more powerful proponents of the project as well as the (ultimately prevailing) elected officials who supported the project. The proponents tended to be the community elites; their process was centralized and based on a closed and stable policy network (the city mall network) in coalition with the majority in the city council and the large interests groups in the city. The opposition no-mall coalition claimed to represent the public interest in defending the architectural history of the city. The opposition group was obviously not effective because Helsingør now displays a pedestrian mall in the old part of the city.

Sehested was clear on the stakes for democratic theory. Those who see a new governance mode, in which pluralistic interests gain access to decision-making power, focus their attention on the negotiation processes and network relationships among politicians, administrators, private businesses, citizens, and local pressure groups. The unresolved theoretical problem is to determine where the public interest lies, because factions often disagree as they did in Helsingør. From an elitism lens, however, the problem is quite different. The dispersion of power into local issue networks is only apparent; developers, city officials, and politicians continue to possess superior institutional power. Economic growth, a legitimating rationale, established itself as the name of the public interest, and hierarchy remained the technically superior social formation for the local community elites to accomplish their purposes.

As Sehested reminds us, the centralized, elitist governance process does not undermine representative democracy. To the contrary, representative democracy evolved into an aggregative version of network democracy. The public dialogue, the formal complaints, and the various challenges to the decision to proceed with the mall did not render the decision undemocratic, even though the integrative/deliberative model of democracy was not effectuated. Yet animosity to the mall project lingered long after the battles were won and lost.

Facilitators and Entrepreneurs

Marshall and Ozawa show in chapter 8 that it does not have to be that way. They found that the participants in the Johnson Creek Corridor Committee, located in the area of Portland, Oregon, emerged from their water-policy processes with strong mutual respect over a period of five years. The meetings that took place cultivated a climate of tolerance and acceptance for sometimes volatile, emotional disagreements. At precisely the points where participants expressed their passions and flashed their tempers, the presence of a mediator served to turn the passion into constructive energy. Marshall and Ozawa claim that public decision making supported by facilitative mediation can advance the practice of democratic governance. Among the important dynamics of such facilitation are mediated negotiation, inclusiveness (to avoid elitism), and relationships. Skilled mediators can steer the process away from opportunistic deal making while enhancing personal and societal development.

While it is far from obvious that facilitation will always yield democratic outcomes, the focus on mediation and facilitation directs the researcher's attention to the actual social practices that are entailed in deliberative democracy. The focus on relationships—also emphasized by Kensen and Tops in chapter 9—relieves the researcher of the heavy burden of uncovering motivations and intentions. While these remain important, they bias the observer to adopt an "exchange theory" view of the policy network in question, wherein rational, utility-maximizing self-interest is projected onto all participants. While such a frame is, no doubt, useful sometimes, it might also be useful to open one's eyes to the transformational potential of deliberative processes.

If facilitators and mediators can help groups make transformational changes, social entrepreneurs help set the agenda. The activities of Hulgård's social entrepreneur, as reported in chapter 6, are embedded in community. This sort of entrepreneur generates currency for ideas, which then circulate among governmental institutions and within political conversations. Social entrepreneurs participate in governance networks and often serve as mediators between segregated communities. Relying solely on the constructs of rational economics—such as the self-interested utility-maximizing individual—leads to a neglect of the many facets of entrepreneurship that inform innovative practices of democratic social action. Feelings of community and value orientation are among the noneconomic factors that are associated with social entrepreneurship.

Conclusion

The point of this book, then, has been to show that there are forms of democracy, such as the direct democracy of smaller social groupings or vaguely defined concepts such as social entrepreneurship, that deserve our attention. Images of ancient Greek city-states and bucolic New England town meetings present only part of the picture and do not capture the multitudinous venues for the local practice of democracy. These practices are infused with normative meaning and transformational potential. Public administration, under democratic norms, would share "power with" its fellow citizens rather than exercise "power over" its disempowered clients. Because of the discretion that is now explicitly handed to administrators, these new practices and norms can generate role uncertainty. They also indicate a challenge to the formalism of public policy formation and implementation.

Legitimacy is no longer framed in terms of elected officials, political ideology, or sovereign authority. Political issues that gain salience are about the capacity of governing institutions (public agencies, nonprofit organizations, cultural institutions, ad hoc social formations, relations among social entrepreneurs, etc.) to solve public problems. Governing, in this usage, does not refer to "the government." It refers to social practices that regulate conduct and social intercourse. These practices are institutionalized to a degree—some more, some less. Meanwhile, the art of governance is no longer about legitimizing the state or about state sovereignty or framing a constitution. Nor is it, by intention, a way of putting into place ancient concepts about citizen participation and direct democracy. In modernity politics has changed, and the locus of tension has shifted away from structural formulae that serve the purpose of legitimation. Political tension and conflict aims more toward the arena occupied by pragmatic public administration, a power-exercising citizenry, and a domain of public problems that can be found in everyday life.

Note

1. One can argue that the systems are there to control the population, and I would not necessarily disagree with this view. But from Foucault's (1991) presentation of his ideas on governmental rationality, we can see that a social system's rationality emanates from within the population being controlled. For example, a fearful population willingly (more or less) accepts some amount of coercion in response to its demand for security.

References

Abma, Tineke A. 1997. "Playing with/in Plurality, Revitalizing Realities and Relationships in Rotterdam." *Evaluation* 5 (1): 25-48.

Andersen, Johannes, Ann-Dorte Christensen, Kamma Langberg, Birte Siim, and Lars Torpe. 1993. *Medborgerskab—demokrati og politisk deltagelse*. Herning, Denmark: Systime.

Anderson, D.K. 2002. "A Psychodynamic Analysis of Discourse Theory: Understanding the Influence of Emotions, Regression, and Change." *Administrative Theory & Praxis* 24 (1): 3-24.

Argyris, C., and D. A. Schön. 1978. *Organizational Learning: A Theory of Action Perspective*. Reading, Mass.: Addison Wesley.

Baldersheim, Harald, and Krister Ståhlberg, eds. 1994. *Towards the Self-Regulating Municipality. Free Communes and Administrative Modernization in Scandinavia*. Aldershot U.K.: Dartmouth.

Bang, Henrik P., and Eva Sørensen. 1999. "The Everyday Maker: A New Challenge to Democratic Governance." *Administrative Theory and Praxis* 21 (3): 325-341.

Bang, Henrik P., Allan D. Hansen, and Jens Hoff. 2000. *Demokrati fra neden. Casestudier fra en dansk kommune*. Copenhagen, Denmark: Jurist- og Økonomforbundets Forlag.

Barber, Benjamin. 1984. *Strong Democracy: Participatory Politics for a New Age*. Berkeley: University of California Press.

Beck, Ulrich, Anthony Giddens, and Scott Lash. 1994. *Reflexive Modernization. Politics, Tradition and Aesthetics in the Modern Social Order*. Cambridge: Polity Press.

Beierle, T. 2000. "The Quality of Stakeholder Based Decisions: Lessons from the Case Study Record." Resources for the Future Discussion. Paper 00-56. Washington, D.C., November.

Bella, Robert Neely, ed. 1996. *Habits of the Heart: Individualism and Commitment in American Life*. Berkeley: University of California Press.

Bellah, Robert N., et al. 1992. *The Good Society*. New York: Alfred A. Knopf.

Bengtsson, Steen, and Lars Hulgård. 2001. " Denmark: Cooperative Activation and Community Development." Pp. 65-82 in Carlos Borzaga and Jaques Defourny, eds. *Social Enterprises in Europe*. London: Routledge.

Benhabib, Seyla. ed. 1996. *Democracy and Difference: Contesting the Boundaries of the Political*. Princeton, N.J.: Princeton University Press.

Bevir, M., and R. A. W. Rhodes. 1998. "Public Administration without Foundations: The Case of Britain." In *Administrative Theory & Praxis* 20 (1): 3-13.

Bingham, Gail. 1984. *Resolving Environmental Disputes: A Decade of Experience*. Washington, D.C:. The Conservation Foundation.

Blaakilde, A. L. 1998. "A Vision of 21st Century Folkloristics: Difference, Coherence, and Interpretation." Pp. 107-16 in *ARV Nordic Yearbook of Folklore*. Uppsala, Sweden: The Royal Gustavus Adolphus Academy.

Boer, Nico de, 2001. "De opkomst van de wijkaanpak als dominante strategie in het sociaal beleid." Pp. 29-50 in Lex Veldboer and Jan-Willem Duyvendak, eds., *Meeting Point Nederland*. Amsterdam: Boom.

Boer, Nico de, Jan-Willem Duyvendak. 2001. *Buurten in wijken: Verslag van een onderzoek*. The Hague: Ministerie van Buitenlandse Zaken en Koninkrijksrelaties.

Bogason, Peter. 1990. "Danish Local Government: Towards an Effective and Efficient Welfare State." In, Jens Joachim Hesse, ed., *Local Government and Urban Affairs in International Perspective. Analysis of Twenty Western Industrialised Countries*. Baden-Baden: Nomos.

_____. 1992. "Strong or Weak State? The Case of Danish Agricultural Export Policy 1849-1906." *Comparative Politics* 24: 219-27.

_____. 1996. "The Fragmentation of Local Government in Scandinavia." *European Journal of Political Research* 30 (1): 65-86.

_____. 1998. "Changes in the Scandinavian Model. From Bureaucratic Command to Interorganisational Negotiation." *Public Administration* 76 (2): 335-54

_____. 2000. *Public Policy and Local Governance. Institutions in Post Modern Society*. Cheltenham, U.K.: Edward Elgar.

_____. 2001. *Fragmenteret forvaltning. Demokrati og netværksstyring i decentraliseret lokalstyre*. Århus, Denmark: Systime.

Bohman, James. 1996. *Public Deliberation: Pluralism, Complexity and Democracy*. Cambridge, Mass.: MIT Press.

Borzaga, Carlos, and Jacques Defourny, eds. 2001. *Social Enterprises in Europe*. London: Routledge.

Bout-Saari, R., and W. Groenewold. 2001. *Onderzoek naar de structuur en werkwijze van de Rotterdamse wijkaanpakorganisatie*. Rotterdam:

Gemeentelijke Bestuursdienst.

Box, R. C. 1998. *Citizen Governance: Leading American Cities in the 21st Century.* Thousand Oaks, Calif.: Sage Publications.

Box, Richard C., and Deborah A. Sagen. 1998. "Working with Citizens: Breaking Down Barriers to Citizen Self-Governance." Pp. 158-74 in Cheryl S. King and Camilla Stivers, *Government Is Us: Public Administration in an Anti-Government Era.* Thousand Oaks, Calif.: Sage Publications.

Breton, Margot. 1994. "On the Meaning of Empowerment and Empowerment-Oriented Social Work Practice." Pp. 23-27 in *Social Work with Groups.* 17(3). Binghamton, N.Y.: The Haworth Press.

Bryner, Gary C. 1995. *Blue Skies, Green Politics: The Clean Air Act of 1990 and Its Implementation.* Washington, D.C.: CQ Press.

Bush, Robert Baruch, and Joseph Folger. 1994. *The Promise of Mediation: Responding through Empowerment and Recognition.* San Francisco: Jossey-Bass.

Carpenter, Susan, and W.J.D. Kennedy. 1988. *Managing Public Disputes: A Practical Guide to Handling Conflict and Reaching Agreements.* San Francisco: Jossey-Bass Publishers.

Chaskin, R. J., P. Brown, S. Venkatesh, and A. Vidal. 2001. *Building Community Capacity.* New York: Aldine de Gruyter.

Chaskin, Robert J., ed. 2001. *Building Community Capacity.* New York: Aldine de Gruyter.

Clark, Terry Nichols, and Ronald Inglehart. 1998. "The New Political Culture: Changing Dynamics of Support for the Welfare State and Other Policies in Postindustrial Societies." Pp. 9-72 in Terry Nichols Clark and Vincent Hoffmann-Martinot, eds., *The New Political Culture.* Boulder, Colo.: Westview Press.

Clift, S. 2002. *The Future of E-Democracy: The Fifty Year Plan.* http://www.publicus.net/articles/future.html

Cohen, Jean L. 1997. Working Paper #6. University of Maryland. *American Civil Society Talk.* College Park, Md.: The National Commission on Civic Renewal.

Cooper, Terry L. 1984. "Public Administration in an Age of Scarcity: A Citizenship Role for Public Administrators." Pp. 297-314 in Jack Rabin and James S. Bowman, eds., *Politics and Administration: Woodrow Wilson and American Public Administration.* New York: Marcel Dekker.

Cooper, Terry L. 1984. "Citizenship and Professionalism in Public Administration." *Public Administration Review* 44: 143-49.

Couto, R. A., and C. S. Guthrie. 1999. *Making Democracy Work Better: Mediating Structures, Social Capital, and the Democratic Prospect.* Chapel Hill: University of North Carolina Press.

Cox, A., and J. K. Scott. 1999. "Measuring the Economic Importance of Health Care in Rural Communities: The Role of Local Stakeholders." Presented at the Annual Meeting of the Center for Health Statistics. Washington, D.C.

Crowfoot, James E., and Julia M. Wondolleck. 1991. *Environmental Disputes: Community Involvement in Conflict Resolution*. Washington, D.C.: Island Press.

Dahl, Robert A. 1961. *Who Governs? Democracy and Power in an American City*. New Haven, Conn.: Yale University Press.

Dees, Gregory J. 1998. "The Meaning of Social Entrepreneurship." Paper. Stanford, Calif.: Stanford University Kauffman Center for Entrepreneurial Leadership.

Defourny, Jacques. 2001. "From Third Sector Concepts to a Social Enterprise" Pp. 1-29 in Carlos Borzaga and Jacques Defourny, eds. *Social Enterprises in Europe*. London: Routledge.

DeLeon, P. 1997. *Democracy and the Policy Sciences*. Albany: State University of New York Press.

Deleon, Richard E. 1991. "San Francisco: Postmaterialist Populism in a Global City." Pp. 205-215 in H.V. Savitch and J.C. Thomas, eds., *Big City Politics in Transition, Urban Affairs Annual Reviews* 38. Newbury Park, Calif.: Sage Publications.

Denhardt, Robert B., and Janet Vinzant Denhardt. 2000. "The New Public Service: Serving Rather than Steering." *Public Administration Review* 60 (6): 549-59.

Dewey, John. 1927. *The Public and Its Problems*. Athens: Ohio University Press.

Dongen, H. J. van, W. A. M. de Laat and A. J. J. A. Maas. 1996. *Een kwestie van verschil*. Delft: Eburon.

Dryzek, J. S. 1990. *Discursive Democracy: Politics, Policy, and Political Science*. Cambridge: Cambridge University Press.

———. 2000. *Deliberative Democracy and Beyond: Liberals, Critics, Contestation*. Oxford: Oxford University Press.

Dryzek, J. S., and D. Torgerson. 1993. "Democracy and the Policy Sciences: A Progress Report." *Policy Sciences* 26 (3): 127-49.

Dukes, E. Franklin. 1996. *Resolving Public Conflict: Transforming Community and Governance*. Manchester: Manchester University Press.

Duyvendak J.W. 2001. *Opbouwwerk in Zeeburg in het nieuwe millennium: Onderzoek naar kansen en mogelijkheden*. Utrecht: Verwey-Jonker Instituut.

Elshtain, Jean B. 1997. "Civil Society Creates Citizens. It Does Not Solve Problems." *The Brookings Review*. 15(4). http://www.brook.edu/pub/review/oldtoc.htm# FAL97.

Elster, Jon, ed. 1998. *Deliberative Democracy*. Cambridge: Cambridge

University Press.

Engbersen, R., and A. Sprinkhuizen. 1998. *In de ban van de buurt: Over lokaal sociaal beleid in de buurt: ondersteunende teksten.* Utrecht: NIZW.

Eriksen, Erik Oddvar. 1995. "Introduktion til en deliberativ politikkmodell." Pp. 11-29 in E.O. Eriksen, ed., *Deliberativ politikk. Demokrati i teori og praksis.* Oslo: Tano.

──────. 2000. *Is Democracy Possible Today?* Århus, Denmark: Magtudredningen.

Eriksen, Erik Oddvar, and Jarle Weigaard. 1999. *Kommunikativ handling og deliberativt demokrati.* Bergen: Fagbokforlaget Vigmostad og Bjørke AS.

Erlandson, D. A., E. L. Harris, B. L. Skipper and S. D. Allen. 1993. *Doing Naturalistic Inquiry.* Newbury Park, Calif.: Sage Publications.

Etzioni, Amitai. 2000. *The Limits of Privacy.* New York: Basic Books.

Etzioni-Halevy, Eva. 1993. *The Elite Connection.* Cambridge: Polity Press.

Evers, Adalbert, and Matthias Schulze-Böing. 1998. "Mobilizing Social Capital—The Contribution of Social Enterprises to Strategies against Unemployment and Social Exclusion." Paper presented at the EMES-network, December 10-13. European Centre for Social Welfare Policy and Research, Vienna

Evers, Adalbert. 2001. "The Significance of Social Capital in the Multiple Goal and Resource Structure of Social Enterprises." Pp. 273-95 in Carlos Borzaga and Jacques Defourny, eds., *Social Enterprises in Europe.* London: Routledge.

Fairclough, N. 1995. *Discourse and Social Change.* Cambridge: Polity Press.

Ferman, Barbara, 1996. *Challenging the Growth Machine: Neighborhood Politics in Chicago and Pittsburgh.* Lawrence: University Press of Kansas.

Fischer, Frank. 1999. *Citizens, Experts, and the Environment: The Politics of Local Knowledge.* Durham, N.C.: Duke University Press.

──────. *The Politics of Local Knowledge.* Durham, N.C.: Duke University Press.

Fishkin, J.S. 1991. *Democracy and Deliberation.* New Haven, Conn.: Yale University Press.

Flex, Kenneth. 1993. "Municipalities, Counties and the Danish Social Development Programme." In Birgit Jæger, ed., *Developmental Programmes as a Strategy to Innovate Social Policy.* Copenhagen: AKFs Forlag.

Flyvbjerg, Bent. 2001. *Making Social Science Matter: Why Social Inquiry Fails and How It Can Succeed Again.* Cambridge: Cambridge University Press.

Forester, John. 1999. *The Deliberative Practitioner: Encouraging Participatory Planning Processes.* Cambridge, Mass.: MIT Press.

Fortuin, K., P. van der Graaf en K. van Vliet. 2002. *"Eendjes voeren": Verkenning sociale component Singelplan.* Utrecht: Verwey-Jonker Instituut.

Foucault, Michel. 1991. "Governmentality." Pp. 87-104 in Graham Burchell, Colin Gordon and Peter Miller, eds., *The Foucault Effect: Studies in Governmentality*. Chicago: University of Chicago Press.

Fountain, J. 2000. *Building the Virtual State*. Washington, D.C.: Brookings Institution.

Fowler, R. 1991. *The Dance with Community: The Contemporary Debate in American Political Thought*. Lawrence: University Press of Kansas.

Fox, Charles J., and Hugh T. Miller. 1995. *Postmodern Public Administration: Toward Discourse*. Thousand Oaks, Calif: Sage Publications.

Gadamer, Hans-Georg. 1996. *Truth and Method*. 2nd rev. ed. Translation revised by Joel Weinsheimer and Donald G. Marshall. New York: Continuum.

Garreau, Joel. 1992. *Edge City: Life on the New Frontier*. New York: Anchor Books.

Gayle, Mike. 1999. *Mr. Commitment*. London: Flame.

Gibbons, M., C. Limoges, H. Nowotny, S. Schwartsman, P. Scott, and M. Trow. 1994. *The New Production of Knowledge. The Dynamics of Science and Research in Contemporary Societies*. London: Sage Publications.

Giddens, Anthony. 1984. *The Constitution of Society. Outline of the Theory of Structuration*. Cambridge: Polity Press.

Gittell, Ross and Avis Vidal. 1998. *Community Organizing. Building Social Capital as a Development Strategy*. London: Sage Publications.

Gramsci, Antonio. ca. 1969. *Soviets in Italy*. Nottingham: Institute for Workers' Control.

Greve, Carsten. 1998. *Den grå zone—fra offentlig til privat virksomhed*. Copenhagen: Jurist- og Økonomforbundets Forlag.

Guba, E. G., and Y.S. Lincoln. 1985. *Naturalistic Inquiry*. Newbury Park, Calif.: Sage Publications.

⸺. 1989. *Fourth Generation Evaluation*. London: Sage Publications.

Gundelach, Peter, and Lars Torpe. 1997. "Social Reflexivity, Democracy and New Types of Citizen Involvement in Denmark." Pp. 47-63 in Jan W. van Deth, ed., *Private Groups and Public Life. Social Participation, Voluntary Associations and Political Involvement in Representative Democracies*, London: Routledge.

Gutmann, A., and D. Thompson. 1996. *Democracy and Disagreement*. Cambridge, Mass.: Harvard University Press.

Haack, Susan. 1993. *Evidence and Inquiry: Towards Reconstruction in Epistemology*. Cambridge, Mass.: Blackwell.

⸺. 1997. "Vulgar Rortyism." *The New Criterion* 16 (November): pp. 67-70.

⸺. 1998. *Manifesto of a Passionate Moderate: Unfashionable Essays*. Chicago: University of Chicago Press.

Habermas, Jürgen. 1995. "Tre normative demokratimodeller: Om begrepet deliberativ politikk." In E.O. Eriksen, ed., *Deliberativ politikk. Demokrati i teori og praksis*, Oslo: Tano.

———. 1996. "Three Normative Models of Democracy." In, Seyla Benhabib, ed., *Democracy and Difference. Contesting the Boundaries of the Political.* Princeton, N.J.: Princeton University Press.

———. 1996. *Between Facts and Norms.* Cambridge: Polity Press.

Hajer, M., and H. Wagenaar, eds. 2003. *Deliberative Policy Analysis: Understanding Governance in the Network Society.* Cambridge: Cambridge University Press.

Hamed, M. 1998. "The Role of Agriculture and Agricultural Processing in Saline County, Missouri." Columbia, Mo. Community Policy Analysis Center Research Report.

Hamed, M., T.G. Johnson, and K. Miller. 1998. "The Impacts of Animal Feeding Operations on Rural Land Values." Community Policy Analysis Center Research Report R-99-02. May.

Hansen, Allan D. 1999. "Demokrati og medborgerskab." Pp. 350-74 in Uffe Jakobsen and Morten Kelstrup, eds., *Demokrati: teorier og begreber*, Copenhagen: Forlaget Politiske Studier.

Harding, Allan. 1995. "Elite Theory and Growth Machines." Pp. 35-53 in, David Judge and Gerry Stoker, eds., *Theories of Urban Politics.* London: Sage Publications.

Harmon, Michael. 1981. *Action Theory for Public Administration.* Burke, Va.: Chatelaine Press.

Harter, Phillip. 1982. "Negotiated Regulations: A Cure for the Malaise." *Georgetown Law Journal* 71: 1-117.

Hatch, Mary Jo. 1997. *Organization Theory. Modern, Symbolic and Postmodern Perspectives.* Oxford: Oxford University Press.

Healey, Patricia. 1997. *Collaborative Planning—Shaping Places in Fragmented Societies.* London: Macmillan.

Heinrich, Carolyn J., and L. E. Lynn, Jr., eds. 2000. *Governance and Performance.* Washington, D.C.: Georgetown University Press.

Held, David. 1996. *Models of Democracy,* 2nd ed. Stanford, Calif.: Stanford University Press.

Hendriks, Frank, and Pieter W. Tops. 2001a. "De paradoxale praktijk van de wijkaanpak in Rotterdam." Pp. 5-70 in *Stadsbespiegelingen, deel B. Ervaringen en observaties uit het stedennetwerk.* M. Boogers, F. Hendriks, S. Kensen, P.W. Tops, R. Weterings en S. Zouridis. Tilburg, Netherlands: KUB

———. 2001b. "Tussen hard en zacht in Den Haag." Pp. 45-94 in ,M. Boogers, F. Hendriks, S. Kensen, P.W. Tops, R. Weterings en S. Zouridis, *Stadsbespiegelingen, deel A. Ervaringen en observaties uit het stedennetwerk.* Tilburg, Netherlands: KUB.

———. 2002. "The Quest for Interaction, The Reinventing of Consensus

Democracy and Its Critics." In *Dutch Crossing: A Journal of Low Countries Studies* 26 (1): 9-27.

Henton, Douglas, John Melville, and Kimberly Walesh. 1997. *Grassroots Leaders for a New Economy—How Civic Entrepreneurs Are Building Prosperous Communities.* San Francisco: Jossey Bass.

Hirschman, Albert O. 1972. *Exit, Voice, and Loyalty: Responses to Decline in Firms, Organizations, and States.* Cambridge, Mass.: Harvard University Press.

Hirst, Paul. 1994. *Associative Democracy. New Forms of Economic and Social Governance.* Cambridge: Polity Press.

Hogan-Esche, Tom. 2002. "Recapturing Suburbia: Urban Secession and the Politics of Growth in Los Angeles, Boston, and Seattle." Unpublished Dissertation. University of Southern California.

Hood, Christopher. 1991. "A Public Management for all Seasons?" *Public Administration* (6): 3-19.

Howarth, D. 1995. "Discourse Theory." Pp. 115-33 in, D. Marsh and G. Stoker, eds., *Theory and Methods in Political Science.* Basingstoke: David Macmillan Press.

Hulgård, Lars. 1995. "Den lokale ildsjæl og det polycentrerede samfund." *Politica* 27 (1): 38-53.

_____. 1997. *Værdiforandring i Velfærdsstaten—et weberiansk perspektiv på sociale forsøgsprogrammer.* Copenhagen: Forlaget Sociologi.

Hull, C., and B. Hjern. 1982. "Helping Small Firms Grow: An Implementation Analysis of Small Firm Assistance Structures." *European Journal of Political Research* 10 (2): 187-98.

Hunter, J. D., and T. Fessenden. 1994. "The New Class as Capitalist Class: The Rise of the Moral Entrepreneur in America." in, Kellner and Heuberger, eds., *Hidden Technocrats. The New Class and New Capitalism.* New Brunswick, N.J.: Transaction Publishers.

Jaeger, Birgit. 2001. "The E-Government of the Future." Pp. 13-8 in, P.W. Tops, B. Jaeger, en S. Kensen, *Reader voor de opleidingsdag Sociaal en Fysiek in Cohesie.* Tilburg, Netherlands: KUB.

Jaja, Cheedy, and Hugh T. Miller. 2003. "Public Administration Theory and Scholarship: A Narrative Analysis of Symposia Genre." *American Review of Public Administration.* Forthcoming.

Janoski, Thomas. 1998. *Citizenship and Civil Society.* Cambridge: Cambridge University Press.

Jansson, Torkel. 1988. *State, Local Government and Voluntary Associations. A Triangular Drama in 19th Century Scandinavia.* Uppsala: University of Uppsala, Department of History. Mimeo.

Jessop, Bob. 1998. "The Rise of Governance and the Risk of Failure: the Case of Economic Development." *International Social Science Journal.* 50 (1): 29-45.

Jordan, Grant, and Klaus Schubert. 1992. "A Preliminary Ordering of Policy Networks Labels." *European Journal of Political Research.* 21 (1): 7-21.
Judge, David. 1996. "Pluralism." in *Theories of Urban Politics.* David Judge, Gerry Stoker and Harold Wolman, eds. London: Sage Publications.
Kamarck, E. C., and J.S. Nye, eds. 2000. *Democracy.com.* Cambridge: Harvard University Press.
Keane, John. 1998. *Civil Society—Old Images, New Visions.* London: Polity Press.
Kellner, Hansfried, and Frank W. Heuberger, eds. 1994. *Hidden Technocrats— The New Class and New Capitalism.* New Brunswick and London: Transaction Publishers.
Kensen, Sandra. 1999. *Sturen op variatie. Sociale vernieuwing en de Deense variant als bronnen van inspiratie.* Den Haag: VNG Uitgeverij.
_____. 2000. "The Dialogue as Basis for Democratic Governance." *Administrative Theory & Praxis*, 22 (1): 117-131.
_____. 2002a. "Sociaal en fysiek in cohesie: een leer-werk programma in Amsterdam." Pp. 241-271 in *Stadsbespiegelingen, deel A. Ervaringen en observaties uit het stedennetwerk.* M. Boogers, F. Hendriks, S. Kensen, P.W. Tops, R. Weterings en S. Zouridis. Tilburg, Netherlands: KUB.
_____. 2002b. *Opleidingsdag sociaal en fysiek in cohesie. Een verslag van een leerproces.* Dongen, Netherlands: Pijnenburg.
_____. 2002c. *Opleidingsdag Sociaal en Fysiek in Cohesie: Een spannende ontmoeting tussen hard en zacht. Het uitbreiden van netwerken.* Tilburg, Netherlands: Stichting KINO.
Kensen, Sandra, and Peter Bogason. 1999. "Two Approaches of Narrative Policy Evaluation Compared. Evaluating a Danish Neighborhood Council Twice." Pp. 79-108 in Tineke A. Abma, ed., *Advances in Program Evaluation.* Greenwich, Conn.: JAI Press.
Kickert, Walter, and E.K.J. Koppenjan. 1997. *Managing Complex Networks.* London: Sage Publications.
King, Cheryl S., Camilla Stivers, et al.. 1998. *Government Is Us: Public Administration in an Anti-Government Era.* Thousand Oaks, Calif.: Sage Publications.
Kingdon, J.W. 1984. *Agendas, Alternatives and Public Policies.* Boston, Mass.: Little Brown.
Kooiman, Jan. 1993. "Governance and Governability: Using Complexity, Dynamics and Diversity." Pp. 35-50 in *Modern Governance.* Jan Kooiman, ed. London: Sage Publications.
_____. 1993. "Social-political Governance: Introduction." Pp. 1-9 in Jan Kooiman, ed., *Modern Governance. New Government-Society Interactions.* London: Sage Publications.
_____. 1993. "Findings, Speculations and Recommendations." Pp. 249-62 in Jan Kooiman, ed. *Modern Governance. New Government-Society*

Interaction. London: Sage Publications.
Kovalyova, A., A. Cox, and T.G. Johnson. 1999. "Saline County Retail Trade Analysis: Sales, Employment and Income." Columbia, Mo.: Community Policy Analysis Center Research Report R-99-03. July.
Kristiansen, Bente, and Lars Hulgård. 2002. *Demokratiets rodent*. Copenhagen: JL-Foundation.
Kuhn, Thomas S. 1962/1970. *The Structure of Scientific Revolutions*. Chicago: Chicago University Press.
Laclau, Ernesto, and Chantal Mouffe. 1985. *Hegemony and Socialist Strategy*. London: Verso.
Lakoff, G., and M. Johnson. 1983. *Metaphors We Live By*. Chicago: University of Chicago Press.
Lang and Hornburg. 1998. "What Is Social Capital and Why Is It Important to Public Policy." *Housing Policy Debate* 9 (1).
Latour, B. 1997. *Guust Flater als technologiefilosoof, De Berlijnse Sleutel en andere lessen van een liefhebber van wetenschap en techniek*. Amsterdam: Van Gennep Amsterdam.
Leadbeater, Charles. 1997. *The Rise of the Social Entrepreneur*. London: Demos.
Lenin, V. I. 1924/1976. Letter to M. Sokolov, published in Pravda in 1924. P. 20 in Andras Hegedus *Socialism and Bureaucracy*. New York: St. Martin's Press.
Lepsius, M. Rainer. 1988. *Interessen, Ideen und Institutionen*. Opladen, Germany: Westdeutscher Verlag.
Levine, P. 2001. "Civic Renewal and the Commons of Cyberspace." *National Civic Review* 90 (3): 205-12
Lijphart, Arend. 1999. *Government Forms and Performace in Thirty-Six Countries*. New Haven, Conn.: Yale University Press.
Lindblom, Charles E. 1959. "The Science of Muddling Through." *Public Administration Review* 19: 79-99.
Lindblom, Charles E., and E. J. Woodhouse. 1993. *The Policy-Making Process*. 3rd ed. Englewood Hills, N.J.: Prentice Hall.
Lipsky, Michael. 1980. *Street-Level Bureaucracy: Dilemmas of the Individual in Public Services*. New York: Russell Sage Foundation.
Logan, J., and H. Molotch. 1987. *Urban Fortunes: The Political Economy of Place*. Berkeley: University of California Press.
Lowi, Theodore J. 1967. "Machine Politics—Old and New." *The Public Interest* (9): 83-92.
———. 1969. *The End of Liberalism: Ideology, Policy and the Crisis of Public Authority*. New York: Norton.
———. 1993. "Legitimizing Public Administration: A Disturbed Dissent." *Public Administration Review* 53 (3): 261-64.
Lowry, K., P. Adler and N. Mildner. 1997. "Participating the Public: Group

Process, Politics, and Planning. *Journal of Planning Education and Research* 16(3): 177-87.
Luke, J.S. 1998. *Catalytic Leadership: Strategies for an Interconnected World.* San Francisco: Jossey-Bass.
Lyotard, Jean-François. 1984. *The Postmodern Condition: A Report on Knowledge.* Translated by Geoff Bennington and Brian Massumi. Minneapolis: University of Minnesota Press.
March, J. G., and J. P. Olsen. 1989. *Rediscovering Institutions. The Organisational Basis of Politics.* New York: The Free Press.
_____. 1995. *Democratic Governance.* New York: The Free Press.
Matthews, D., and N. McAfee. 1999. "Making Choices Together: The Power of Public Deliberation." The Kettering Foundation. Report no. 9942.
Mayntz, Renate, and Bernd Marin. 1991. "Introduction: Studying Policy Networks." Pp. 11-25 in Renate Mayntz and Bernd Marin, eds., *Policy Networks. Empirical Evidence and Theoretical Considerations.* Frankfurt and Boulder CO: Campus Verlag and Westview Press.
Mayntz, Renate. 1999. "New Challenges to Governance Theory." Unpublished paper.
McNamee, S., and K. J. Gergen. 1999. *Relational Responsibility. Resources for Sustainable Dialogue.* London: Sage Publications.
McSwain, Cynthia. J. 1985. "Administrators and Citizenship: The Liberalist Legacy of the Constitution." *Administration & Society* 17(2), 131-48.
Michels, Robert. 1962/1984. "Political Parties." Reprinted as "Oligarchy," in Frank Fischer and Carmen Sirianni, eds., *Critical Studies in Organization & Bureaucracy,* revised and expanded editions. Philadelphia, Pa.: Temple University Press.
Miller, Hugh T. 1994. "Post-progressive Public Administration: Lessons from Policy Networks." *Public Administration Review* 54 (4): 378-386.
_____. 1997. "Why Teaching Theory Matters," *Journal of Public Administration Education* 3 (3): 363-73.
_____. 2000. "Rational Discourse, Memetics, and the Autonomous Liberal Human Subject." *Administrative Theory & Praxis* 22 (1): 89-104.
_____. 2002. *Postmodern Public Policy.* Albany: State University of New York Press.
Miller, Hugh T., and Charles J. Fox. 2001. "The Epistemic Community." *Administration & Society* 32 (6): 668-85.
Miller, Hugh T., and Cheryl S. King. 1998. "Practical Theory." *American Review of Public Administration* 18 (1): 43-60.
Milward, H. Brinton, and Keith Provan. 1992. "Institutional-Level Norms and Organizational Involvement in a Service Implementation Network." *Journal of Public Administration Research and Theory* 1 (4): 391-417.
Mollenkopf, John. 1983. *The Contested City.* Princeton, N.J.: Princeton University Press.

Morone, James A. 1990. *The Democratic Wish*. New York: Basic Books.
Mundell, M., A. E. Kovalyova, and T. G. Johnson. Forthcoming. "The Regional Economic Contributions of Kingdom City Businesses." Community Policy Analysis Center Studies Report.
Musso, Juliet. 1999. "Federalism and Community Governance: Can Los Angeles Neighborhoods Help Govern Gargantua?" *Public Administration Theory and Praxis* 21 (3): 342-54.
Nagel, Thomas, and Richard Rorty. 1998. "Truth and Progres." Philosophical Papers 3. Cambridge, Mass.: Cambridge University Press.
Noordegraaf-Eelens, L. 2002. *Het Overspelige Subject*. Rotterdam: Erasmus Universiteit Rotterdam.
Oliver, T. R. 1996. "Conceptualizing the Challenges of Public Entrepreneurship." In *The Integration of Psychological Principles in Policy Development*. Westport, Conn.: Praeger.
Organization for Economic Cooperation and Development (OECD). 2001. "Engaging Citizens in Policy Making: Information, Consultation and Public Participation." PUMA Policy Brief No. 10. http://www.oecd.org/pdf/M00007000/M00007815.pdf.
Osborne, David, and Ted Gaebler. 1992. *Reinventing Government. How the Entrepreneurial Spirit Is Transforming the Public Sector*. New York: Plume.
Ostrom, Vincent. 1989. *The Intellectual Crisis in American Public Administration*. Rev. ed. Tuscaloosa: University of Alabama Press.
―――. 1991. *The Meaning of American Federalism: Constituting a Self-Governing Society*. San Francisco: Institute for Contemporary Studies Press.
O'Toole, Laurence J. 1997. "Treating Networks Seriously: Practical and Research-Based Agendas in Public Administration." *Public Administration Review* 57 (1): 45-52.
Ozawa, Connie P. 1991. *Recasting Science: Consensual Procedures in Public Policy Making*. Boulder, Colo.: Westview Press.
―――. Forthcoming. "Johnson Watershed Management Plan: An Example of Mediated Negotiation." In. Peter Adler and Kem Lowry, eds., *Finding Common Ground: Case Studies in Consensus-Building and the Resolution of Natural Resource Controversies*. Newbury Park, Calif.: Sage Publications.
Ozawa, Connie P., and Peter Adler. Forthcoming. *Dealing with Scientific Complexity and Uncertainty*.
Pateman, Carole. 1970. *Participation and Democratic Theory*. London: Cambridge University Press.
Pedersen, A.R. 1999. *Den udfoldende praksis*. Roskilde, Denmark: Roskilde Universitetscenter.
Pestoff, Victor A. 1992. "Third Sector and Co-operative Services—An

Alternative to Privatization." *Journal of Consumer Policy* 15: 21-45.
Peterson, Paul. 1981. *City Limits*. Chicago, IL: University of Chicago Press.
Pierre, Jon, ed. 2000. *Debating Governance. Authority, Steering and Democracy*. Oxford: Oxford University Press.
Pine, J., and J. Gilmore. 1999. *The Experience Economy. Work Is Theatre and Every Business a Stage*. Boston: Harvard Business School Press.
Pressman, Jeffrey, and Aaron Wildavsky. 1984. *Implementation*. Berkeley: University of California Press.
Putnam, Robert D. 1993a. *Making Democracy Work. Civic Traditions in Modern Italy*. Princeton, N.J.: Princeton University Press.
_____. 1993b. "The Prosperous Community: Social Capital and Public Life." *The American Prospect*. 13. (Spring 1993). http://epn.org/prospect/13/13/putn.html.
_____. 1995a. "Bowling Alone: America's Declining Social Capital." *Journal of Democracy* 6 (1): 65-78.
_____. 1995b. "Bowling Alone: An Interview with Robert Putnam about America's Collapsing Civic Life." Copyright: American Association for Higher Education. Washington, D.C.
http://xroads.virginia.edu/~ HYPER /DETOC/assoc/aahe.html
_____. 1996a. "The Strange Disappearance of Civic America." *The American Prospect*, (winter): Pp. 34-48.
_____. 1996b. "Unsolved Mysteries. The Tocqueville Files." *The American Prospect* 25: 26-28.
_____. 2000. *Bowling Alone: The Collapse and Revival of American Community*. New York: Simon and Schuster.
Putnam, Robert D., R. Leonardi, and R. Y. Nanetti. 1993. *Making Democracy Work: Civic Traditions in Modern Italy*. Princeton, N.J.: Princeton University Press.
Quinn, R. E. 1984. "Applying the Competing Values Approach to Leadership: Towards an Integrative Framework." Pp. 10-27 in J. G. Hunt, et al. eds., *Leaders and Managers: International Perspectives on Managerial Behavior and Leadership*, Elmsford, N.Y.: Pergamon Press.
Rappaport, J. 1985. "The Power of Empowerment Language." *Social Policy* 16(2): 15-21.
Rhodes, R.A.W. 1997. *Understanding Governance. Policy Networks, Governance, Reflexivity and Accountability*. Buckingham: Open University Press.
_____. 2000. "The Governance Narrative: Key Findings and Lessons from the ESRC's Whitehall Program." *Public Administration*. 78 (2): 345-64.
Roe, Emery. 1994. *Narrative Policy Analysis*. Durham, N.C.: Duke University Press.
Rohr, John A. 1986. *To Run a Constitution: The Legitimacy of the Administrative State*. Lawrence: University Press of Kansas.

Rorty, Richard. 1979. *Philosophy and the Mirror of Nature*. Princeton, N.J.: Princeton University Press.

———. 1999. *Philosophy and Social Hope*. Middlesex: Penguin Books.

Sandel, Michael J. 1996. *Democracy's Discontent: America in Search of a Public Philosophy*. Cambridge, Mass.: Belknap Press of Harvard University Press.

Savitch, H. V., and J. C. Thomas. 1991. "Introduction: Big City Politics, Then and Now." Pp. 10-27 in *Big City Politics in Transition. Urban Affairs Annual Reviews*. Newbury Park, Calif.: Sage Publications.

Scharpf, Fritz W. 1994. "Games Real Actors Could Play: Positive and Negative Coordination in Embedded Negotiations." *Journal of Theoretical Politics*. 6 (1): 27-53.

———. 1999. *Governing in Europe: Effective and Democratic?* Oxford: Oxford University Press.

Schluchter, Wolfgang. 1979. *Die Entwicklung des okzidentalen Rationalismus— Eine Analyse von Max Webers Gesellschaftsgeschichte*. Tübingen, Germany: J.C.B. Mohr (Paul Siebeck)

Schneider, Mark, and Paul Teske. 1992. "Toward a Theory of the Political Entrepreneur: Evidence from Local Government." *American Political Science Review* 86 (3): 737-47.

Schneider, Mark, Paul Teske, and Michael Mintrom. 1995. *Public Entrepreneurs*. Princeton, N.J.: Princeton University Press.

Scott, Allen, ed. 2001. *Global City-Regions, Trends, Theory, Policy*. Oxford: Oxford University Press.

Scott, J. K., T. G. Johnson, and M. Mundell. 2000. *Community Memory: An Internet-Based Approach to Enhancing Community Learning, Knowledge Management and Public Participation in Local Governance*. Unpublished manuscript.

Sehested, Karina. 2002. *Netværksstyring i byer. Hvad med planlægningen og demokratiet?* Copenhagen: Jurist- og Økonomforbundets Forlag.

Siegel, Fred. 1997. *The Future Once Happened Here: New York, DC, LA and the Fate of America's Big Cities*. New York: Free Press.

Simpson, Ian. 2001. "The Clark Fork Settlement Agreement: An Example of Civic Environmentalism's Collaborative Process at Work." Working Paper. Portland, Oregon: Portland State University.

Skocpol, Theda. 1996. "Unravelling from Above." *The American Prospect* 25: 20-25.

———. 1997. "Building Community Top-down or Bottom-up?" *The Brookings Review* 15 (4).
http://www.brook.edu/pub/ review/oldtoc.htm# FAL97.

Sørensen, Eva. 1995. "Democracy and Regulation in Institutions of Public Governance." Ph.D.-Publications 1995/2. Copenhagen, Department of Political Science, University of Copenhagen.

Sørensen, Eva, and Jacob Torfing. 2002. "Network Politics, Political Capital and Democracy." *International Journal of Public Administration* 26 (6): 609-34.
Southern California Studies Center. 2001. *Sprawl Hits the Wall: Confronting the Realities of Metropolitan Los Angeles*. Los Angeles: University of Southern California.
Spano, Shawn. 2001. *Public Dialogue and Participatory Democracy*. Cresskill, N.J.: Hampton Press.
Staples, Lee H. 1990. "Powerful Ideas about Empowerment." *Administration in Social Work* 14(2): 29-42.
Stivers, Camilla M. 1990. "Active Citizenship and Public Administration." Pp. 246-73 in Gary L. Wamsley, Charles T. Goodsell, John Rohr, Phillip Kronenberg, Orion F. White, James F. Wolf, and Camilla M. Stivers, *Refounding Public Administration*. Newbury Park, Calif.: Sage Publications.
_____. 1990. "The Public Agency and Polis: Active Citizenship in the Administrative State." *Administration and Society* 22(2): 86-105.
Storing, Herbert J. 1981. *The Complete Anti-Federalist*. Chicago: University of Chicago Press.
Stout, Chris E. ed. 1995. *The Integration of Psychological Principles in Policy Development*. Westport: Praeger.
Sullivan, William M. 1997. "Making Civil Society Work: Democracy as a Problem of Civic Cooperation." Working Paper no. 3.: The National Commission on Civic Renewal University of Maryland. College Park, Maryland.
Susskind, Lawrence, and Jeffrey Cruikshank. 1987. *Breaking the Impasse*. New York: Basic Books.
Susskind, Lawrence, and Liora Zion. 2001. "Strengthening the Democratic Process in the United States: An Examination of Recent Experiments." Consensus Building Institute. Draft Working Paper. Cambridge, Massachusetts.
Susskind, Lawrence, Sarah McKearnan and Jennifer Thomas-Larmer. 1999. *The Consensus Building Handbook: A Comprehensive Guide to Reaching Agreement*. Thousand Oaks, Calif.: Sage Publications.
Thomas, J.C. 1995. *Public Participation in Public Decisions*. San Francisco: Jossey-Bass.
Tiebout, Charles M. 1956. "A Pure Theory of Local Expenditures." *Journal of Political Economy* 64: 416-24.
Tomlinson, J. 1999. *Globalisation and Culture*. Cambridge: Polity Press.
Tonkens, E. H. 2000. "Het isolement van het emancipatiebeleid." *Socialisme en democratie* 57 (11): 500-06.
Tops, P. W., F. Hendriks, E. Knippers, A. Spapens and J. Verduin. 1998. *Verlengstuk of spreekbuis: Het wijkbureau als schakel in het Utrechts*

besturingsmodel. Tilburg, Netherlands: KUB.
Tops, P.W. 2002. "Introductie: Het stedennetwerk en interactie-onderzoek ." Pp. 5-18 in M. Boogers, F. Hendriks, S. Kensen, P.W. Tops, R. Weterings and S. Zouridis, *Stadsbespiegelingen, deel A. Ervaringen en observaties uit het stedennetwerk,* Tilburg, Netherlands: KUB.
Toregas, C. 2001. "The Politics of E-Gov: The Upcoming Struggle for Redefining Civic Engagement." *National Civic Review* 90(3): 235-240.
Torfing, Jacob. 1999. *New Theories of Discourse. Laclau, Mouffe and Zizek.* Cambridge: Blackwell Publishers.
Twist, M.J.W. van. 1994. *Verbale vernieuwing. Aantekeningen over de kunst van bestuurskund.* The Hague: VUGA.
Villadsen, Søren. 1986. "Local Corporatism? The Role of Organizations and Local Movements in the Local Welfare State." *Policy and Politics* 14(2): 247-66.
Waldo, D. 1984. *The Administrative State. A Study of the Political Theory of American Public Administration:* 2nd ed. New York: Holmes and Meier.
Weber, Max. 1973. *Die protestantische Ethik II. Kritiken und Antikritiken.* Hamburg: Siebenstern Taschenbuch Verlag.
_____. 1985. *Wirtschaft und Gesellschaft.* Tübingen, Germany: J.C.B. Mohr (Paul Siebeck).
_____. 1989. *Gesamtausgabe Band 19: Die Wirtschaftsethik der Weltreligionene, Konfuzianismus und Taoismus.* Tübingen, Germany: J.C.B. Mohr (Paul Siebeck).
Wenger, Etienne. 1998. *Communities of Practice: Learning, Meaning, and Identity.* Cambridge, New York: Cambridge University Press.
White, J.D. 1999. *Taking Language Seriously. The Narrative Foundations of Public Administration Research.* Washington, D.C.: Georgetown University Press.
White, Orion F. 1990. "Reframing the Authority/Participation Debate." Pp. 182-245 in Gary L. Wamsley, Charles, T. Goodsell, John Rohr, Phillip Kronenberg, Orion F. White, James F. Wolf and Camilla M. Stivers, *Refounding Public Administration.* Newbury Park, Calif.: Sage Publications.
Wilson, Patricia. 1997. "Building Social Capital: A Learning Agenda for the Twenty-first Century." *Urban Studies* 34 (5-6): 745-60.
Witt, Matthew. 2000. "Dialectics of Control: The Origins and Evolution of Conflict in Portland's Neighborhood Association Program." Ph.D. Diss., School of Urban Studies and Planning, Portland, Oregon, Portland State University.
Wolin, Sheldon S. 1960. *Politics and Vision: Continuity and Innovation in Western Political Thought.* Boston: Little, Brown and Company.
Wuthnow, Robert. 1997. "The Role of Trust in Civic Renewal." Working Paper no. 1. The National Commission on Civic Renewal. University of

Maryland. College Park, Maryland

Yankelovich, D. 1991. *Coming to Public Judgment: Making Democracy Work in a Complex World.* Syracuse, N.Y.: Syracuse University Press.

_____. 1999. *The Magic of Dialogue: Transforming Conflict into Cooperation.* New York: Simon and Schuster.

Index

accountability, 12, 19, 65, 132, 143-44
action research, 151, 162, 164, 168, 176
activism, 35, 54
activist, 56, 125
ad hoc political, 5
agency, 6, 7, 99, 133-34, 136, 139-40, 142, 176; democratic, 6-8
anthropology, 90, 174
anti-foundationalist, 179
arena, 13-14, 51, 58, 60, 66, 70-71, 75, 95, 97, 101-2, 195
Arendt, Hannah, 135

Baldersheim, Harald, 28
bargaining, 3, 147, 187; interest-based, 138
Beck, U., 31
Bengtsson, Steen, 93, 98
Berger, P. L., 90
Bogason, Peter, 1, 8, 23, 61
Britain, 93, 102
bureaucracy, 3, 5-6, 10, 25, 28, 31, 35, 38, 47, 51, 55, 65, 78-79, 84, 108, 109, 114, 121, 186-187, 191-93

change agents, 8, 39-40, 51, 54, 87, 180, 187
citizen, 7, 13-15, 19, 20, 44, 51-53, 55-61, 69, 99, 109, 128, 160, 187, 193; activism, 1, 56; competent, 70, 82, 85; engagement, 4, 5, 23, 46-47, 58-59, 136; governance, 52, 55, 60; groups, 76, 141; participation, 20, 186, 191-92, 195
citizenry, 15, 136-37, 188, 195
citizenship, 11, 37, 135
civic culture, 13, 190
civic education, 13
Cohen, J. L., 104
collaboration, 4, 15, 50, 52, 55, 95-97, 101-2, 131, 141, 146; research, 19
collective, 7, 16-19, 26, 36, 49, 65, 92, 95, 104, 126-27, 133, 146, 183
communitarianism, 5, 56, 187
community, 7-8, 12, 14-16, 19-21, 24-25, 32, 35, 38, 46, 48-51, 55-59, 66-67, 70, 73, 87-88, 90-93, 95-105, 123, 128-29, 133-34, 136-37, 141, 144, 147, 151, 153-54, 159, 167, 174-76, 180-84, 189, 193-94; advisory panel, 19, -based problem

215

solving, 51, 55; building, 88, 90, 93, 101, 104; development, 87, 93, 98, 100, 102, 104; governance, 5, 53; individual-in-, 101, 103; learning, 21; mediation, 134; members, 16, 49, 133
conflict, 3, 7, 14, 16-17, 24, 35, 48, 54, 68-70, 72, 75-76, 81, 83-85, 116-17, 120-21, 125-26, 146, 177, 183, 195; resolution, 19, 137
confrontation, 81-83
consensus; and collaboration, 131; building, 138, 141
constituency, 25, 32, 133, 143-44
constructivism; social, 5
cooperation, 3, 7, 19, 28, 30-32, 44, 72-74, 76, 97-98, 108, 112-13, 122-23, 128, 142, 153, 166, 168, 171; governmental, 5; institutional, 98
coordination, 44
corporatism, 32, 35, 72
culture, 20, 30, 41, 47, 48, 59, 65, 88, 90, 93, 94, 97, 99, 102, 110, 112-13, 120-22, 136, 177-79, 181-83, 189, 195; civic, 13, 190; class, 100; political, 42, 59

Dahl, Robert A., 57, 110
decentralization, 28, 46-48, 70, 72, 107, 111-12, 191-92
decision-making, 16, 65-66, 108, 110-12, 123, 126, 131, 133, 144, 165, 193; conventional, 142; decision cycle, 17; public, 132, 146-47
deliberation, 5, 7-8, 11-21, 24-26, 35-38, 52, 70-71, 81-83, 85, 104, 136, 145, 147, 187-92, 194; authentic, 20; governance, 11-14, 17-21, 189; partici-

pative, 192; practice of, 11; process of, 18; project, 18; public, 138, 187; technique, 20
democracy, 1, 5-13, 21, 23-24, 26, 30, 32-38, 40, 42, 54, 56-58, 60-61, 64, 66-71, 75, 77, 79-85, 107-11, 119, 123-30, 132, 135-37, 147, 173-74, 177, 180, 182, 185-86, 188-95; ad hoc, 192; aggregative, 60, 127; and governance, 135; associational, 59; ballot box, 5; consensus, 58, 61; deliberative, 5, 8, 13, 24, 70, 105, 137, 145, 187, 189, 190, 192, 194; developmental, 8, 56, 60; direct, 5, 57-58, 185, 195; discursive, 136; electoral, 189; extra-formal, 2, 10, 193; in-direct, 57, 58; integrative, 9, 24, 129; interpretation of, 67, 73, 80, 84; local, 23, 36-37, 42, 59, 85, 160, 171; models of, 7, 9, 27, 56, 60; network, 63, 79-81, 83-85, 194; overhead, 2; parliamentary, 25, 69; partici-patory, 97, 135-36, 142, 192; pendulum, 58, 61; protective, 8, 56; radical, 58; represen-tative, 1-3, 8, 10, 30, 34, 37-38, 64, 67-70, 72, 79-80, 83-85, 109, 124, 126-27, 129, 133, 193-94; research on, 173-74, 177; traditional forms of, 1; urban, 64, 83, 85
democratic, 1-3, 5-12, 14, 23-27, 30, 34-35, 37, 39-40, 42, 51, 56-58, 60-61, 63-64, 67-71, 76-77, 80-85, 88, 108-10, 122, 124, 126-38, 142, 147, 148-49, 152, 155, 161, 173-74, 176-78, 180-95; accountability, 1, 5; agency, 6-8; decision making,

109-10, 129, 133; language, 40; legitimacy, 56, 60, 128
demonstration project, 28
Denmark, 8, 23, 30, 33, 37, 69, 72, 88, 90, 93, 98-99, 104, 131, 191-93
deregulation, 33
Dewey, John, 5
discourse; theory, 5, 26-27, 36, 155
disembedded, 31
disenchantment, 85
diversity; societal, 159
Dobson, Julian, 102
double hermeneutic, 175
Durkheim, Emile, 92

election, 1, 3, 5, 17, 25, 27, 29-31, 38, 42-43, 49, 54, 60, 64-65, 67-71, 73, 84, 117, 127, 133, 140-41, 185, 188-89, 193, 195; day, 7, 35
electoral politics, 1
elite, 8, 35, 38, 64, 67-68, 70, 72, 75, 77, 79-85, 133, 136, 147, 177, 180, 182, 193-94
embedded, 88, 92, 104, 137, 194
empowerment, 29, 32, 60, 90, 99-100, 180, 187, 193
entrepreneurship, 8, 10, 32-34, 36, 87-93, 95-104, 114, 150, 194-95; civic, 88, 96-97; public, 88-89; social, 88, 90, 98, 101-4, 185, 195; theory of, 88-89, 92
epistemology, 4, 173, 175, 178-80, 190
Eriksen, Erik O., 27, 69, 70
European Union, 28, 99
evaluation; responsive, 162, 166
everyday maker, 5, 31-35, 55

Flex, Kenneth, 29
fragmentation, 23, 28, 30, 41, 47, 65
fragmented, 8, 23, 30, 38, 41, 47, 64, 66, 68, 70, 84, 104, 107, 125-26, 151, 170, 192

Gaebler, Ted, 108
Giddens, Anthony, 31, 36
Gittell, Ross, 87, 104
governance, 8, 11-14, 17-21, 23, 30, 35, 41-42, 53-55, 59-61, 63-68, 70-71, 73, 77-81, 83-87, 107-9, 111, 113-16, 118, 125-26, 128, 130-31, 136-38, 149-50, 192-93; administrative, 114, 117; and democracy, 64, 68, 86; approach to, 12, 97; art of, 186-87, 195; central, 112, 114; citizen, 52, 55, 60; city, 49; community, 5, 53; deliberative, 11-14, 17-21, 189; democratic, 8, 12, 14, 34, 83, 88, 126, 128, 132, 134-35, 147, 149, 152, 192, 194; elitist, 67-68, 77, 79, 80, 83-84, 194; for democracy, 64; local, 9, 41, 44, 50, 59, 88, 98, 104-5, 111, 140, 154, 171 neighborhood, 39, 42-43, 50, 53, 58-61, 187; network, 87, 99, 104, 115, 192-93, 195; of a city, 155; process, 3, 20, 59, 64-66, 68, 71, 75, 77-79, 83-85, 115, 118, 136, 192; self-, 7, 51, 55, 59; societal, 3, 108-9; structure, 47-49, 59, 107, 109, 114-15; system, 8, 12, 24, 35, 107-11, 113, 116, 126-27, 130, 192; theory of, 5; through policy, 64; urban, 40, 64, 67, 79, 83, 85, 98
government, 1-3, 12-13, 17, 21, 29, 41-42, 50, 54-55, 59-60, 65-66, 97, 102, 118, 132, 136-37, 139-40, 142-43, 146-47, 186,

195; activities, 142; local, 2, 6, 8, 14, 16, 23, 27-29, 34-35, 37, 73-74, 78-79, 84, 91, 95-96, 100, 139-40, 151, 160, 192; national, 45; neighborhood, 43; system of, 3, 23, 30, 37, 107-8, 110, 113, 130

Greve, Carsten, 108

Gundelach, Peter, 33

Hansen, Allan D., 70, 110

Hatch, Mary Jo, 28, 30

Healey, Patricia, 87, 104

hegemony, 133

Held, David, 56, 135-36

Henton, Douglas, 88, 95-97, 103

Heuberger, Frank W., 91

Hewitt, Patricia, 102

hierarchy, 3-4, 8, 10, 28, 36-37, 52, 65-67, 71, 77-79, 83-84, 107-8, 115, 117-18, 120, 122-24, 128, 177, 189-92, 194

Hirst, Paul, 33

Hogan-Esche, Tom, 48

Hulgård, Lars, 8, 31, 87, 93, 97-98, 192, 194

Hume, D., 177

Hunter, J. D., 88, 105

identity, 5, 9, 11, 72-74, 77, 84, 101, 108, 120, 124

ideology, 26, 177, 186, 195

individual, 18, 29-31, 33-35, 60-61, 87-92, 94-97, 101, 103-5, 126-27, 138, 146, 154-55, 165, 181, 183, 188, 195; administrator, 9, 108, 109, 111, 114-26, 129-30, 134, 159-60, 166-67, 187, 191-93; citizen, 4, 47, 53, 60, 109, 119, 122; institutions, 111; level, 1-3, 8, 12-13, 20, 29-37, 39, 41-47, 51, 54, 56, 58-61, 65, 88, 91, 97, 104-5, 109, 120-21, 123, 127, 129, 131, 137, 140, 142, 144, 145, 147, 186, 192-93; liberty, 127; perspective, 1, 4, 13, 24-25, 30, 32, 34, 36, 51, 64, 67-71, 80-83, 85-86, 92, 94, 116, 122, 128-29, 132-33, 135, 153, 157, 163, 175, 189; researcher, 1, 2, 4, 7, 9, 37, 67, 75, 110, 150-59, 161-62, 164, 166-71, 173-78, 180-83, 190, 194

individualism, 7, 9, 19, 24-25, 27, 30-31, 33-34, 38, 56, 59, 61, 87-89, 91, 104, 134, 136, 142-43, 151, 158, 170, 188, 193; methodological, 104

influence, 1-4, 11, 20, 26, 31-32, 35, 37-39, 49, 58, 63, 68-69, 74, 76, 78-81, 85, 87, 89, 92, 98, 102, 104, 113, 123-24, 126-27, 131, 133, 140, 144, 145, 161, 182; channels of, 31, 69, 70, 79, 129; citizens', 1; decision making, 8; democratic, 3, 34, 70; distribution of, 9, 128-29; participation and, 69; the political decisions, 123

Inglehart, Ronald, 30

institutional, 2, 5-9, 11, 23-26, 34-37, 39-45, 47-48, 50, 52-54, 56-60, 67, 69, 86-87, 104-5, 107-8, 111-12, 114-17, 119, 121-22, 126-27, 133, 137-38, 144, 147, 150-51, 160-61, 163, 170-71, 177, 181-83, 187-88, 192-95; change, 23, 30, 37, 39, 40, 52-53, 59-60, 187, 192; configuration, 94, 98; environment, 41, 122, 192; fragmentation, 47, 59; innovation, 42, 45, 60; power, 100, 194; reform, 8, 39, 54; separation, 115, 117, 126, 193; setting, 58-59, 111, 130, 171; shift, 192; structure, 41, 188

integration, 7-9, 24-26, 29, 35, 37-38, 44-47, 51, 57-58, 60, 69-71, 77, 79, 81-83, 85, 98-99, 118, 123, 128-29, 147, 184, 194; integrative democracy, 9, 24, 129
interaction; adversarial, 24, 38
intermediary, 8, 24-25, 38, 192-93

Jansson, Torkel, 33
Jessop, Bob, 107-8
joint action, 9, 52, 151
Jordan, Grant, 66

Keane, John, 104
Kellner, Hansfried, 91
Kettering Foundation, 14-16
Kickert, Walter, 107
Kristiansen, Bente, 97

Laclau, Ernesto, 86
Lash, Scott, 31
Leadbeater, Charles, 88, 101
leadership, 6, 16, 20, 24, 26, 95, 111-12, 114, 116, 117-18, 127, 132, 136
learning; organizational, 21
legitimacy, 2, 7, 38, 69-71, 73, 77-79, 81, 84, 103, 108-9, 119-20, 122-25, 127, 129, 144, 178, 183, 186-88, 191, 195; constitutional, 5; democratic, 56, 60, 128; gaining, 51, 125; of the network, 78
Leonardi, R., 33
Lepsius, Rainer M., 90, 92
Lewcock, Tom, 96
Lindblom, Charles, 3
Lipsky, Michael, 109, 186, 192
local government, 43, 46, 51
local knowledge, 16
Lynn Jr., L. E., 107-8

management, 18, 32-33, 40, 44-46, 58, 65, 66, 73, 78, 91, 93, 96, 99, 131, 138, 139-42, 144-46, 157-59, 165-66, 168, 170, 186; adaptive, 146
Marshall, Donald G., 9, 97, 131, 190-91, 194
Mawson, Andrew, 102
Mayntz, Renate, 66, 107
mayor, 2, 31-32, 43, 48, 54-55, 59, 61, 73, 78-79, 91, 99, 112, 114-15, 162
mediation, 9, 13, 19, 68-69, 83, 85, 97, 101-2, 104, 118, 132-34, 137-38, 141, 144-48, 194; mediated negotiation, 9, 131-135, 137-41, 143-44, 146-47, 185, 194
Melville, John, 95
method; discursive, 184
Miller, Hugh, 1, 10, 173, 185
Milward, H., 2
model; monistic rational, 3
modernism, 24, 28, 31, 92, 104, 136, 187, 191, 195
Molotch, H., 67
motivation, 50, 80, 84, 87, 89-90, 92, 95, 97, 101, 110, 134, 145, 147
Mouffe, Chantal, 86
muddling through, 3
Musso, Juliet, 8, 39, 61

negotiation, 3, 8, 9, 13, 27, 32, 36, 38, 58, 66, 67, 74, 108, 125, 131-35, 137-38, 143, 145, 147-48, 153-54, 167, 193
neighborhood; council, 48-51, 54-56, 58-60, 187; council movement, 55-56, 187; fixation, 42, -governance, 8; mobilization, 50, -oriented reform, 39-40, 42-43, 45-47, 50, 56-58

Netherlands, 8, 42, 45, 50, 60-61, 131, 149, 157, 163, 187, 190-91
network, 3-4, 7-8, 20, 32, 39, 43, 45, 47, 50-51, 55, 60, 63-71, 73-86, 93, 95-96, 98-99, 101-2, 105, 108, 112, 114-15, 118-25, 127-29, 133, 150-52, 154, 156, 158, 161, 187, 192-94; activity, 3, 124; administration, 127; administrative, 121, 129, -based democracy, 8; builder, 119, 120-21, 124; corporative, 69, 79; fluid, 42-43; gover-nance, 59, 87, 104, 192, 195; participant, 108, 121, 129; process, 65, 67; social-physical, 163, 164, 167; supporter, 119-21, 124;
new public management, 12, 32, 186
Nietzsche, Friedrich, 175

organization; hybrid forms of, 7
Osborne, David, 108
Ozawa, Connie P., 9, 97, 131, 133, 142, 144, 146, 190-91, 194

participation, 1, 6-8, 13, 15, 17-20, 24-25, 33-35, 37, 46-47, 60, 68-71, 79, 81-82, 85, 88, 93, 104, 109, 128-29, 132-33, 135-37, 139-40, 142-44, 158, 187-89, 191; active participant, 173; democratic, 26, 30, 69, 136, 183, 186; quality of, 138, 147, 159; reflective, 6
partnership, 17, 28, 66, 69, 104, 108, 156, 159, 163-64
pluralism, 3, 8, 67-68, 70, 186
politicians, 3, 5, 7-8, 28, 34, 37-38, 40, 53-54, 63, 65-71, 73, 76, 80-83, 85, 108-10, 112, 114-18, 121-28, 193

postmodernism, 30, 48, 64, 65, 104
power, 1, 6, 19-20, 28-29, 33, 35-36, 38, 49, 61, 66-72, 82, 89, 117, 133, 141, 151, 177, 180-81, 185, 187-88, 193, 195; decision-making, 108; institutional, 100, 194; political, 56, 112; public, 7, 26
pragmatism, 5-6, 9, 184, 186
process; deliberative, 11-13, 17-21, 194
professionals, 5, 8, 28, 40, 45-47, 53, 58-60, 87, 109, 133, 155, 157, 167, 187
project; deliberative, 18
public dialogue, 16, 21, 71, 81-82, 85, 194
public involvement, 13, 19, 98
public action, 5-6, 16, 26, 135, 145; collective, 7
public administration, 2, 6, 12-13, 18, 28, 42, 52, 59, 87-88, 127, 131-32, 135, 137, 150, 155, 164, 174, 185-88, 191, 195
public decision-making, 132, 146-47
public policy, 132, 134
public-private consortia, 14

rationality, 3, 71, 85, 136, 187, 192, 196
reflexivity, 31
reform, 8, 27-30, 34, 37, 39-42, 45-51, 53-60, 69, 108, 111-12, 114-15, 149-50, 152, 187
reorganization, 111, 130, 161
representation; appropriateness of, 143
research, 1, 2, 4, 7, 11, 15, 17, 20-21, 61, 87, 91-93, 96, 149-57, 159-62, 164-71, 173-78, 180-84, 186, 192-93; action, 151, 162, 164, 168, 176; constructionist, 151, 162-63; demo-

cratic, 9, 161, 173-74, 176-78, 180-82, 184, 189-90; empirical, 138, 173, 189; interaction, 9, 150-51, 155-57, 161-62, 166, 169-71, 190; narrative, 151, 162, 164-65; pragmatic, 178, 184; project, 93, 110, 151, 153-54, 156-57, 160-62, 173, 176, 180, 182, 193; relationship, 162, 174; responsive, 151; tradition, 151, 162; value-neutral, 177
responsibility, 7, 15, 17-18, 33, 38, 44-45, 55, 59, 61, 65, 82, 91, 94-96, 117, 128, 139, 140-41, 155, 162, 168, 181, 191
Rousseau, Jean-Jacques, 135-36
Rousseauean, 136

Savitch, H. V., 67
Scharpf, Fritz W., 65, 107
Schluchter, Wolfgang, 92
Schneider, Mark, 87-92, 104
Schubert, Klaus, 66
Sehested, Karina, 8, 63, 86, 193-94
self-governance, 7, 51, 55, 59
services, 11, 12, 23, 27-35, 37, 43, 46-47, 51, 54-55, 58, 61, 88, 94-95, 98, 101, 109, 112, 114, 150, 160-61, 191
Skocpol, Theda, 104
social capital, 5, 13, 17-19, 21, 33-34, 44, 47, 88, 101, 103-5
social cohesion, 33, 95
social movements, 49, 59-60, 69, 91, 104, 187
social renewal, 151
sociology, 88, 90, 92, 149, 175
Sørensen, Eva, 5, 9, 29, 31, 68, 107, 110, 192-93
sovereignty, 36, 65, 107, 128, 186, 195
Spano, Shawn, 97

Ståhlberg, Krister, 28
structuration, 6, 9, 38, 42-44, 48, 50, 53, 55, 59, 60, 98, 103-4, 107-8, 110, 112, 114, 115, 117-18, 121-24, 134, 143, 146-47, 174, 183, 187
sustainability, 64, 66, 70-71, 74, 77, 79, 103-4, 137, 174
Sweden, 72

technique; deliberative, 20
Teske, Paul, 88-90
theory, 1, 6-8, 11, 20, 45, 47, 64-65, 71, 76, 79, 83, 104, 151, 162, 165, 171, 177-80, 182, 184, 186-88, 191, 193-94, democratic, 24, 57, 135-36, 138, 188, 193; discourse, 5, 26, 27, 36, 155; of entrepreneurship, 88, 89, 92
Thompson, D., 13, 105
Tocqueville, de, Alexis, 33
Torfing, Jacob, 70, 110
Torgerson; D., 13
Torpe, Lars, 33
transaction costs, 17-18
trust, 11-12, 19, 25-26, 30, 66, 74, 85, 92, 116, 125

undemocratic, 82-83, 85, 194
ungovernability, 67
United States, 7-9, 19, 21, 24, 48, 61, 104, 131-32, 135-36, 147, 191
urban development, 31, 40, 64, 80, 99, 157
utilitarian, 92

Villadsen, Søren, 32
voters, 1, 2, 26, 30, 31-33, 35, 41, 49, 58, 74, 127, 139-40, 188, 192

voting, 1, 5, 8, 27, 30, 33, 58, 68-69, 136, 188-89

Walesh, Kimberly, 95
weaver, 99
Weber, Max, 92

Weberian, 88, 90, 92
Weigaard, Jarle, 70
welfare, 27-29, 33-34, 36, 38, 46, 91, 98, 100, 138, 191
Wilson, Patricia, 87, 88, 101, 103-5
Wittgenstein, 175

About the Contributors

Guy B. Adams is professor and associate director of the Harry S Truman School of Public Affairs at the University of Missouri-Columbia. Adams's research has focused on organizational symbolism and culture, and on public service ethics, history and theory.

His book, *Unmasking Administrative Evil*, with Danny A. Balfour, won the 1998 Louis Brownlow Book Award: the National Academy of Public Administration's highest award for excellence in public administration scholarship, as well as the two other national book awards from sections of the Academy of Management. Adams also coauthored *The Tacit Organization* and has over fifty scholarly publications, including books, book chapters, and articles in the top national public affairs journals. He currently serves as co-editor-in-chief of the *American Review of Public Administration*.

Peter Bogason is professor in public administration in the Department of Social Sciences, Roskilde University, Denmark. He has published on public administration in general and specializes in intergovernmental relations, policy analysis, democracy, and in research methods. He was a member of the Danish National Social Science Research Council and was also deputy editor of the journal *Public Administration 1998-2001*. He is a member of the editorial board of the journals *Governance, Administrative Theory & Praxis* and *Scandinavian Political Studies*.

Recent books include: *Forvaltning og stat, Fragmenteret forvaltning. Demokrati og netværksstyring i decentraliseret lokalstyre; Public Policy and Local Governance: Institutions in Postmodern Society*, and *Comparing Networks*, a special issue (guest editor with Theo A. J. Toonen) of Public Administration.

Frank Hendriks is currently associate professor of public administration at Tilburg University and is presently a staff member of the department of public administration at Tilburg University, the Netherlands. He holds a Ph.D. from Leiden University in the Netherlands and specializes in comparative politics, interactive governance and urban policy.

The books Hendriks has published in English include: *Public Policy and Political Institutions: The Role of Culture in Urban Policy* and *Polder Politics: The Reinvention of Consensus Democracy in the Netherlands* (coedited with Theo A. J. Toonen).

Lars Hulgård is associate professor and director of MPP, University of Roskilde in Denmark. He was a research consultant for social development programs at the Danish Ministry of Social Affairs. He was also a member of the executive committee in the National Association on Social Policy, and president of the Danish Sociological Association.

Among his recent publications are: *Weak Ties in Strong Welfare States, Social Capital, Trust and Networks*; *Civilsamfund eller social kapital? En institutionel kritik af Habermas og Putnam inspirerede civilsamfundsteorier*; and *Cooperative Activation and community Development in Denmark*.

Hulgård is a reviewer of Sociology for the Danish National Radio Broadcasting Network and has reviewed books regarding Erving Goffman, Anthony Giddens, C. Wright Mills, and Robert Putnam.

Sandra Kensen holds a Ph.D. in public administration from the Erasmus University Rotterdam in the Netherlands and is presently a staff member of the department of public administration at Tilburg University, the Netherlands. Since 2001, Sandra has led the research program *Relational Thinking in Urban Policy*, which is being carried out in Amsterdam and other cities in the Netherlands and Denmark. She is presently writing a book about this research and hopes to publish her findings next year.

She recently coordinated a symposium on Administrative Theory and Praxis on The Theory and Practice of Community Democracy for which she wrote her article "Playing with Boundaries as Democratic Scholars."

Gary S. Marshall is associate professor of public administration at the University of Nebraska at Omaha. He holds a Ph.D. in public administration from Virginia Tech's Center for Public Administration and Policy. Professor Marshall teaches in the areas of public administration theory, organization theory and behavior, organization development, and public policy mediation. His work has been published in leading academic journals such as *Public*

Administration Review, *The American Review of Public Administration*, and *The American Behavioral Scientist*.

Professor Marshall works closely with the Nebraska Office of Dispute Resolution and the Nebraska Mediation Center Association. He is a trained mediator and is a board member of the Concord Center in Omaha, Nebraska.

Hugh T. Miller is professor of public administration and director of the School of Public administration at Florida Atlantic University. He is the author of *Postmodern Public Policy*.

Juliet Musso is associate professor of public policy at the School of Policy, Planning and Development, University of Southern California. She holds a Ph.D. from the Goldman School of Public Policy, University of California, Berkeley. Professor Musso has expertise in urban policy, with specific research interests in community governance, local institutional reform, and federalism. She has written on the political economy of city formation, on metropolitan fiscal disparity, and currently is researching the development of neighborhood councils in the City of Los Angeles. Other research topics include local government use of advanced telecommunications technologies to improve participation and service delivery, and intergovernmental finance in California.

Recent publications include *Faith Organizations and Neighborhood Councils in Los Angeles*, with Alicia Kitsuse and Terry L. Cooper, and *The Distributive Impact of Federal Fiscal Policy: Federal Spending and Southern California Cities*, with Pascale Marcelli.

Connie P. Ozawa, Ph.D., is professor of urban studies and planning at Portland State University. She is associate editor of the *Negotiation Journal* and a member of the Editorial Board of the *Journal of the American Planning Association* and of the Governing Board of the Association of Collegiate Schools of Planning.

Recent publications include *Mediated Negotiation and Democratic Theory: Implications for Practice*, with Gary Marshall; *Clear Signals: Moving On to Planning's Promise*, with Ethan P. Seltzer; and *Making the Best Use of Technology*.

James K. Scott, Ph.D., is associate professor and director of policy programs at the Harry S Truman School of Public Affairs, University of Missouri-Columbia. Dr. Scott also serves as director of the European Union Center at the University of Missouri. His current research focuses on the changing nature of local governance and on the role of social trust and social networks in the production of public goods and services.

He has published numerous articles and research reports on local public involvement and local public decision-making. He has worked with dozens of community groups and state and local government officials to assess the economic, fiscal and social impacts of proposed or expected changes.

Karina Sehested, Ph.D., is associate professor and a full-time researcher at the Danish Building and Urban Research Institute. She is consultant for The Danish Board Of Technology on the project: *New Forms of Participation in Urban Planning*.

Among her latest publications are: *Netværksstyring i byer - hvad med planlægningen og demokratiet?*; *Bypolitik mellem hierarki og netværk*; and *Cross-sector Partnerships as a New Form of Local Governance*.

Eva Sørensen is a Ph.D. in political science and professor in public administration and democracy at the Department of Social Science, Roskilde University, Denmark. She is leader of the research program *Roles in Transition: Politicians and Public Administratior between Hierarcy and Networks* (www.ssc.ruc.dk/freja/), and member of the Center of Democratic Network Governance (www.demnetgov.ruc.dk).

Recent publications are *The Future of PA in Denmark: Projections, Prospects and High Hopes*, with Lotte Jensen and Asbjørn Sonne Nørgaard; *Network Politics, Political Capital and Democracy*, with Jacob Torfing; *Democratic Theory and Network Governance*, and *Studies of Power and Democracy: Towards a Constructivist Analysis of Governance from Below*.

Pieter Tops is a professor of public administration at Tilburg University in the Netherlands. His publications, books, and articles cover a wide range of subjects related to local democracy, urban politics, multilevel government, and political change and renewal.

He is actively involved in several national and international research groups including the EGPA research group on Informatization and Public Administration (1991-1997), the COST-research group on Government and Democracy in the Information Age (1996-2001) and the Demo-net research group (2000 -).

Barton Wechsler, Ph.D., is professor and director of the Harry S Truman School of Public Affairs. Professor Wechsler's research, largely concerned with public leadership and strategy, has been published in the *Public Administration Review*, *Administration and Society*, *Journal of the American Planning Association*, *Public Performance and Management Review*, and numerous other academic and practitioner journals and edited books.

Before coming to the Truman School, Wechsler was dean of the Edmund S. Muskie School of Public Service at the University of Southern Maine and a faculty member at the University of Illinois and Florida State University.